VIRGINIA WATERWAYS

— and the —

UNDERGROUND RAILROAD

VIRGINIA WATERWAYS
— *and the* —
UNDERGROUND RAILROAD

CASSANDRA L. NEWBY-ALEXANDER, PhD

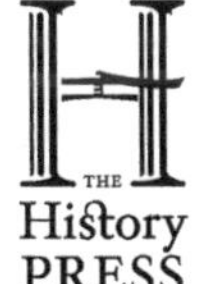

Published by The History Press
Charleston, SC
www.historypress.net

First published 2017

ISBN 978-1-5402-2782-9

Library of Congress Control Number: 2017953905

Notice: The information in this book is true and complete to the best of our knowledge. It is offered without guarantee on the part of the author or The History Press. The author and The History Press disclaim all liability in connection with the use of this book.

DEDICATION

To my ever-patient and supportive husband, William, whose love lifts me up every day;

To my mother, who will always be the wind beneath my wings;

To my deceased father, who continues to be an ever-present force in my life;

To my niece Nicole, whose heart and character are my inspiration;

To my family—brothers, sisters-in-law, nieces, nephews, aunts, uncles and cousins—whose strength, talents and support are always appreciated and never forgotten.

And to "my spies" in the Archives at the Slover Public Library in Norfolk—Troy Valos and Bill Inge—who continually amaze me with their research acumen and generous hearts.

CONTENTS

INTRODUCTION

"For some years before escaping," thirty-one-year-old Portsmouth native John Atkinson was "a prisoner of hope." Hiring out his time for $120 annually, Atkinson labored "to support his drunken and brutal master," twenty-six-year-old James Ray, a sailor who lived at the U.S. Navy Yard in Gosport. Atkinson declared Ray to be "a worthless sot" with a character that was "too disgusting for record." Eventually, the horrors of his situation and his expectation of imminent sale on the auction block compelled Atkinson to leave, even though that meant abandoning his free black wife, Mary Atkins, without a word, fearing knowledge would implicate her in his escape.[1]

This sudden departure from his wife, parents and friends must have been particularly painful for Atkinson, who was described as a highly intelligent and ambitious individual. And as a slave who hired out his own time, Atkinson used his mobility to arrange for passage aboard a vessel bound for the North once it was clear to him that he would be sold to the Deep South. So in the summer of 1854, he connected with one of the Underground Railroad's most dexterous and active conductors in Virginia, Henry Lewey, alias "Bluebeard," who arranged with twenty-nine-year-old John Minkins, a steward aboard the *City of Richmond*, to hide him in a secret compartment for a two-day journey to Philadelphia. Minkins was plugged into the Philadelphia Underground Railroad and frequently connected "passengers" who escaped aboard his ship with William Still, an Underground Railroad stationmaster. As secretary of the Philadelphia Vigilance Committee, Still arranged for the passengers' resettlement in northern communities—especially after the

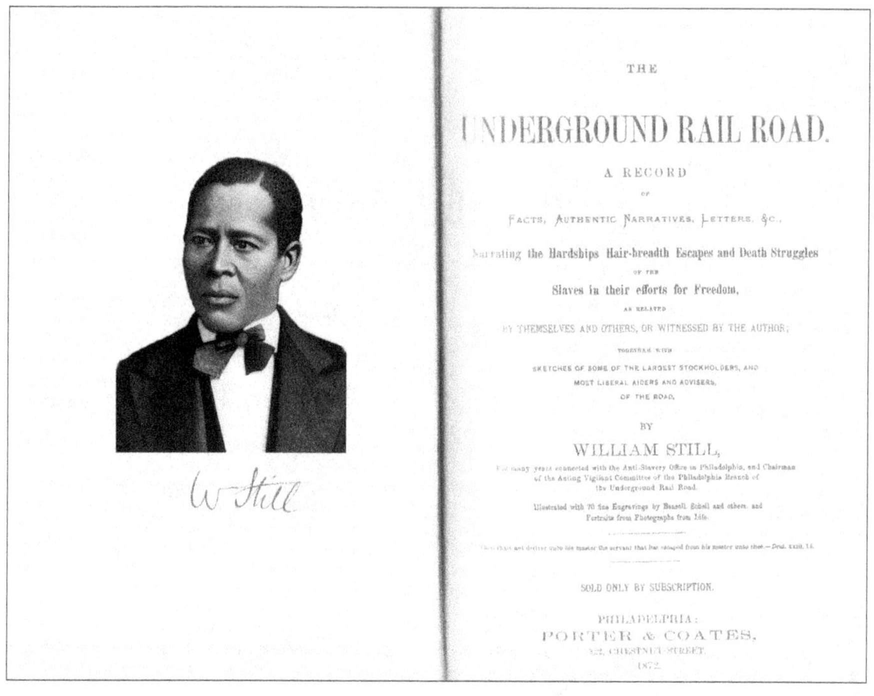

THE

UNDERGROUND RAIL ROAD.

A RECORD

OF

FACTS, AUTHENTIC NARRATIVES, LETTERS, &C.,

Narrating the Hardships Hair-breadth Escapes and Death Struggles

OF THE

Slaves in their efforts for Freedom,

AS RELATED

BY THEMSELVES AND OTHERS, OR WITNESSED BY THE AUTHOR;

TOGETHER WITH

SKETCHES OF SOME OF THE LARGEST STOCKHOLDERS, AND MOST LIBERAL AIDERS AND ADVISERS, OF THE ROAD.

BY

WILLIAM STILL,

For many years connected with the Anti-Slavery Office in Philadelphia, and Chairman of the Acting Vigilant Committee of the Philadelphia Branch of the Underground Rail Road.

Illustrated with 70 fine Engravings by Bensell, Schell and others, and Portraits from Photographs from Life.

SOLD ONLY BY SUBSCRIPTION.

PHILADELPHIA:
PORTER & COATES,
CHESTNUT STREET.
1872.

William Still's book, *The Underground Railroad*, originally published in 1872, told the story of many runaways from the Upper South, although there were some examples of those who escaped from other areas. The recorded accounts were of those individuals who passed through William Still's station in Philadelphia. *William Still,* The Underground Railroad, *1872.*

1850 Fugitive Slave Act—in cities and towns that protected fugitives, such as New Bedford, Massachusetts, and those in Canada's Ontario Province.[2]

Shortly after arriving in Philadelphia, Atkinson was ferried to St. Catharines, a city in Ontario (Canada West) and home to numerous fugitives, including Harriet Tubman. Reunited with his brother and probably others that he knew from the Norfolk-Portsmouth area, Atkinson soon found a job and a place to live. Yet despite achieving freedom, Atkinson was unhappy because he left so much behind, including clothing that he worked so hard to procure. In a letter to William Still, Atkinson wrote, "I hope you will intercede for my clothes and as soon as they come please to send them to me.…[And] tell [Henry Lewey] to give [my letter] to my wife." He added, "Brother sends his love to you and all the family and he is overjoyed at seeing me arrive safe, he can hardly contain himself; also he wants to see his wife very much, and says when she comes he hopes you will send her on as soon as possible."[3]

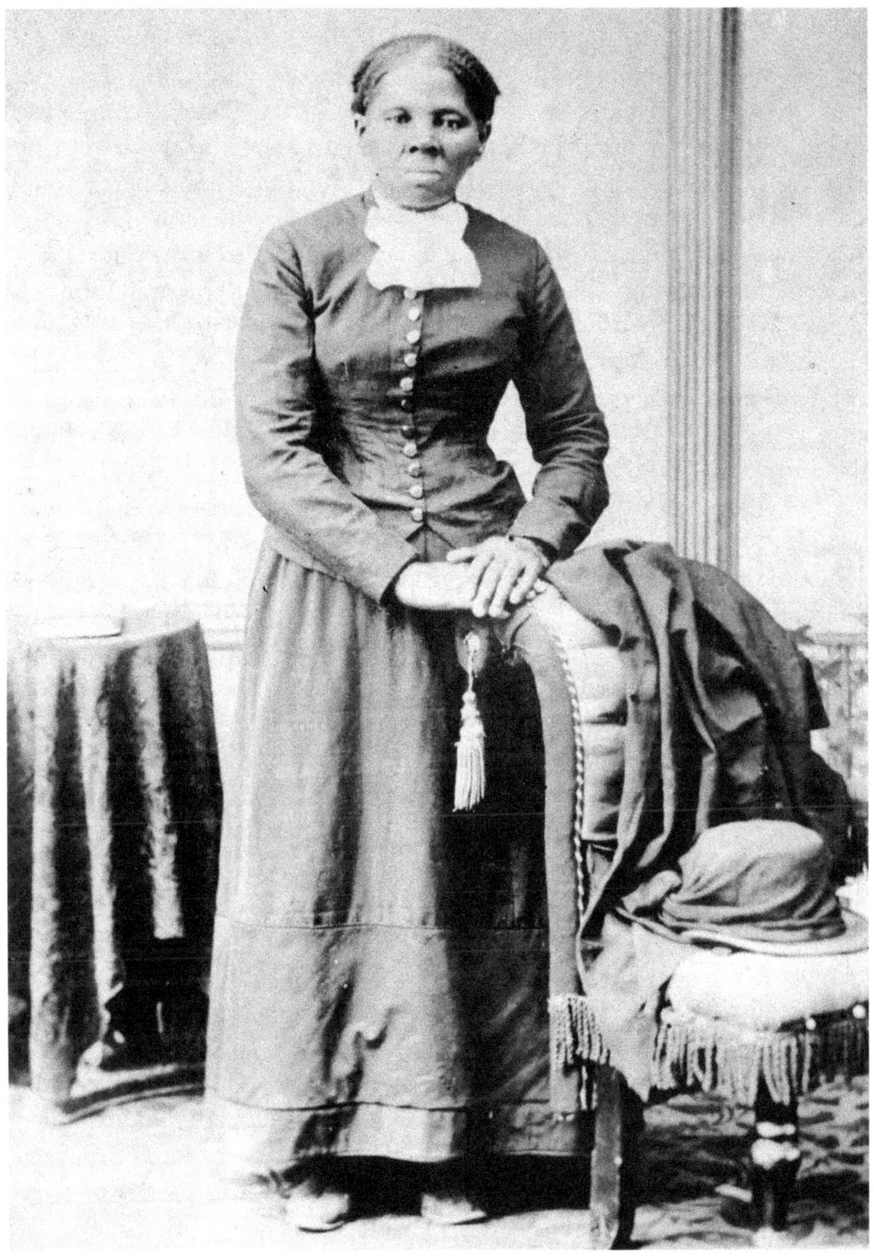

This iconic portrait of Harriet Tubman, taken sometime between 1871 and 1876 by photographer Harvey B. Lindsley, symbolizes the strength and unassuming pose of one of the most noted Underground Railroad conductors, whose life spanned from 1823 to 1913. *Library of Congress.*

In his last recorded letter to William Still, in October 1854, Atkinson, who changed his name to John Atkins, remarked that a friend of his, Richmond Bohm, had transferred his clothes to Philadelphia and was asking that Dr. Benjamin Lundy forward them as soon as possible to his friend Hiram Wilson, a noted missionary and veteran of the Underground Railroad network in Canada West. He also wanted a letter to his wife to be forwarded to Henry Lewey. In the letter, he expressed his enduring love for her and his relatives. He wanted Mary to pass on his love and thoughts to her mother and cousin and his mother and father. Atkinson also wanted his wife to write to him and reminded her "to be of good courage, that I love her better than ever…[and that he] would like for her to come on as soon as she can, but for her to written [*sic*] and let [him] know when she is going to start."[4]

From Atkinson's experiences, it is clear why the Underground Railroad occupies a romantic place in America's imagination. Rife with intrigue, desperation, betrayal, loss of family and danger, the story of the Underground Railroad was the passage to freedom for some and hope for others. The Underground Railroad flourished in Virginia's cities, where the maritime industry and a cosmopolitan atmosphere dominated. The multitude of port cities and towns, the dominance of slaves for hire, the existence of black churches and neighborhoods and the presence of a sizeable free black population allowed slaves to have secret meetings for religious purposes and for planning escapes. Those who fled included some of the most nationally known fugitives in the 1850s, including Henry "Box" Brown, Shadrach Minkins, George Latimer and Anthony Burns.

Even though Virginia was the center of freedom-seeker activity, public memory redirected attention from the East Coast to the Ohio region, in part because of *Uncle Tom's Cabin* and the sensationalized escape of Eliza across the Ohio River and into the waiting arms of abolitionists. Fergus Bordewich's 2005 book *Bound for Canaan* added to this perspective while simultaneously dispelling the romanticized, stereotyped and exploited perceptions of previous Underground Railroad interpretation. Bordewich relayed the story from a broader perspective, integrating stories of well-known fugitives with the activities of both black and white operatives in the South and North who assisted freedom seekers in their escapes. Yet Bordewich's comprehensive analysis focused primarily on the most famous fugitives and those who escaped to the Ohio region, leaving as a sidebar the activity of fugitives and agents along the Eastern Seaboard, and particularly along the waterways in Virginia. Nevertheless, Bordewich

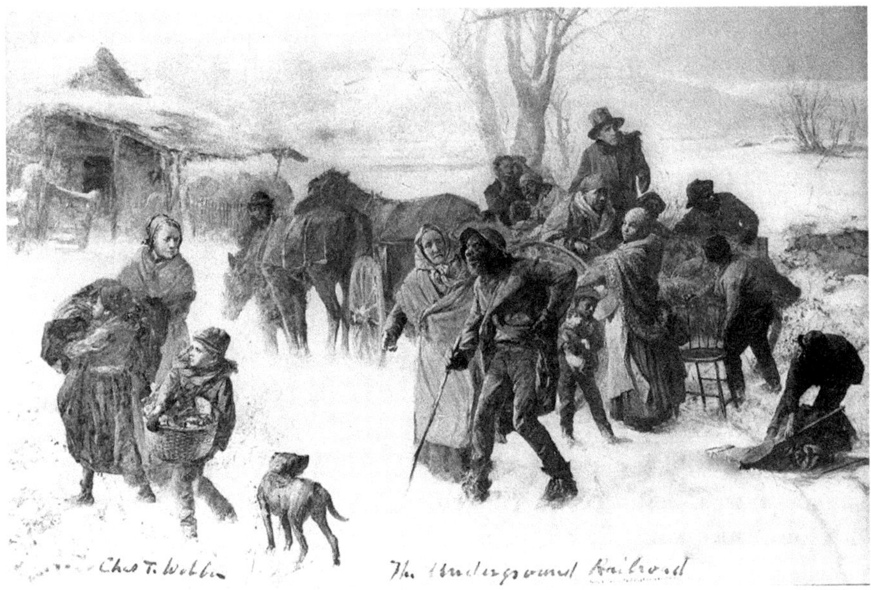

This iconic 1893 image of freedom seekers by Charles T. Webber titled *The Underground Railroad* is typically what many imagine when they envision how many freedom seekers left. The painting dramatizes African American families escaping on foot and by wagon at night and in challenging weather conditions. *Library of Congress.*

successfully wove the various accounts into a broader narrative and understanding of the nation's most secret of operations.[5]

It was along the thousand miles of tidal rivers, which included the James, Elizabeth, York, Susquehanna, Rappahannock and the Potomac, that uncounted freedom seekers made their escape. These rivers were some of the most important water routes along the Atlantic Seaboard that earlier brought Africans to their fate as enslaved laborers. It is ironic that these rivers would also be part of a waterway network that took many to freedom. Flowing into the Chesapeake Bay and the Atlantic Ocean, these rivers provided access to fugitives aboard small vessels and steamships because of the vibrant trade between Virginia's cities and global trade communities. Smaller rivers that were tributaries to the larger tidal rivers allowed freedom seekers using skiffs and other small watercraft as their vehicles of escape additional passageways.[6]

Some freedom seekers followed river valleys eastward to the coastal ports in Virginia, while others journeyed on land, crossing Free State borders and connecting with abolitionist cells. Those in Appalachia escaped over land into Lancaster and Chester Counties in Pennsylvania or across the Ohio

River. Those who escaped through Loudoun and Fauquier used routes that traversed the Catoctin and Bull Run Mountains, Short Hill Mountain and the Blue Ridge. Others traveling from Culpeper County were assisted by free black communities. Culpeper's Chinquapin Neck, which separated the Rapidan and Rappahannock Rivers, was also used by fugitives. So as freedom seekers plied the smaller rivers in the northern regions and in the western sections, they used wagons or horses to escape across the smaller shallow rivers. However, the largest numbers left aboard ships from Richmond, Norfolk and Alexandria.[7]

And while the true numbers of those who escaped will never be known, Virginia's leaders were concerned because of the loss of revenue and the perception that they had lost control of their enslaved populace. Even in the early 1800s, Thomas Jefferson and James Madison estimated that as many as thirty thousand enslaved men, women and children escaped either with the British forces or on their own. By the 1840s and 1850s, Virginia officials passed legislation to make it harder for enslaved people to escape. Yet estimates of similar numbers from Virginia continued being reported. Despite their best efforts, Virginia officials were unable to prevent the invasive impact of this secret network because of the dedication of those seeking freedom and those determined to assist.

This work seeks to begin refocusing attention on the East Coast and especially Virginia, where many of America's most famous freedom seekers departed on their journey to liberty. It is often forgotten that Virginia had the largest population in the South and, until the early 1800s, the largest populace in the nation. And it continued through the beginning of the twentieth century to have the largest African American population in America. It was in Virginia that the struggle for black freedom began as laws were passed establishing slavery and denying to all blacks their basic human and political rights, including the right to protect themselves and their families. And yet, even as whites set up these artificial barriers to self-determination, blacks constructed rivers of resistance, as historian Vincent Harding so eloquently discussed in his book *There Is a River*.[8]

This book seeks to underscore the importance of these individuals who risked life and limb to escape from the center of slavery's power, despite the best efforts of slave owners, who used legislation, public and private funds and the force of law to prevent escapes. The accounts of fugitives suggest that many were successful in obtaining freedom from slavery. Even when individuals did not succeed, their efforts inspired generations to understand

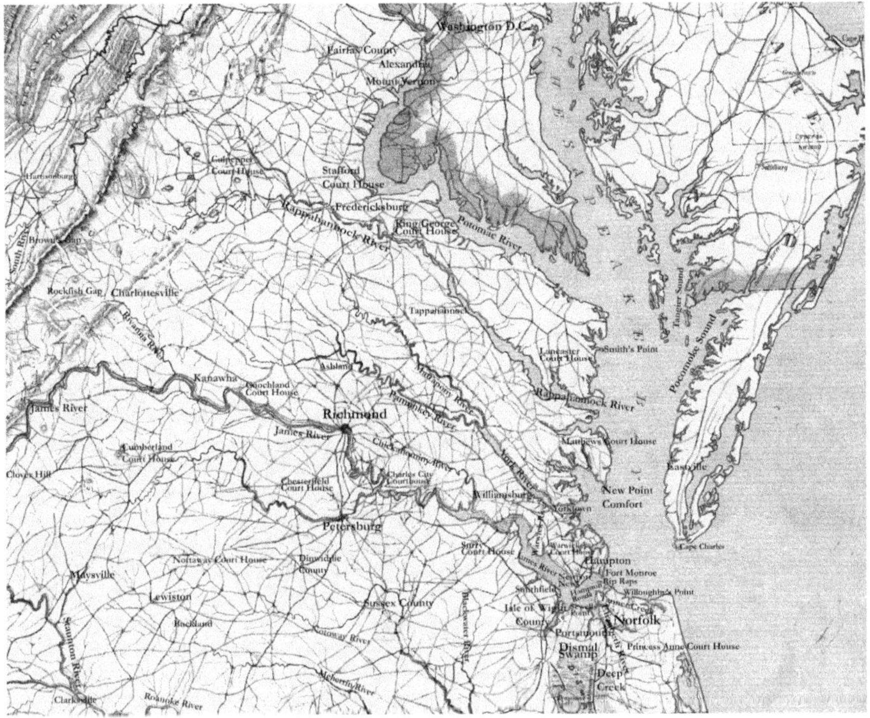

This 1862 J.H. Colton map of Virginia illustrates the various topographies of the state. Central to this map is the dominance of the waterways along the Eastern Seaboard, where the rivers emanate from the Chesapeake Bay, pushing their way into the interior up to the fall line (where the Appalachian Mountain range begins). In the western sections, a more complicated topography is evident, illustrating how freedom seekers needed various methods to secure liberty from bondage. *Library of Congress.*

that the desire for freedom is a human story and part of an enduring quest by all Americans.

The story of freedom seekers began long before the period typically designated as the Underground Railroad. Indeed, all acts of self-emancipation that spanned from the earliest period—the arrival of the first Africans at Point Comfort in the Jamestown Settlement in 1619—through the end of the Civil War were part of a continuing ebb and flow of resistance to any barriers to liberty. And this meandering river metaphor, used by Harding to describe black resistance, is appropriate to this examination. For in Virginia, the rivers became not only a metaphor for self-determination but also actual pathways to liberty for countless thousands who sought to achieve what was promised in America: life, liberty and the pursuit of happiness.

1

BACKGROUND OF SLAVERY AND FLIGHT IN COLONIAL VIRGINIA

John Willoughby was a member of one of the oldest families in Virginia. Serving as the county lieutenant of Norfolk and chair of the Norfolk County Committee of Safety, it was certain that he was a supporter of the patriot cause. However, rumors spread that his loyalties lay with the British, and in 1775, he was brought before a board of inquiry to prove his innocence. Barely a year later, in April 1776, suspicion reemerged about Willoughby and he was ordered to move thirty miles from the shoreline with his eighty-seven slaves. By May, those suspicions had been confirmed when Willoughby's slaves were sighted getting aboard a boat and rowing to the British warship HMS *Roebuck*, one of the vessels in Lord John Dunmore's fleet, when it was in the vicinity of Willoughby's Point. Two years later, Willoughby's son unsuccessfully attempted to sue for compensation for the loss of the enslaved people from the Virginia legislature, believing that the state's actions resulted in those enslaved men, women and children being left unguarded and able to flee to the British. The *Virginia Gazette* reported on May 10, 1776, that sixty to seventy blacks fled to Lord Dunmore's fleet.[9]

Mary Perth was one such refugee who ended up aboard one of Dunmore's ships. Before the war, she was John Willoughby's slave on his Princess Anne County plantation. Mary and her daughter Patience were among the slaves who left the area aboard the British fleet and were transported to New York City. There she married Caesar Perth, a former Norfolk slave. At war's end, when the British evacuated New York, the couple, Mary's daughter Patience and two orphans from the Willoughby plantation sailed aboard *L'Abondance* to Nova Scotia. They settled at Birchtown, but they regarded their conditions as no better than when they were enslaved. Nine years later, in 1792, because of the poor conditions for blacks in this newly established English colony, Mary, Caesar and Patience immigrated to Sierra Leone. Caesar died shortly afterward, and Mary supported her family as the housekeeper for Governor Zachary Macaulay and as a teacher of African children.[10]

An Inventory of John Willoughby's Slaves

Females	Age	Offspring	Males	Age	Occupation
Plana	55	1 girl	Saser	60	sawyer
Nancy	46	4 girls	Toby	54	
Mary	40	2 girls, 2 boys	Ned	44	
Judy	28	3 girls, 2 boys	Peter	37	half carpenter
Lucy	25	1 girl, 8 boys	James	35	shoemaker
Keziah	23	3 boys	Robin	24	sawyer
Cate	30	2 girls, 1 boy	Bob	30	
Rachel	25	4 boys	Charles	24	
Easter	27	4 boys	Glasgow	21	
Sesise	23	1 girl	Wills	21	
Jenny	42		Anthony	19	
Lindah	27	2 girls, 2 boys	George	18	
Manda	25	3 boys	Jacob	20	
Dinah	26	2 girls	Isaac	16	
Lydia	26	2 girls, 1 boy	Brister	20	sawyer
Abby	29	3 boys	Moses	25	house servant
Beth	23	1 girl			
Jenny	30				
Jessie	16				
Nell	25	2 girls			
Peg	18				

This listing of fugitives was an example of how enslaved African Americans often fled in family groups aboard British vessels early in the war. From the Willoughby petition, *Journal of the House of Delegates of the Commonwealth of Virginia* (Richmond, 1827), 55.

Caesar and Mary Perth were among the thousands waiting to evacuate New York at war's end. And despite strong objections from General George Washington and the U.S. Congress, British commander Sir Henry Clinton, who had promised the former slaves protection and liberty, transported them to Nova Scotia in 1783. These self-emancipating freedom seekers' singular goal was freedom, and the Loyalist cause was seen as their avenue to liberty from slavery. It was from Virginia—the colony often called the "mother of the nation" by writers because it was the first and most populous colony in America—that many of these freedom seekers fled. Yet the American Revolution was only one of many events used by freedom seekers in their quest for independence.[11]

Freedom Seekers, 1783

Examples of Black Loyalists Leaving from New York to Nova Scotia in 1783

Taken from the *Book of Negroes*.

Peter Moses, 27, stout man, (Pioneer, KAD). Formerly the property of General Balford of Hampton, Virginia, says that at his death got his freedom about 8 years ago.

London Jackson, 32, stout fellow, pilot by order (Capt. Mowat). Formerly slave to William Ballad, Hampton, Virginia; left him two years past.

Nelly Jackson, 33, stout wench. Formerly slave to Hampstead Bailie, Hampton, Virginia; left him two years past.

Nancy Walker, 21, likely wench, M, (on her own bottom). Formerly slave to Col. Cornel, Hampton, Virginia; left him two years past.

Lewis Moore, 50, stout fellow, (Engineer Department). Formerly slave to Mr. Moore, Hampton County, Virginia; left him 3 years ago. GBC.

Joe, 26, stout fellow, B, (Peter Parker). Formerly slave to William Bennet, Hampton, Virginia; left him 3 years ago.

Hannah his wife, 21, stout wench, B, 2 small children, (Peter Parker). Formerly slave to Ned Cooper, Hampton, Virginia; left him 3 years ago.

Nancy McKay, 20, stout wench, formerly the property of Francis Ballard of Hampton, Virginia; left him 3 years ago. GBC.

Hannah Miller, 21, stout wench & child 1 year old. Formerly the property of Colonel Carnel of Hampton, Virginia; left him 4 years ago.

Jonathan Glasgow, 39, stout man. Formerly the property of William Curle, Hampton, Virginia; left him 3 years ago.

Pamela Glasgow, 30, stout wench with a girl 8 years old. Formerly the property of James Barrow, Hampton, Virginia; left him 3 years ago.

James Thompson, 25, stout fellow. Formerly the property of Edward Cooper, Hampton, Virginia; left him 3 years ago.

Hannah Johnson, 40, stout wench, (Thomas Cartwright). Formerly the property of Simon Hallyar, Hampton, Virginia; left him 4 years ago. GBC. J

James With, 24, stout fellow, (Col. Stewart). Formerly slave to George With, Hampton, Virginia; left him in 1779. GMC.

Rachel Wilson, 34, stout wench, (Wagon Master General Department). Formerly the property of William Curl of Hampton, Virginia; left him 5 years ago.

Pomp Wilson, 54, stout fellow, (Wagon Master General Department). Formerly the property of William Curl, Hampton, Virginia; left him 5 years ago. GMC.

Charles Sweeney, 40, stout fellow. Formerly slave to Major Sweeney, Hampton, Virginia. GMC.

Richard Price, 30, stout fellow. Formerly slave to James Price, Hampton, Virginia; left him in 1776. GMC.

Charles Barren, 25, stout fellow. Formerly slave to James Barren, Hampton, Virginia; left him in 1778. GMC.

The emerging slave system in the burgeoning colony of Virginia set a pattern for the original settlement design in the Tidewater region, which spanned from Richmond to Norfolk. The tobacco plantations located along the James and York Rivers prospered in the eighteenth century while the Lower Tidewater area grew based on its maritime industry. In Norfolk's port, enslaved men operated boats, barges and ferries in addition to being trained as ship artisans and pilots. Eventually, this became a lucrative source of revenue for white owners, who then hired out slaves skilled in the shipbuilding trades, helping Norfolk to become a prominent maritime center prior to the American Revolution. However, the time of slaveholders' greatest prosperity also spurred increased flight from slavery—particularly with the threat of being sold down South—especially from those who hired out their own time, because of their mobility. This relative liberty allowed some to connect with ship captains and crews who plied the seas. By the mid-eighteenth century, slaveholders and colonial leaders noted that these waterways, avenues for prosperity in trade, were also routes to freedom and a source of angst for those intending to maintain a system of enslavement.[12]

The Jamestown settlement, founded in 1607 as "a profit-oriented trading station," was populated initially by an immigrant elite who created a self-governing colony where half the population were servants. Although there was no initial plan to follow the example of Portugal and Spain to establish an economy or society based on slavery, the shift from "collective farms to private gardens" encouraged English privateers and traders to bring Africans into English North America as a supplement to its workforce, beginning in 1619. By 1625, ten of the elite members who governed the colony owned half of all the servants, creating a society that was clearly divided between the very wealthy and the extreme poor. As a result, for some decades, white indentured servants worked alongside black servants until black servitude proved more economical and posed fewer problems for landowners. Yet almost immediately, this unfree labor group experienced efforts by whites to make their bondage permanent, resulting in the evolution of a system of enslavement by the 1650s.[13]

Beginning with the arrival of the first recorded Africans from Angola in the Virginia colony, the English colonists enacted laws restricting the rights and freedoms of Africans that also enhanced their own wealth. From the beginning, Africans were considered "unfree" but not yet legal slaves. Unlike England's West Indian colonies, which were not seen as an extension of English society but rather a purely economic enterprise, Virginia was both an extension and an economic venture.[14]

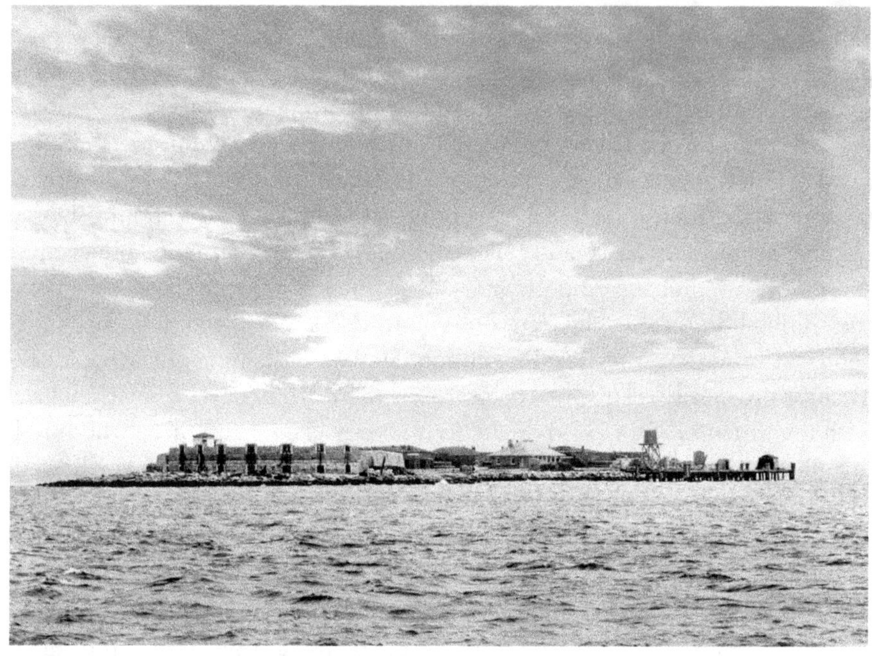

This image, circa 1900–1920, looking toward the Rip Raps from Fort Monroe in Hampton, Virginia, shows Virginia's inspection station. In the mid-1850s, officials were on the lookout for fugitives on ships bound for northern ports. The goal was to capture any enslaved persons seeking freedom aboard these vessels. The body of water where all the major rivers in Tidewater Virginia flow into the Chesapeake Bay and Atlantic Ocean is called the Hampton Roads. *Library of Congress.*

Throughout the 1630s and 1640s, court cases and local ordinances in Virginia, Maryland and Massachusetts highlighted how African servants were not treated the same as English (or European) servants. Frequently, last names of Africans were not recognized. Laws were passed forbidding Africans to bear arms, and they were restricted from having sexual contact with whites (presumably to protect whites from any legal rights of inheritance claims from blacks). By the 1640s, colonial courts and legislatures began to make legal distinctions between whites and backs. Bills of sale placed a higher value on black servants, illustrating that Africans were, no doubt, held permanently in bondage. These bills of sale also declared that the children of these Africans were to be slaves for life.[15]

All these things occurred twenty-five years before blacks would comprise even one-fifth of the population of Virginia and before slavery or black labor became an important part of the southern economy. It seemed that across all classes of white colonial society, negative feelings toward Africans and

African Americans grew, in part, propelled by court cases and the passage of restrictive laws. The very existence of black slavery provided a sense of separateness and unity to whites of gentry, middling or commoner classes.[16]

Throughout the colonial and early antebellum years, the settlement pattern was focused along the waterways of the York and James Rivers, where the great plantations with their wharves and industries were based. During this period, the wealthier areas of the Tidewater region became the "emergent black belt." Yet even with the Tidewater's development, settlements were scattered, with the primarily enslaved labor force dispersed throughout the region on the plantations of the elite. The exception was the port town of Norfolk. But even there, most of the handful of blacks were usually sailors on foreign and domestic ships or were brought to Norfolk as servants from the West Indies, especially the Spanish Caribbean. Between 1630 and 1660, one hundred officeholders owned a small number of black servants or slaves. According to historian John Coombs, the most affluent white planters owned between ten and twenty blacks. For example, Samuel Matthews in Warwick County (Newport News today) owned "40 Negro servants" in the late 1640s. That number did not change significantly during this period. In 1669, David Fox and Colonel John Carter of Lancaster County owned a total of seventy-six laborers, with forty-three of that number being enslaved black people. Clearly, slaveholding was the prerogative of the elites, despite the annual arrival of nearly ten thousand enslaved people after 1660.[17]

By the 1690s, the gentry's workforce was almost entirely enslaved, while 25 to 40 percent of ordinary planters had white servants until the eighteenth century. Not until 1720 did blacks make up 20 percent of the population (30,600 blacks out of a total population of 158,600). After the 1730s, Africans and African Americans would make up 40 to 45 percent of the population (138,000), but by 1763, the populations were equal (170,000 each). In 1775, some 500,000 black people lived in Virginia, with 50 percent free and enslaved Africans. That number would soon be over half, with blacks increasing by 18,000, while the white population remained constant.[18]

Population density was even low in heavily populated towns, such as Gloucester, Elizabeth City, York and James City. Yet even though the population was small, many of these towns, and later cities of Hampton and Norfolk, were magnets for runaways because of their proximity to the waterways and to the colony's main port. Runaway advertisements provide clues about this activity beginning in the 1730s. But perhaps what is most surprising about these early decades was that the majority of runaways were white servants rather than black enslaved men and women. That would quickly change, however, by the 1740s, as the numbers of the enslaved grew in size. And unlike the Caribbean, the enslaved were distributed among the areas settled by white Virginians, especially along the major rivers of the James, York and Rappahannock.[19]

Historian Gerald Mullin provided clues as to why fugitives were attracted to the port areas, estimating that approximately one-fourth of all runaways in Virginia were mariners (between 1736 and 1801). Mullin said, "The small sloops conducting Chesapeake Bay's internal commerce, according to Virginia's Governor William Gooch in 1730, relied on 'planters with negroes.'" When tobacco regulation began in 1730, new laws were established that expanded trade and created public warehouses and tobacco inspections. The hogsheads of tobacco, previously hauled to the plantations located at the tributaries, were now moved to the seaports, such as Norfolk, in bay craft manned by slaves.[20]

In fact, eighteenth-century Lower Tidewater Virginia witnessed the dominance of the maritime industry, a business that eventually depended heavily upon the presence of slave watermen. On many of the large plantations along the James and York Rivers, owners trained almost all their male slaves as watermen and for general plantation work. This was especially true in Norfolk, Virginia's primary port, where slaves operated boats, barges and ferries in addition to being trained as ship artisans and pilots. Many whites also apprenticed their slaves to white shipbuilders to learn the trade of ship ironers, blacksmiths, carpenters, sawyers, axe men and ship riggers. This became a lucrative source of revenue for the white owners, who then hired out slaves skilled in the shipbuilding trades and helped Norfolk to become a prominent maritime center prior to the American Revolution.[21]

While the maritime industry was expanding in Lower Tidewater, London merchants' grip was loosening on trade and being supplanted by merchants in Norfolk, Annapolis and Charleston. The creation of a Virginia-owned Chesapeake merchant fleet helped Norfolk's emergence as a maritime center, replacing Philadelphia as the shipbuilding center second only to New England. This mercantile prominence bolstered the maritime experience of blacks and their acquaintance with the area's rivers and creeks. Most shipwrights became significant employers of black skilled laborers (carpenters, lather workers and blacksmiths), resulting in the domination of certain industries by blacks, such as Virginia's ironworks.[22]

In 1637, Philip Lightfoot reported the escape of Tidewater resident Amos. Described as a mulatto who resembled someone from Madagascar, Amos was last seen offering "a Reward to an Oysterman to transport him across the Bay." More than likely, the objective was to get to a place where he could disappear within one of the cities or secure passage on a ship leaving the area.[23] There were also accounts of free blacks who were helping enslaved men, such as Warrah, an enslaved African who had only been in Virginia for four years, to escape. His owner, Andrew Giles from Warwick County, remarked that Warrah's escape was assisted by a free black. Giles also provided a very detailed physical description of Warrah, who had attempted to escape but was subsequently caught and locked up in the Isle of Wight courthouse until his owner secured him.[24]

What was unclear from some of the advertisements published in the 1730s was where the runaways would go. Most headed where they might disappear within a city or town. That would change beginning in 1751, as illustrated in the runaway slave advertisements, with many escaping to port cities in the hopes of leaving the colony. In that year, twenty-nine slaves and thirty-nine indentured servants were advertised for recovery. Presumably, all of the servants were white and the slaves black—although there may have been a few exceptions. The following year would see even more servants and slaves escaping, with thirty-eight slaves and fifty-three servants leaving plantations along Virginia's Tidewater waterways spanning from the mouth of the Chesapeake Bay and along the major rivers, including the James, York, Rappahannock and Potomac. While most of the runaways were Virginians, some also came from North Carolina, such as an enslaved family of five (Mingo, Phillis, Peter, Judy and Fanney) who escaped from Thomas Willis and were caught in Williamsburg, either trying to blend into that town's free population or attempting to flee farther north. It is unknown what happened to this family. By 1767, clearly the majority of those escaping were enslaved (seventy-five slaves and twenty-seven servants), illustrating not only Virginia's shift in its labor force but also its natural increase in the numbers of enslaved people.[25]

In May 1751, Charles escaped from his owner in York County by hiding out in Hampton or Jamestown. Presumably, he went toward Hampton because of the numerous black sailors and seamen who worked aboard vessels along the wharves and in the vicinity of this important seaport. Likewise, Dick escaped from Williamsburg in September of that same year and was thought to be working as a ferryman in Hampton. There were others, such as George and Boatswain, who escaped from their owner from Sarah's Creek in Gloucester County while visiting Hampton in August 1752. No doubt, Boatswain, probably named because of his skill in sailing, thought it more possible to escape aboard a ship destined for freedom from

Hampton than farther inland. Similarly, Mingo from Yorktown pretended to be on business from his owner to secure passage aboard ships departing from Hampton. One can only speculate that many of these freedom seekers, who took the opportunity to escape to Hampton, thought that the shipping traffic would provide opportunity and cover for their escape within or from that region.[26]

A decade later, running away became even more intense, with primarily enslaved men fleeing to port cities and towns in Tidewater. In 1761, Christopher Wright of Norfolk advertised that his sister's thirty-three-year-old Virginian slave Ned was a tall, "grim countenanced, obstinate man who was apt to give surly answers" and had been allowed to hire himself out for several years. Wright thought that he was attempting to pass for a freeman, and since he was accustomed to the maritime trade and had a wife on the Eastern Shore, no doubt he would be found there. In August 1772, slave owner Josiah Riddick of Suffolk advertised that a white man, James Nickolas, carried away his slave Boson and a flat containing forty barrels of tar that was to have been delivered to Norfolk. Riddick noted, "I have heard that such a Flat, and Hands, were seen going up the Bay, and on the eastern shore of Maryland."[27]

Demographic changes fueled by frequent sales spurred more frequent escapes by freedom seekers. As the population increased, lucrative slave sales separated or threated to separate families. From 1650 to 1671, Virginia's African population jumped from three hundred to two thousand. Ten years later, the African population was three thousand. By 1699, twelve thousand Africans, out of a population of seventy thousand people, inhabited Virginia. The rising black population also created uneasiness among Virginia's white population, resulting in repressive legal measures and increased plantation discipline. In fact, according to historian Lorena Walsh, "The society became enmeshed in an ever-tightening spiral of racism and repression that left slaves few hopes for gaining their freedom or improving their status."[28]

By 1770, the population in Virginia had risen to about 437,000; in Hampton Roads, it was approximately 20,000, with 42 percent of African descent.[29] This demographic reality became a particular problem for the white colonists at the start of the Revolutionary conflict. For example, twenty-six-year-old Bob, who was enslaved on a plantation near the southern branch of the Meherrin River in Mecklenburg County, had apparently attempted to escape on several occasions. A skilled fiddler and singer, Bob frequently passed himself off as a freeman named Robert Chavers, according to his owner. Clearly, this was his name, a fact that his owner refused to acknowledge. In June 1774, he was caught in Norfolk but managed to break out of the city's jail and was last seen on Craney Island making his way toward Hampton, doubtless in an effort to disappear as a free person or to connect with British ships or Loyalists.[30]

It was common for many to run away to Hampton Roads with the hope of passing for free persons by disappearing among the black populace. John Emanuel, a sailor who for years had passed as a freeman in Norfolk, often told the curious that he was part of a crew recently shipwrecked on the seacoast nearby. However, Emanuel, like many other runaways, was unsuccessful in maintaining this ruse, and he was eventually apprehended and returned to his owner in 1774. Another slave, a mulatto woman named Peg, from Essex County, was seen hailing a ship anchored off the banks of the Rappahannock River near Layton's warehouses. She reportedly told the

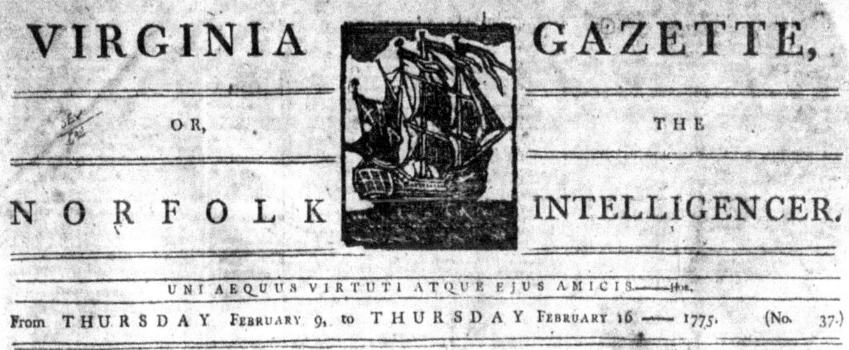

VIRGINIA GAZETTE,
OR, THE
NORFOLK INTELLIGENCER.
UNI AEQUUS VIRTUTI ATQUE EJUS AMICIS.—Hor.
From THURSDAY FEBRUARY 9, to THURSDAY FEBRUARY 16 — 1775. (No. 37.)

RUN AWAY

From the Brig INNERMAY lying at Brandon; on James river the 27th of December laſt, an Apprentice lad named William Johnſton about 17 or 18 years of age five feet ſix inches high, ſwarthy complexioned and a little pitted with the ſmall pox, knock-knee'd, he was born in or near Williamſburg, where it is ſuppoſed he is now harboured, he carried with him a new ſailors Jacket, blue duffle breetches lined with white plaid and white metal buttons, a green cloth ... quet pretty much wore, a blue and white broad flapp'd cloth coloured thread under Jacket, country made ſhoes and ſtockings, one or two pair of ſailors trowſers, and his bed clothes. Whoever ſecures him ſo that I get him again, ſhall have Fifteen Shillings reward. All Captains of Ships, or Maſters of Veſſels, are forewarned from carrying him out of the Country or employing him.

JAMES BELCHES.

CABIN-POINT, January 3d, 1775. 35

This is a typical advertisement seen in the *Virginia Gazette* during the eighteenth century. *From the* Virginia Gazette.

skipper that she wanted to go to Norfolk. He promptly sent his flat and two black crewmen to carry her aboard, and she was not heard from again.[31]

Other freedom seekers had even better luck—although not without demonstrating considerable determination. Amelia County fugitive Dick fled to Portsmouth in May 1774 and lived as a freeman working as a carpenter until he was captured and taken to Charles City County. However, even recapture did not deter Dick, who soon escaped again, returning to the Hampton Roads area by the summer of 1775. At that time, Dick enlisted with the Princess Ann County militia under the alias Will Thompson. When his company came to the capital of Williamsburg, he was discovered by his owner, recaptured and jailed. Ever persistent, Dick escaped one final time, returning to Princess Ann County and disappearing, seemingly achieving his goal of boarding a ship and leaving the colony.[32]

With the outbreak of the American Revolution at Lexington and Concord in April 1775, Virginia was quickly on the side of the Patriots, with the exception of the Lower Tidewater region, where Loyalist support centered in the Norfolk port area. Hearing of the rising tide of support for rebellion against England, Lord John Dunmore, governor of the largest colony in America, quickly left the capital in Williamsburg to set up a defense perimeter in anticipation of war with the American colonists. Dunmore attempted to take advantage of the large population of enslaved blacks in Virginia, issuing a proclamation in November promising freedom in exchange for bearing arms against the Rebels. The governor believed this would be especially effective in Tory-friendly towns such as Norfolk, which soon became the center of early fighting. Approximately three hundred Tidewater slaves joined Lord Dunmore in Norfolk one week after the November proclamation, while a total of eight hundred joined him prior to his leaving the area. During this attack, Norfolk was burned, convincing Virginians that no compromise was possible with the British. Ironically, by the end of the Revolution, Norfolk's Tory merchants, anticipating British victory, fostered Norfolk's rebuilding.[33]

The year after Dunmore's proclamation was issued, the Virginia Council decreed that counties with navigable waters should position guards around all boats that blacks might use to escape. Virginia's Governor Patrick Henry asked the council to advise him on how to restrict blacks from fleeing from Northampton and Accomack Counties. So desperate were Virginia's slave owners to secure the return of the freedom seekers that the Virginia Council permitted two American officers to board British ships at York and Hampton to request their return.[34]

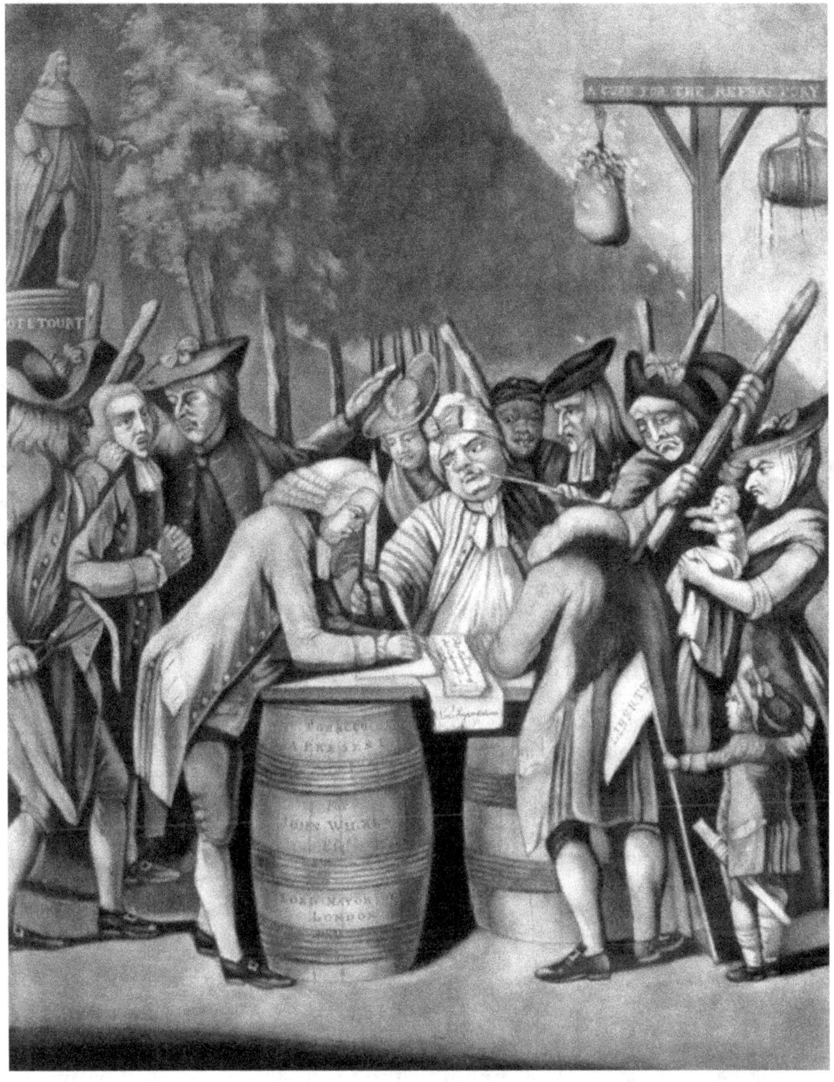

This Philip Dawe print illustrates the conflict between the Loyalists in Lower Tidewater and the larger group of Patriots. In this 1775 depiction, the Loyalist is being forced to sign a pledge by a club-wielding mob. At the same time, the other is being led to the gallows while on the right is a sack of feathers and a barrel of tar. *Library of Congress.*

Not surprisingly, the issues of freedom and slavery became an important component in the national debates at the start of the American Revolution, especially as activities by freedom seekers increased because of disruptions caused by the war. Some took advantage of the British invasion of the

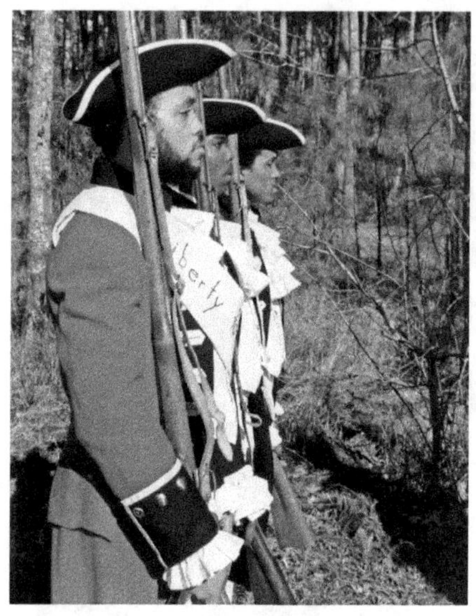

This image depicts a modern-day reenactment of the December 1776 Battle of Great Bridge in which Portsmouth native William Flora (1755–1820) stood his ground, defending against the British attack. Flora's bravery was credited with an American victory that forced the British to withdraw from Hampton Roads, taking a number of black and white Loyalists with them. He was rewarded with freedom and a one-hundred-acre land bounty. *Portsmouth Public Library and Mae Breckenridge-Haywood.*

area by joining Lord Dunmore's Ethiopian Regiment or one of the other British units that sought to take advantage of the enslaved manpower. For example, twenty-four freedom seekers from Hampton alone were listed in the *Book of Negroes* as departing aboard British vessels bound for Halifax, Nova Scotia, and presumably freedom. The numbers departing from Norfolk and Portsmouth were even higher. What is interesting about these records is that almost all of those who departed were not listed with first and last names (which enslaved people had but slaveholders refused to acknowledge because it would bestow the very humanity that slavery was designed to strip away). Moreover, similar to runaway slave accounts, these individuals were described by age and physicality (height, distinguishing marks, body type, how long ago they left their owners and gender).[35]

Blacks were fully aware of the hypocrisy and shortsightedness inherent in the whites' reasoning for revolution. They knew that white Virginians did not plan to extend basic rights and freedoms to slaves and did not question the injustice of African enslavement in the myriad speeches and pamphlets condemning oppression and tyranny. Still, blacks took heart as the words *independence* and *liberty* became common currency.[36] And while the colonial press tagged the British as "oppressors" and "tyrants," most slaves saw them as potential saviors. Their enslavers' enemy had to be their friend. Likely, they also knew about the celebrated decision of Britain's high court in the Somerset case, a ruling that raised fundamental questions about slavery because of the growing fear by slaveholders throughout the British Empire of what they perceived as the abolitionist threat. Virginia newspapers, such as the *Virginia Gazette*, published a long account of the 1771 trial of

James Somerset, an enslaved man from Jamaica who was visiting London with his owner. While in the capital city, Somerset escaped from his owner but was recaptured and forcibly returned to Jamaica. Somerset's interests were championed by abolitionist Granville Sharp. Eventually, Chief Justice Lord Mansfield ruled that slaveholders could not sell an English slave to another country. Slaveholders pushed back, claiming that this decision would effectively overrun England with poor and idle blacks, thus setting a pattern for the fear-mongering that accompanied the presence of free blacks in communities throughout English America.[37]

Regardless of efforts to deter freedom seekers, historian Cassandra Pybus observed that fugitives premeditated their escapes, using a well-organized communication network to assist in connecting with British ships in the area. When British ships returned to the Chesapeake region between 1779 and 1781, slaves continued their flight whenever British ships or troops appeared. Charles ran away from his owner Robert Brent from Stafford County in 1775 to join Lord Dunmore. His owner believed his departure was "long premeditated." Still others used the disruptions to reconnect with family or to obtain freedom on their own terms. In 1779, for example, a young boy named George escaped from his master in Hampton with a captain named Lee, who ferried people and goods between Hampton and Philadelphia. George's owner believed he was trying to make it to the Eastern Shore in Maryland, no doubt because he had family there. Unlike George, a year later, twenty-one-year-old runaway Isaac was believed to be seeking work in Hampton, Portsmouth or Richmond. A skilled ship carpenter, Isaac probably believed he could pass as a freeman or gain passage aboard one of the ships departing Virginia. Precept from Pungoteague in Accomack County on the Eastern Shore also escaped in 1780. His owner, William Walker, noted in an advertisement that he believed Precept would try to connect with the British fleet and eventually return to his home in the French West Indies.[38]

Alan Kulikoff's *Tobacco and Slaves* asserted that as many as 3,000 to 5,000 black men joined the British throughout the war, taking advantage of the conflict to obtain freedom. Yet even these figures represent a small portion of the colony's 250,000 slaves. Tom, a thirty-two-year-old slave who was described in a runaway advertisement as having "remarkable red eyes," ran off from Goochland County owner Francis Boykin in September 1775 and joined the British forces. By January of the following year, he had left Dunmore's "crew" and sought his freedom elsewhere. Others sought escape in the general instability. Will, "very sensible, and a great Rogue," broke jail in Brunswick County in September 1776. Jailer George Walker

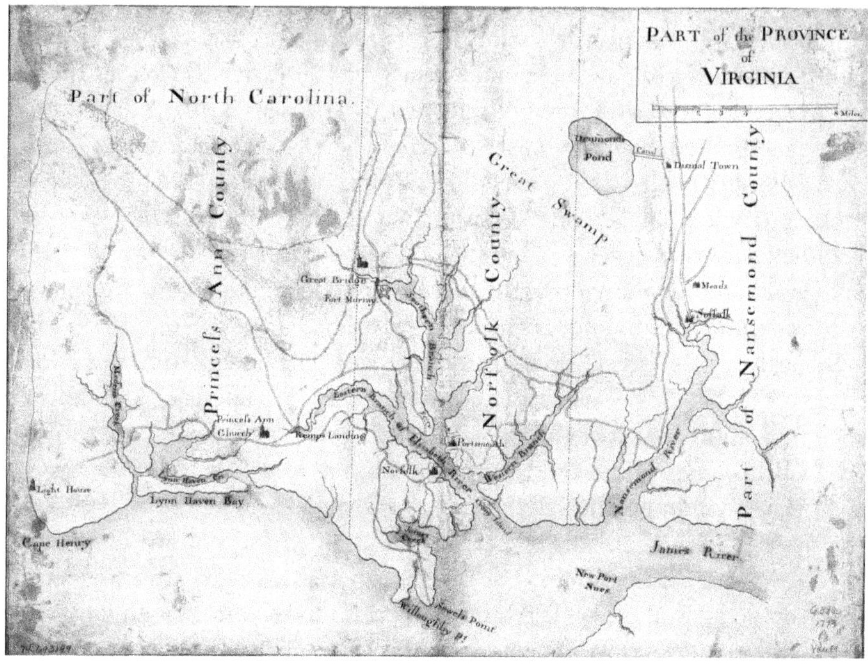

This map of Lower Tidewater includes portions of "Princess Anne" and Norfolk Counties, where much Loyalist and British activity occurred during the American Revolution. The map points out military action sites during the early days of the Revolutionary War, including the Battle of Kemp's Landing, the Battle of Great Bridge, the Burning of Norfolk and the Battle of the Chesapeake. *Library of Congress, Geography and Maps Division.*

advertised that Will was "well acquainted with Nansemond, Norfolk, and Elizabeth City Counties," and he believed the runaway would make for "the Frontiers, as he was seen lately going upwards, had an Axe with him, and declared he would leave the Country." Walker concluded with a warning to slave catchers to "iron him well," as Will "expects to be hanged" and was "dexterous at breaking Doors, &c." Whether Will intended to join the British is uncertain. What was clear during this period was the ongoing and persistent efforts exhibited by enslaved persons to be free. In fact, a number of slaves who ran off to join Dunmore had already run for freedom once, and their actions provided ample testimony that the bondsmen who joined the British possessed a sincere desire for freedom.[39]

Ithiel Town's account, *A Detail of Some Particular Services Performed in America During the Years 1776–1779*, noted that hundreds of enslaved African Americans fled plantations in Norfolk, Nansemond and Princess Anne

Counties during the British attack on Hampton Roads that eventually destroyed both Norfolk and Portsmouth. In May 1779, British vice admiral Sir George Collier dispatched a fleet of ships under the army detachment of General Edward Matthew to launch a punitive raid on the tobacco warehouses in Portsmouth, Norfolk and Norfolk County at large. Gathering his forces on Craney Island, Collier reported that most of the fugitives had kinship ties to a charismatic Methodist slave preacher named Moses Wilkinson, who had joined Lord Dunmore's Ethiopian Regiment after the November 7, 1775 proclamation was issued, which called upon all enslaved men to join Dunsmore to fight against the American Rebels in exchange for freedom. Assisted by John Goodridge's privateer ships, the British removed 256 men, 135 women and 127 children who were held as slaves in the area following this raid. Eventually, this group was taken to New York, and some became members of Reverend Wilkinson's Methodist congregation in New York.[40]

At the conclusion of the war, and after the Treaty of Paris was signed in 1783 following the protracted peace negotiations, the British made preparations to evacuate all personnel from New York. Some 750 black men, women and children who had sided with the British were transported by ships to Nova Scotia, including Reverend Wilkinson's congregants, with as many as 374 of the expatriates coming from the Norfolk area. Contrary to the anti-British propaganda spread by the Patriots, British officers gave refuge to fugitive women and children as well as men of fighting age. Of that number, 166 of the local émigrés were men; 137 were women, and 71 were children.[41]

Although conditions were harsh in the frigid climate of Nova Scotia, many Hampton Roads refugees made the province their new home, while others disliked the conditions that too closely resembled those from which they escaped—namely conditions of slavery. It seems that Nova Scotia was not altogether unfriendly to slaveholding. Because the newly formed colony was predominantly homogeneous, this sudden influx of people of color was met with prejudice and resentment. Many quickly found that their only employment opportunities resembled those during slavery. Household labor appeared to be the dominant occupation for many of the refugees, although limited opportunities for tradesmen existed. Consequently, in 1792, 1,190 people, including Reverend Moses Wilkinson's Methodist congregation, embarked on a forty-day journey to Sierra Leone, where ongoing hardships and challenges met this fledging group of pioneers who sought a life free from prejudice and enslavement.[42]

From the first forced arrival of Africans to the Americas, the quest for freedom guided their journey and defined a spirit of black agency and self-emancipation. This journey emerged stronger following the American Revolution, a robust and ongoing river that unleashed egalitarianism sentiment that would drive freedom seekers to find avenues to liberty, despite ongoing and state-sponsored barriers. In spite of persistent efforts by national and regional agencies to stymie those efforts to achieve freedom, black agency endured and expanded by force and by flight in an effort to realize freedom—in what was ironically called the "land of the free"—through the eventual formation of a national system called the Underground Railroad.

2

ORIGINS OF ABOLITIONISM AND THE EMERGING UNDERGROUND RAILROAD IN VIRGINIA

With only a few months left in office, President George Washington faced a conundrum that other slaveholders, lawmakers and supporters of slavery faced. His slave Ona Judge Staines took the opportunity to flee to Portsmouth, New Hampshire, while serving in the Executive Mansion in Philadelphia. Undoubtedly, her proximity to a state that had recently abolished slavery and her impending return to Mount Vernon, Virginia, the nation's slaveholding capital, prompted her escape. Staines was the daughter of a white servant, Andrew Judge, and an enslaved seamstress, Betty. Following in her mother's footsteps, Ona Staines was also an accomplished seamstress and therefore considered an asset to the first family. At the age of fifteen, she was forced to leave her family in Mount Vernon and travel to Philadelphia during Washington's tenure in office. Fearing that this was her last chance at freedom, toward the end of Washington's second term, Staines boarded a ship captained by John Bowles bound for Portsmouth, New Hampshire, with the assistance of some members of Philadelphia's African American community. However, word soon reached Washington of her whereabouts, and he quickly wrote letters soliciting help in securing her return.[43]

Frustrated with his inability to secure the return of Staines, Washington wrote to Joseph Whipple, whom he had appointed as Portsmouth, New Hampshire's customs collector:[44]

> *However well disposed I might be to gradual abolition, or even to gradual emancipation of that description of people (if the latter was in itself*

> *practicable) at this moment it would neither be politic nor just to reward unfaithfulness with a premature preference, and thereby discontent beforehand the minds of all her fellow serv'ts, who, by their steady attachment, are far more deserving than herself of favor.*[45]

Clearly, the antislavery sentiment was growing in northern states, and Washington was unwilling to make his efforts public, which would have been required to secure Staines's return. Eventually Staines found a new life, love and freedom in Greenland, New Hampshire.[46]

Ona Staines was like many black freedom seekers during the era who, with some assistance, sought liberty. Following the American Revolution and the departure of thousands of enslaved men, women and children who supported the English Crown during the war, the British abandoned the trans-Appalachian West per the 1783 Treaty of Paris, fueling efforts by land-hungry white settlers to occupy this land. Their efforts triggered an

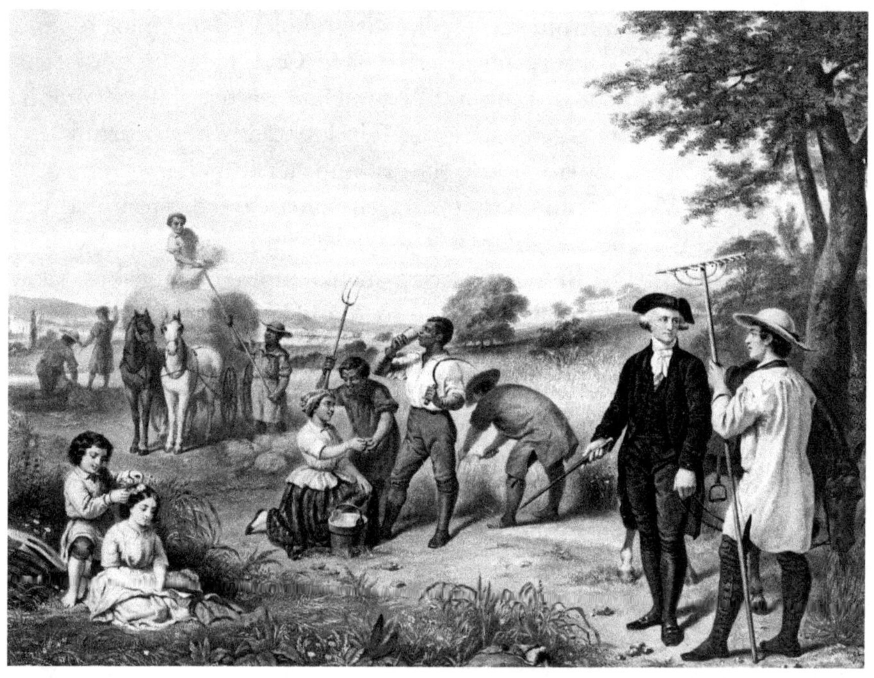

This 1853 painting by Junius Stearns provides an idyllic portrayal of George Washington's life on his Mount Vernon plantation. Rather than depicting the true horrors of slave life, this image casts Washington as almost an aloof master focusing on ensuring that the grain is harvested while African American slaves are seen leisurely going about their work. *Library of Congress.*

increased demand for enslaved labor, particularly young men. In addition, the invention of the cotton gin relaunched the cotton industry and generated a dire need for enslaved labor. Yet at the time when America's economy most needed increased numbers of enslaved workers, America's participation in the transatlantic slave trade would end by constitutional edict in 1808.[47]

Not to be deterred by these challenges, America's white planters stepped up the transmigration of enslaved Africans from the Caribbean, especially Cuba. They also put in place policies that would increase domestic reproduction of enslaved workers, pressuring enslaved women to have children because their value in the Chesapeake region was now focused on their breeding capabilities, reducing their worth to the most basic of functions: propagation.[48]

From the 1790s to the end of the Civil War, the separation of African American families became the norm in America; this separation was the flame that fueled innumerable insurrections and flights.[49] Indeed, as historian Ira Berlin commented, the Revolution "initiated significant changes in black life, unleashing radical egalitarianism upon which the abolitionist movement, the wartime expansion, the promise of Reconstruction, and the long struggle against Jim Crow rested."[50]

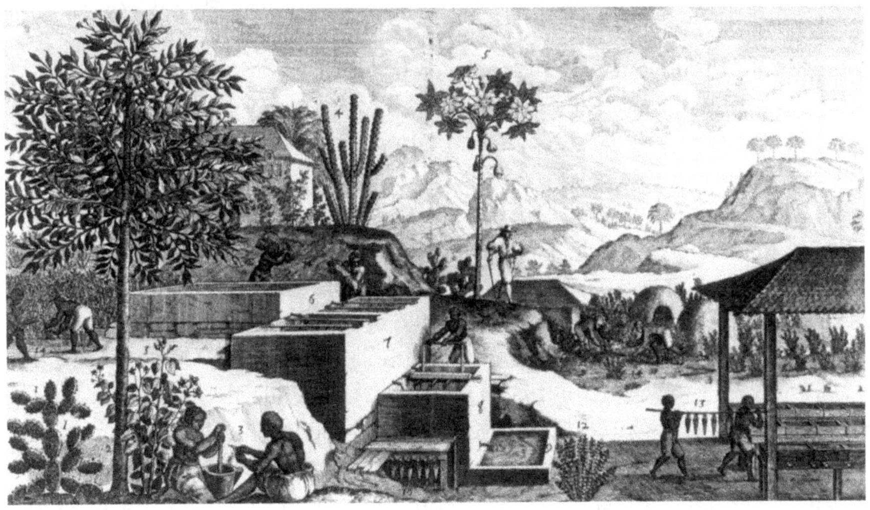

The transatlantic slave trade dominated the global economy from the sixteenth through the first part of the nineteenth centuries. The trade was particularly influential in the West Indies, where the African populations replaced most of the indigenous peoples and produced needed products for Europe, such as indigo, featured in this 1667 engraving. *Library of Congress.*

It was in this period that a fleeting but widespread abolitionist tone emerged, briefly resulting in a movement that would push for immediate or gradual emancipation of slavery. Vermont abolished slavery in its constitution in 1777, and Massachusetts declared, in its 1780 constitution, that all men were born equal and free. Yet these measures did not result in emancipation until prompted by a lawsuit that same year. Other New England states gradually followed suit, but the fight to end slavery took longer in the Mid-Atlantic states because of their vested interest in the institution. In the Upper South, manumission acts allowed individual slaveholders to free their slaves, but in the Lower South, slavery remained an important avenue for economic prosperity and social management.[51]

Beginning in the 1780s, the spiritual movement known as the Second Great Awakening swept through Virginia. Local officials began complaining that the white Baptists and Methodists, two denominations that developed primarily from this spiritual revival, were secretly meeting at night with slaves, sometimes in integrated religious services. One reason many African Americans—free and bond—were attracted to these two denominations was because the religious message was different. The focus was on the afterlife—heaven was preached as a place of peace, rest and freedom—not on obedience here on earth. In addition, the Baptists encouraged the ministries of people called "Negro exhorters," whose credentials lay more in their belief of whether they were called to preach as opposed to formal ministerial training. The Great Awakening also transformed established religious groups, such as the Quakers, into social activists.[52]

This abolitionist spirit affected the Upper South. Virginia passed a 1782 manumission law that allowed individual slaveholders to petition the state legislature to free their slaves. However, with the cotton gin's creation and ease of reproduction, slavery was once again seen as profitable. Cotton production in Georgia, South Carolina, Virginia and other southern states reinvigorated the institution and redirected attention to cultivating a powerful domestic trade. This resulted in the inevitable hardening of slavery and the separation of thousands of black families. And while it would be initially enslaved men who would be sold from the Upper to the Lower South, the lure of money ensured that enslaved women and children would also be part of this devil's bargain as America's economy turned toward dependence on cotton production and an enslaved labor force.[53]

Championed by the Quakers in Virginia, a precedent-setting manumission statute in Virginia that resulted from this revolutionary and evangelical spirit sweeping the nation was passed on May 6, 1782. The result was the liberation of fifteen thousand of Virginia's slaves between 1782 and 1810. Of these, 35 percent were freed through the purchase by other blacks of friends and relatives. This statute authorized the manumission of slaves by their owners and gave blacks the opportunity, for the first time since the early seventeenth century, to take advantage of the law by working together to buy the freedom of their relatives, create social spheres, become educated and own businesses. Throughout Virginia, the appearance of large numbers of blacks as part of the free community allowed for the rapid growth and stabilization of free African American communities, especially because the creation of churches provided a safe space for them to gather and commune.[54]

This increasing presence of free blacks, however, created a problem for slaveholders; they felt it encouraged discontent and changes to the status quo. Complaints about free blacks socializing with slaves or harboring runaways were common. Whites also complained that free blacks were instrumental in teaching slaves how to read and write. Many free blacks even married and did business with slaves. Free blacks, for example, were credited with selling housing and other amenities to slaves. So it was in Virginia's emerging free black communities that enslaved bodies found a life apart from their masters and an environ that disseminated different concepts of freedom. Moreover, many of Virginia's enslaved populace learned about the burgeoning antislavery sentiment in the North through abolitionist newspapers and contacts with travelers with antislavery views. Eventually, the message was clear to most freedom seekers that safety lay in areas beyond Virginia, especially as northern states passed legislation ending slavery within their territories.[55]

In northern communities, emancipation laws led to the emergence of black communities that would also provide support and sanctuary to those fleeing slavery. The growth of a vocal and organized antislavery northern free black population paralleled the expansion of Virginia's slave trade economy, following the shift from a tobacco to a grain-based economy. After 1800, it was more difficult to obtain freedom, as slavery expanded west of the Appalachian Mountains, an essential component to economic survival of the white working classes.[56]

The growing internal slave trade and the passage of emancipation laws in the north led many freedom seekers to no longer see residing freely in urban areas within their states as a possibility. Instead, fleeing to northern states that had abolished slavery was the goal. And as the federal government took it upon itself to protect the institution, using the power of the courts and law enforcement, some Americans fought the institution and its expansion covertly through a loosely devised system called the Underground Railroad, a term that gained popular currency by the 1840s. Whites, especially Quakers, acted in concert with free blacks and enslaved operatives to smuggle enslaved people to cities and towns in America's north and Ontario, Canada. It is unclear where many of these early nineteenth-century freedom seekers fled, as the only accounts were about their departures. However, their quest to board ships bound for northern ports suggests that they understood their chances to secure permanent freedom rested beyond Virginia's borders.[57]

Virginia found itself in the unenviable position of having a large enslaved and free black population following the end of the American Revolution and the passage of a manumission act. Slaveholders were still angry about the successful invasion by the British of the area during the American Revolution and the participation of some blacks. Virginia officials wanted to make sure that all of its port areas, but Norfolk in particular, would be secured. And because of its location, the decision was made for Norfolk to serve as the linchpin for the Chesapeake region's defenses with the establishment of the Gosport Navy Yard.[58]

These maritime advancements came with a price. The years between 1793 and 1831 were times of unprecedented slave unrest in the Tidewater region because of international trade. During the Haitian Revolution, for example, fleets of refugees began arriving in Norfolk as early as July 1793, bringing news of a successful slave revolt. While initially welcomed, the refugees were soon met with fear that their stories would incite Virginia's slaves to revolt. There was also the belief that enslaved refugees were contributing to the general unrest among blacks in the region. Moreover, hundreds of white and black seamen and enslaved blacks intermingled on the busy streets of town, highlighting the commercial and mercantile prosperity of the area and foretelling of a future growth of freedom seekers coming to the region in search of opportunities to escape aboard ships.[59]

The enactment of the 1793 Fugitive Slave Act, which mandated the capture and return of fugitives anywhere in the nation, spurred freedom seekers to escape on their own. The only difference was that most left for points north, especially Canada. Facilitating this northward migration was the appearance of a strong free black population. Hundreds of Virginia's slaves were the beneficiaries of this organized group's efforts. Passage of the Fugitive Slave Clause in the U.S. Constitution generated fear from many who supported abolitionism that slavery would continue to expand with the support of the federal government. Not surprisingly, early white opponents of slavery associated abolitionism with a moral imperative while others saw

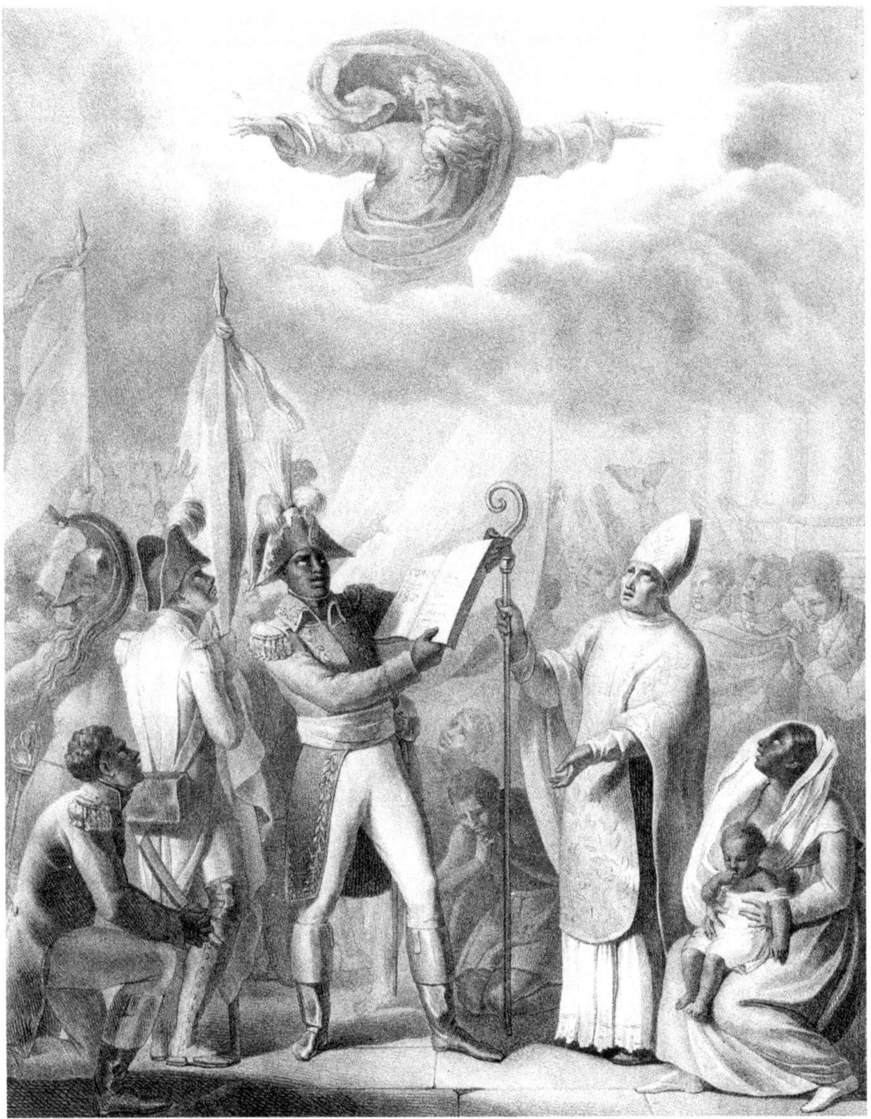

This depiction is an important departure from how Toussaint L'Ouverture and the people of Haiti were represented. *Library of Congress.*

the ideals of the Declaration of Independence reflected in an antislavery spirit. John Woolman, a Quaker from New Jersey, argued "that emancipation of a slave was crucial to personal salvation."[60]

It would be in these formative years of the nineteenth century that a shift in the goals of freedom seekers would reveal itself. In the eighteenth century, the objective was to reach an urban community and disappear among the throngs of people. Passage of emancipation laws and the assistance of free black communities and an emerging abolitionist fever among whites propelled freedom seekers northward, such as nineteen-year-old Daniel, who absconded from his Charleston, South Carolina owner in 1802. Recently purchased in Baltimore, Daniel was clearly familiar with the shipping routes because the runaway slave advertisement indicated that he "procured his passage in some vessel from that place to the Chesapeake, possible to Norfolk or Hampton."[61]

At the start of the antebellum period in 1800, there were 2,294,257 people living in the North. Of that number, only 1.6 percent (36,080) were enslaved, while 38,399 were free blacks. In the South, the population was 2,534,688 people, with slaves making up 34 percent (or 851,532) of the total population. There were also 61,575 southern free blacks—meaning that over one-third of the total population in the South was black. At the height of the Underground Railroad in 1850, there were 472,528 enslaved people in America. Ten years later, that number had grown to 3,953,760 out of a total population of over 31 million people. So it was that Virginia emerged as the state with the largest enslaved population, with 490,845 people. The only states that came close were Georgia with 462,198 and Mississippi with 436,631.[62]

When Britain imposed a blockade on neutral countries, including the United States, in 1803, it initiated a policy of seizing sailors from American ships and impressing them into the British navy, further straining relations. Four years later, an incident in the Tidewater region would foretell of events to come between England and its former colony. In 1807, English admiral George Berkeley, in command of the North American Station, issued instructions to commanders of vessels in his fleet to look out for the American frigate *Chesapeake* and, if they spotted it, to board and search the ship for English deserters. Descriptions of four sailors who were missing from the *Melampus*, lying in Hampton Road, were included in the instructions.[63]

The *Chesapeake* was one of the finest frigates in the U.S. Navy, and when the *Chesapeake* cleared the Hampton Roads—after being outfitted at the Gosport Navy Yard at Norfolk—and passed the Thimble Shoals Channel, headed for the Mediterranean to relieve the USS *Constitution* as flagship of the European station, a British squadron anchored in Lynnhaven Roads caught sight of the vessel. One of the British vessels, the HMS *Leopard*, followed it out to sea and demanded that the ship stand down and surrender the deserters. The *Chesapeake*'s commander, Captain (later Commodore) James Barron, refused, whereupon the *Leopard* fired several broadsides into the *Chesapeake*, killing three men and wounding eighteen. Barron then allowed the officers of the *Leopard* to board and search his vessel for British deserters.[64]

After searching the vessel, the British took out three men they claimed were deserters, plus a fourth man for good measure. Those accused of desertion were William Ware, Daniel Martin, John Strachan, John Wilson and Ambrose Watts. Within a month after their escape from the *Melampus*, the first three of these deserters, who were African Americans, offered themselves for enlistment and were received on board the *Chesapeake*, stationed at Norfolk. The British consul at Norfolk wrote a letter to the American naval officer, requesting the men be returned, but was refused. Subsequently, the British contacted the American secretary of the navy, who declined after discovering that Ware, Martin and Strachan were African American men who had been pressed into British service. They had a right to desert, according to him.[65]

It took four years for the *Chesapeake-Leopard* affair to be resolved. In that time, many other American vessels had been boarded and their

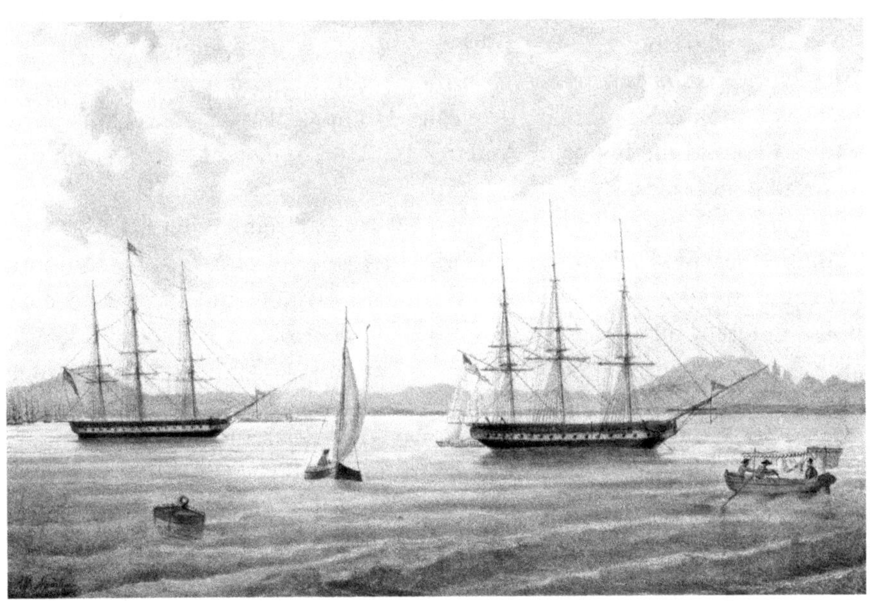

This 1815 drawing depicts the USS *Constitution*'s narrow escape after a sixty-hour chase from a British squadron during the War of 1812. This drawing by Michele Cornè features rowboats towing the USS *Constitution* away from the British fleet as the British frigate HMS *Belvidera* fires its cannons. In the background, rowboats tow the British frigate HMS *Shannon*. Other ships in the British squadron included the HMS *Africa*, HMS *Aeolus* and HMS *Guerriere*. *Library of Congress*.

crew members taken by the British. Angered by this ongoing diplomatic outrage, President James Madison sent a message to Congress on June 1, 1812, declaring, "The impressment of American seamen by the British; the blockade of her enemy's ports, supported by no adequate force, in consequence of which the American commerce had been plundered in every sea, and the great staples of the country cut off from their legitimate markets; and the British orders in council."[66] With the motto "Free Trade and Sailors' Rights," America began its second war with its mother country. Of course, accompanying the unease about trade was the equal anxiety that the British would promote a slave revolt.[67]

As was the case during the American Revolution, ports, such as Hampton Roads, had divided loyalties. Jefferson's Non-Intercourse Act of 1809 devastated the mercantile industry in Virginia, and traders were caught between the French and the British, struggling for dominance. Ships traveling to the Caribbean to trade gave advantage to the British because only 20 percent typically went to the islands while 80 percent went to Britain. If ships went to France, Britain attacked the vessels, took all the goods and imprisoned the captain and crew. If they traveled to Europe, Napoleon's warships seized the vessels. However, traveling to England resulted in American warships seizing them on their return. Such was the situation on the eve of the war's outbreak. Ironically, Hampton Roads' merchants were ready to uphold the honor of America but were reluctant to challenge the powerful British navy.[68]

Despite reservations, in the first year of the war, reinforcing defenses and sending out armed schooners were the first priorities, preventing the port area from suffering economically. By the following year, however, events took a different turn, and the region was forced to clearly choose sides. A large British squadron, commanded by Admiral Sir John Borlase Warren, landed at Bermuda with bombs, Congreve rockets and guns. By February 4, Warren's troops had landed in the area of Seatack, located in what is today Virginia Beach's oldest black community. (Reportedly, the community was so named because of the "sea attack" by the British.) Shortly thereafter, the British controlled the waterways of Hampton Roads, which became the launching point for the British attack on Virginia by cutting off supplies and destroying public works. The fleet consisted of four frigates and a host of other vessels and five thousand troops.[69]

Much was learned by the British during the American Revolution. One such lesson was the effect on the white community when black men were used as soldiers, particularly those who had been enslaved. While Admiral

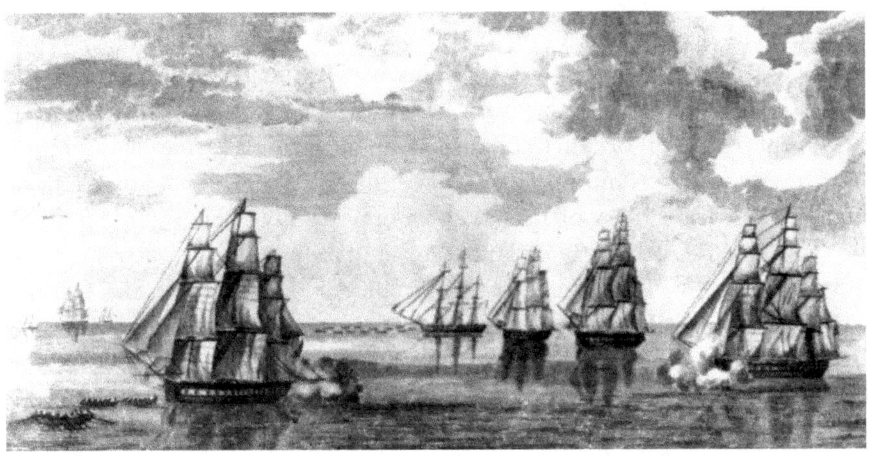

This 1813 painting by London artist Robert Dodd, based on information taken from Captain Falkinir, depicts the capture by British commander Captain P.B.V. Broke of the HMS *Shannon* of the American frigate USS *Chesapeake*. In the image, British seamen and marines are seen boarding and taking down the American flag on the *Chesapeake*. *Library of Congress*.

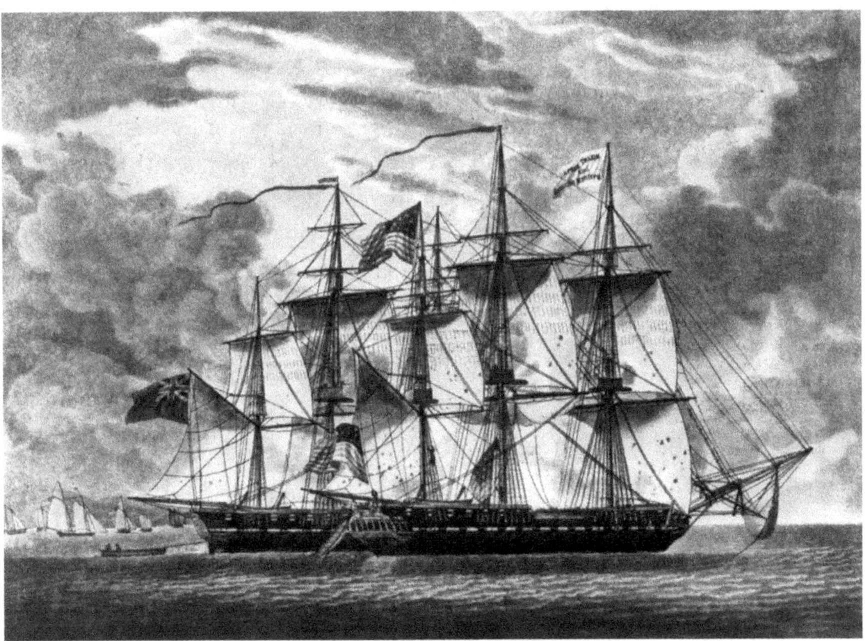

This 1815 William Hoogland painting of the USS *Constitution*'s escape from the British squadron after a chase of sixty hours was designed to highlight the resiliency of the American efforts to thwart British attacks. Seen in the painting are rowboats towing the USS *Constitution* away from the British fleet while the British frigate, HMS *Belvidera*, continues to fire its cannons in the battle. *Library of Congress*.

Warren had been warned not to actively incite a slave rebellion, he was instructed "to receive aboard his ships any blacks who might petition him for assistance." Once aboard, they would be welcomed as free people and were to be sent to any of Britain's colonies. Captain Robert Barnie of the HMS *Dragon* reported to Admiral Warren that enslaved men, women and children had requested sanctuary of him at every opportunity, resulting in a total of 120 refugees, 50 of whom he planned to send to fight in Bermuda.[70]

When the British squadron, commanded by Admiral Sir George Cockburn, sailed through the Virginia Capes to blockade the Chesapeake Bay and raid the coastal settlements, it bottled up the U.S. frigate *Constellation* in Norfolk Harbor. This action became a blessing in disguise, as the officers, sailors, marines, guns and small boats of the frigate helped launch a defense of Norfolk from the blockaders.[71]

For the Americans, recruitment of blacks became a necessity after 1814 because of British policy. In fact, throughout the War of 1812, blacks comprised about one-sixth of the total naval personnel. While derisive at its core, Commodore Perry applauded the valor of these men, stating, "'When America has such tars, she has little to fear from tyrants of the ocean.'"[72] In what would be the only land victory for the Americans in the war, the *Constellation*, regarded as the U.S. Navy's fastest ship, spotted the British entering the Chesapeake Bay and made a run for the Elizabeth River near the Gosport shipyard. When the British noticed the ship, it was already out of reach. Furious, the British followed the vessel, but the Americans raised a chain that ran across the river from Fort Norfolk to Fort Nelson on the Portsmouth side, blocking the British fleet's access. The British turned around and seized Craney Island (a small island, about 900 yards long and 230 years wide), launching their attack against Norfolk and Portsmouth from that point. The intent was to take the ship by going overland from town.[73]

The British sought to stymie America's efforts by attracting runaways concentrated in areas near the mouth of the Chesapeake Bay. The counties of Princess Anne, Northampton and Norfolk were important areas where, by the summer, freedom seekers' numbers surged as word spread that the British welcomed fugitives. Estimates were that the number of runaways was in the hundreds. In fact, a reported 3,580 enslaved people fled Virginia and Maryland during the War of 1812, with most joining the British by getting to the ships that plied the waterways throughout the Chesapeake. By 1814, the British shifted their policy in favor of disrupting the plantation economy by encouraging mass escapes in an effort to increase their war successes.

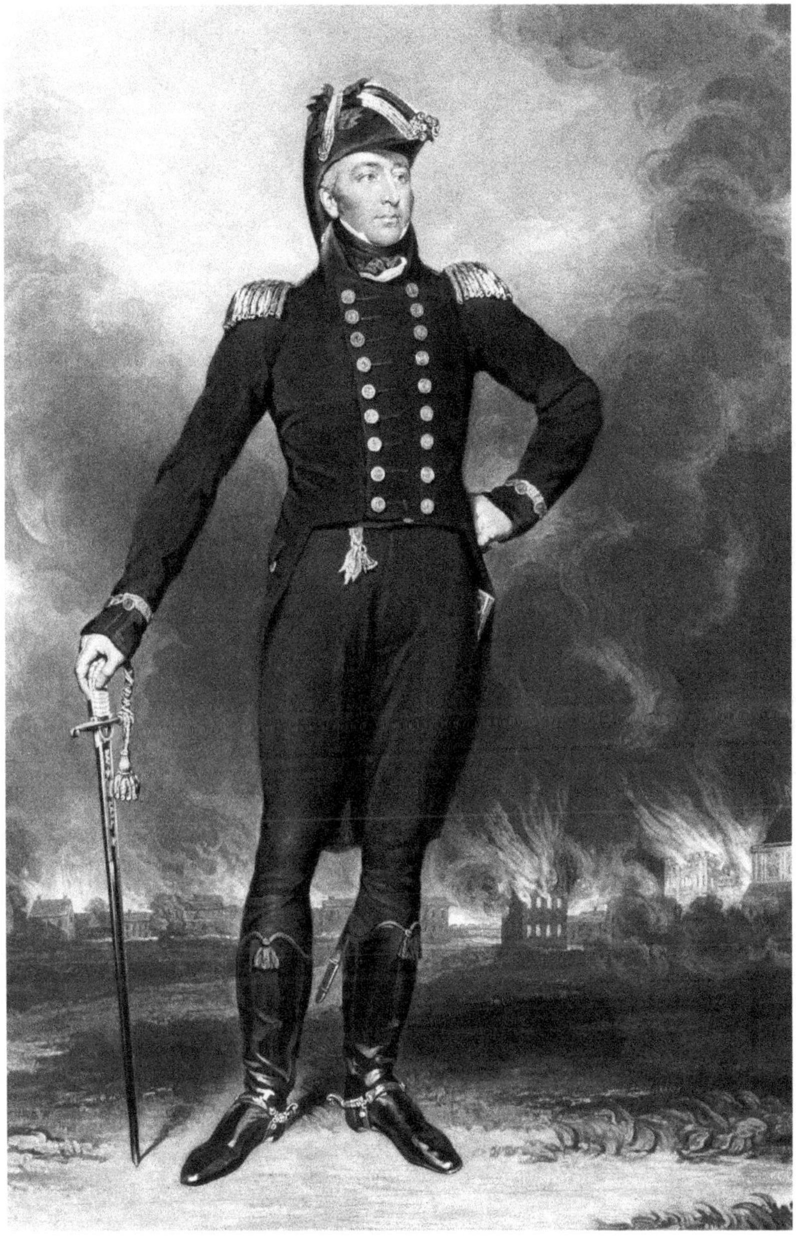

This is an 1819 portrait of Britain's Rear Admiral Sir George Cockburn, who was responsible for organizing raids of cities, towns and plantations along the Chesapeake Bay and the major rivers and tributaries, including Norfolk, Hampton and throughout the Tidewater region. He was regarded by the American officials as a warmonger and savage, especially since most of his raids resulted in the departure of hundreds of enslaved people, who sought refuge aboard British vessels. *Library of Congress.*

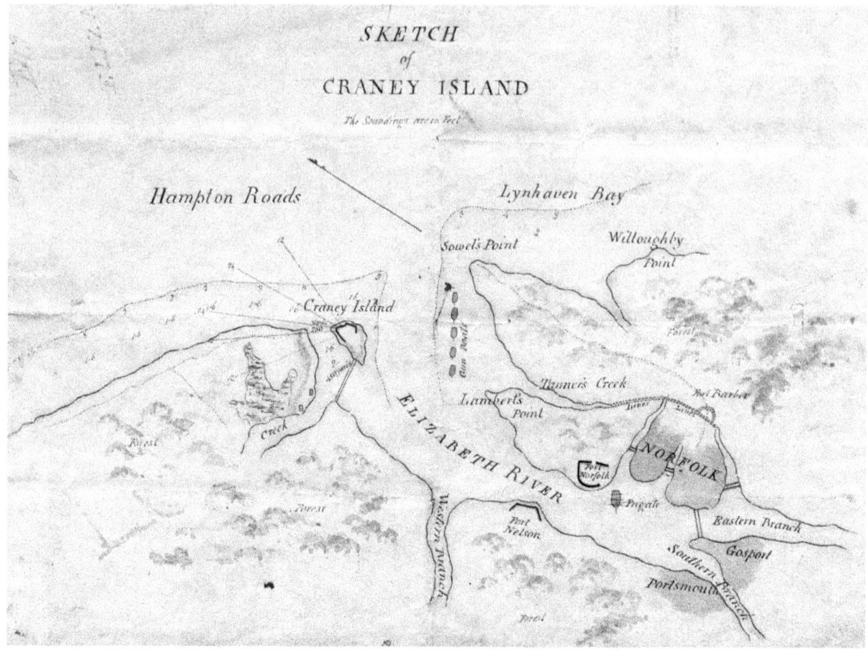

This map of Craney Island in Portsmouth during the War of 1812 depicts that battle that was eventually won by the American forces, resulting in the British retreating from Hampton Roads temporarily in 1813. *Robert Barrie map, David M. Rubenstein Rare Book & Manuscript Library, Duke University.*

And because they understood that many men refused to escape without their families, the British also began accepting women and children.[74]

The expansion of their policy in recruiting enslaved men with their families also allowed the British to make deep incursions into the countryside, with the guidance of black freedom seekers. The result was two-fold for the British because they were able to recruit more enslaved people and plunder plantations for food and supplies. In addition, the British created the Colonial Marines, composed of four hundred male fugitives. Regarded as the best of the British troops, the Colonial Marines wielded tremendous, intimidating power because they stimulated white Americans to imagine that their worst fears had come true: they were about to be destroyed by their enslaved populations.[75]

The account of Moses Grandy, an enslaved man from Lower Tidewater who piloted a boat up and down the Dismal Swamp Canal at the start of the War of 1812, is a telling reminder about how easy it was for the British to take advantage of the divided loyalties of enslaved African Americans, whose focus was on keeping their families together and freedom. The Dismal Swamp Canal, originally built using slave labor from 1793 to 1805, ran twenty-two miles from the southern branch of the Elizabeth River in Virginia to Albemarle Sound in North Carolina. Grandy was allowed by his owner, James Grandy, to transport goods and supplies from Elizabeth City and Hampton Roads. This, no doubt, created concern from slaveholders, who feared a slave absconding or being assisted in his or her escape by another slave.[76]

The end of the War of 1812 on December 24, 1814, prompted Virginia to update its laws concerning fugitive slaves when English soldiers returned, promising freedom similar to what was offered during the American Revolution. Fearing that slaves would assist the British by hijacking smaller vessels to reach the British warships, the Commonwealth responded with two new statutes in 1814 and 1815 that directed militia officers to keep smaller vessels out of reach of enslaved people and to monitor ferries with the intent to prevent escapes.[77]

Moreover, after the war, the majority of enslaved people living around the Chesapeake region were forced to migrate westward with white planters in search of newer farming lands. As many as forty-five thousand were forced westward during the 1810s alone, with about 40 percent going to Kentucky while 60 percent were sent to Alabama, Mississippi and Louisiana. Afterward, a more organized interregional and international trade was in place with professional slave traders whose offices were located in the center of the major port cities from Delaware through Virginia. In Norfolk and Richmond, all the offices of these traders were located on Main Street, near the slave market and the slave jail where those awaiting sale were kept.[78] One Maryland newspaper aptly described what was really happening: "'The selling of slaves [had] become an almost universal resource to raise money.'"[79]

Virginia's 1817 statue, "'An Act to amend the several laws concerning runaways," highlighted how unsuccessful the state was in accomplishing this goal. The preamble confirmed that many slaveholders suffered the loss of their human property because of "the frequent elopement of slaves to states north of the Potowmac [*sic*] and elsewhere."[80] The law had two purposes: provide compensation for those whose slaves escaped and allow compensation for those seeking escaped slaves from anywhere in the nation. Clearly, the law recognized that the borders of Virginia were fluid, making securing slaves extremely difficult. The coastal nature of Virginia, especially the Chesapeake area (centered in Hampton Roads), and the mercantile industry meant that any water conveyance needed to be heavily monitored and runaways needed to be advertised in newspapers throughout the Commonwealth. Virginia even passed a law that set fees for runaway recovery based on where they were recaptured. As comprehensive as this law sought to be, the real difficulty was in enforcement. Obviously, from the history of the Underground Railroad that would emerge by the 1830s, this and other attempts to stave the growing tide of runaways was generally unsuccessful.[81]

One such example was James Harris, a free black from Philadelphia who was kidnapped and sold into slavery as a teenager. While in New Orleans awaiting his sale, he managed to escape and return to Philadelphia. He joined the military and fought against the British during the War of 1812. At the war's end, he sought work with a man in Delaware. Once again, he was kidnapped into slavery, but this time, he was unable to escape before being sold in North Carolina. The Pennsylvania Abolition Society received a letter from him pleading for assistance while he was in Greenville, North Carolina. Before they could locate his free papers, he was sold away. Amazingly, Harris managed to flee and dodge his way through Virginia, bouncing from one jail to the next, eventually ending up in Matthews County, where the law required that if he was not claimed or could not produce free papers within a year, he would be sold as a slave. Unfortunately, the Pennsylvania Abolition Society did not record what his eventual fate was or whether his persistence garnered success. This pattern of kidnapping free blacks and the expanding laws protecting slavery made protections even for the African American veterans of the War of 1812 weak.[82]

Hundreds from the Chesapeake region, which included Maryland and Virginia, seized the opportunity and made their way to British vessels and freedom. This, of course, angered slaveholders, who argued that approximately 2,400 enslaved people were taken from Virginia during the war. Added to their outrage about losing their "property" was the failure by the United States to include what they considered fair compensation in the Treaty of Ghent. So instead of receiving full compensation, Virginians only received remuneration for one-fifth (or 480) of the slaves who escaped. This discrepancy resulted from the ruling that the 1,920 who were taken prior to the treaty's ratification were "the residue of their claims" and therefore were not within the treaty's guidelines. So critical was Virginia in the War of 1812 that the majority of those freedom seekers who joined the British forces and settled in Canada were from Virginia. In the end, a sum of $886,000 was received by the United States from Britain in 1826 to settle all claims, even though the claimants from the Chesapeake region were not asked to submit their evidence prior to the conclusion of negotiations.[83]

So why would America's African American population support an attacking enemy? Perhaps the answer lies in the realities of slavery in post-Revolution America. While some of the names of blacks who fled aboard British vessels were recorded during the Revolution, no such document exists for the War of 1812. This was a different war. It was not one that decided the independence of a nation. Rather, this was a fight for sovereignty, and those who fled seeking freedom did not want their names known, fearing recapture or deportation. This was a complicated war in which people and the nations involved grappled with respecting authority over their geographic space.

3

SLAVERY, POLITICS AND THE UNDERGROUND RAILROAD IN ANTEBELLUM VIRGINIA

It was May 1854 when twenty-two-year-old Portsmouth native Clarissa Davis made her initial attempt to escape. She was scheduled to rendezvous with her brothers—thirty-year-old William, and twenty-eight-year-old Charles—who had secured transit aboard the *Ellen Barnes* from Wareham, Massachusetts, possibly with the assistance of one of Portsmouth's operatives, Eliza Bains or Henry Lewey, also known as Bluebeard in Underground Railroad circles. Lewey was a slave from Norfolk, and Bains was an enslaved housekeeper who worked at the Crawford Hotel, a popular haunt for captains of vessels. Despite her best efforts, Clarissa missed the boat and for seventy-five days hid in "a miserable coop," praying that God would allow her a chance to join her brothers. According to William Still, Philadelphia's Vigilance Committee secretary, word was sent that the steamship, *City of Richmond*, had arrived from Philadelphia and that William Bagnall, a white Norfolk agent, would connect her with the steward, John Minkins. Once aboard, Minkins would hide her in a box.[84]

The trick, however, was how to get to the ship. The docks were closely monitored by night watchmen, and authorities were already alerted to her disappearance. A $1,000 reward had been posted for the return of Clarissa and her two brothers. Clarissa prayed that a heavy rain would reduce the number of people monitoring the docks. Fortunately for her, torrential rains did fall by midnight, allowing Clarissa to embark aboard the ship at the appointed time of 3:00 a.m. dressed in male attire. Once there, Bagnall, a prominent white banking official, hid her in a box, while Minkins made sure that the box was to be delivered to the Vigilance Committee upon arrival in Philadelphia. Once there, the committee took her to their safe house and suggested that Clarissa adopt an alias. Renamed Mary D. Armstead, Clarissa was furnished with a passport and then sent to New Bedford, Massachusetts, at which time she was reunited with her brothers. Meanwhile, her father, Samuel Davis, who was deemed too old to work, was either freed by his owner or able to purchase his freedom for a nominal fee. Leaving Portsmouth after his children's departure, he joined them in New Bedford.[85]

The story of Clarissa's flight illustrated the anxieties and dangers faced by fugitives. And while Clarissa's story was unusual in that her entire family escaped, it was exemplary of the pattern of Underground Railroad activity in Virginia along the Eastern Seaboard. Local operatives—both black and white—secreted fugitives with the complicity of ship captains of schooners

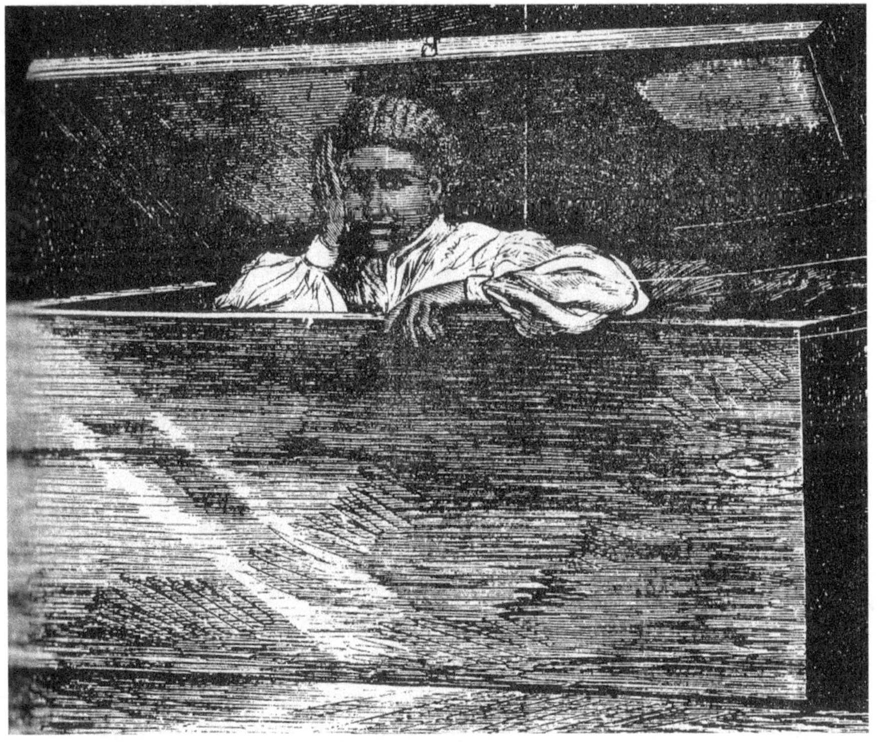

This image of Lear Green of Baltimore was typical of how many freedom seekers went to great lengths to escape their bondage. Like Clarissa Davis, who hid in a box aboard a steamship, in 1854, Green procured a sailor's chest and sailed to Philadelphia. After arriving, the chest was delivered to William Still's residence. *William Still,* The Underground Railroad, *1872.*

and seamen working aboard steamships. It was this local autonomous underground network that worked in concert with northern operations to transport fugitives to freedom.

American slavery created a system of despair and exploitation, but freedom seekers like Clarissa Davis negotiated pathways to hope and possible freedom independently and through a loosely organized method to escape called the Underground Railroad. Those who had established strong family ties were always at risk of being sold on the auction block. These constant disruptions within enslaved family units because of sales to the Lower South prompted increased fugitive activity. For some, the desire for freedom, impending sale because of owner's death or economic hardship or unbearable treatment from their masters prompted their escape. It was Virginia's numerous ports and proximity to northern states that facilitated the successful escapes. And despite how the Underground Railroad is portrayed, these freedom seekers continued their flight throughout the Civil War, forcing changes in the dynamics of the war and of the nation to confront its most divisive, dehumanizing and controversial institution.

At the start of the antebellum period in 1800, there were 2,294,257 people living in the North. Of that number, only 1.6 percent (36,080) were enslaved; 38,399 were free blacks. In the South, the population numbered 2,534,688, with slaves making up 34 percent (or 851,532) of the total population. There were also 61,575 southern free blacks, meaning that over one-third of the total population in the South was black. At the height of the Underground Railroad in 1850, there were 472,528 enslaved people in America. Ten years later, that number had grown to 3,953,760 out of a total population of over 31 million. And of all of the states, Virginia had the largest enslaved population, with 490,845 by 1860. The only states that came close were Georgia with 462,198 and Mississippi with 436,631.[86]

The highest Cash Price will be given for

NEGROES,

By application at No. 89, Church-Street. For tradesmen of every description a more liberal price will be given. January 4. 15t

Advertisements such as this one published on January 9, 1811, in the *Norfolk Gazette* highlight the presence of slave traders in the city of Norfolk a few years before the War of 1812 and the importance of the growing domestic slave trade because of cotton production in the South. *Author's collection.*

These numbers are very telling about the importance of a labor force that was tasked with producing the bulk of agricultural goods. And America's rise as the primary cotton producer in the world (seven-eighths of the world's cotton production) clearly cemented the importance of maintaining slavery and the growing importance of states with a large enslaved population, such as Virginia. While America experienced unprecedented economic growth through slave labor, abolitionism and abolitionist societies appeared and expanded. In the nation's early years, prominent abolitionists were among its leaders, including Benjamin Franklin, who led the Pennsylvania Society for Promoting the Abolition of Slavery—though earlier in his life, he bought and sold slaves. Alexander Hamilton directed slavery opposition in New York along with Governor George Clinton and John Jay, future chief justice of the Supreme Court. Many of these early abolitionist societies emphasized colonization in exchange for freedom, believing that blacks should be resettled in the British colony of Sierra Leone or in the newly founded colony of Liberia. Others pushed for laws allowing for emancipation by slaveholders or through self-purchases.[87]

The antebellum period inherited the strategies and tactics of fugitive slave activity from the colonial years. And while it remains up for debate exactly how many escaped, especially if you include the unsuccessful attempts and the two hundred years prior to 1830, what is clear is that slavery in America went beyond its prominence in southern plantation society. Indeed, the entire nation's economic infrastructure was invested in the continuation and expansion of the institution for the formative years of its existence. And it was only the Thirteenth Amendment's abolition of slavery that ended the work of the Underground Railroad (although many believe it ended with the start of the Civil War).

As antislavery sentiment increased in the North, so did the proslavery faction's determination to enforce the 1793 Fugitive Slave Act, particularly sections 3 and 4, which empowered judges to arrest and order the return of fugitives and made it a punishable crime to assist fugitives. Beginning in the 1820s, influential abolitionists in Connecticut and Indiana responded with the passage of personal liberty laws that provided jury trials for those accused of being fugitive slaves. In the aftermath of the 1842 *Prigg v. Pennsylvania* case, in which the Supreme Court ruled that states could not be forced to litigate fugitive slave cases, Massachusetts, Pennsylvania, Rhode Island, New York and Vermont joined the other states with personal liberty laws, echoing this northern groundswell of dissatisfaction with the Fugitive Slave Act. This polarizing struggle between the pro- and antislavery factions came to a head following the enactment of the controversial 1850 Fugitive Slave Act.[88]

To forestall the work of antislavery sympathizers or those who could be bribed to assist runaways, Virginia, like other southern states, enacted statutes that provided monetary incentives to slave catchers and bounty hunters as well as to workers on railroads, ferries, steamships and the like. The year 1817 witnessed the first such law that provided state-sponsored rewards to slave catchers, as opposed to owner-financed bounties. It also authorized the use of Richmond newspapers to publicize runaway slave advertisements. In fact, the statute noted a "serious inconvenience experienced by Virginians from the frequent elopement of slaves to states north of the Potomac"—no doubt a reaction to increased urbanization and the construction of the nation's capital. Six years later, lawmakers noted the lack of success in preventing escapes. Consequently, they extended their efforts to apprehend fugitives by targeting states with strong abolitionist sentiments.[89]

Private efforts were also exerted in securing the arrest of those who assisted runaways. Slaveholders and officials from Richmond and Henrico County were so concerned about absconding slaves that in 1833 they formed a citizen's organization called the Society for the Prevention of the Absconding and Abducting of Slaves. The society sought to create measures that would "lead to the detection and punishment of evil disposed persons, who, it is believed are aiding and abetting in attempts to destroy all security to that kind of property, have bestowed on the subjects to them committed the attention which their importance requires, as far as they could do so compatibly with a prompt and decisive action on them" and offered rewards based on the level of assistance. They believed this would lead to assistance from an otherwise unconcerned population. While their efforts met with mixed results, between 1830 and 1860, the police and night watch forces in most of Virginia's port areas substantially grew in response to the perception that slaves with industrial experience were more likely to rebel or run away. Consumed by their lack of success, legislators increased the severity of punishment in the vain hope that it would serve as a deterrent.[90]

Meanwhile, abolitionists stepped up efforts to circulate antislavery propaganda and encourage enslaved African Americans to run away through the publication of newspapers and other materials. John Greenleaf Whittier, editor of the *Pennsylvania Freeman* who cut his teeth as a contributing writer for William Lloyd Garrison's column in the *Free Press* of Newburyport in the 1820s, eventually moved to Philadelphia, assuming the job of editor for the *Pennsylvania Freeman* in 1838. Published by the Pennsylvania Anti-

Slavery Society, Whittier's special interest in the fate of runaway slaves in Philadelphia became a preoccupation of the newspaper. Whittier's activities coincided with the Massachusetts legislature's passage of a bill securing the right for accused runaways to a trial by jury and Pennsylvania's rejection of a similar measure.[91] As a result, Whittier decided to "stir the conscience of Philadelphia and to arouse the city to an active sympathy for the refugees he hoped to aid."[92] His first effort, "The Farewell of a Virginia Slave Mother," was appropriate, given the number of runaways from the state with the largest population of enslaved African Americans in the country.[93]

Black bodies chained together during the long walks to the western sections of the state and to the Lower South became an increasingly common sight and powerful indicator of the growing importance of slavery and the role of Virginia in this domestic slave trade. By 1810, the price of slaves in Louisiana had risen to twice that in Virginia and four times what it was in the North. The vibrant slave trade shipments from the Upper South in Virginia and Maryland to the New Orleans markets dominated the landscape. Those who were not carried by ship were taken along roads that took them through Quaker counties in North Carolina. This was where Quaker Levi Coffin first encountered men who were taken from their wives and children to work on the cotton plantations in the Lower South. Coffin recalled one of the men saying to him, "They have taken us away from our wives and children, and they chain us lest we should make our escape and go back to them."[94] The lucrative domestic slave trade soon drowned out opposition to slavery with the assistance of an event that renewed Virginia lawmakers' support for slavery.

The 1831 Nat Turner revolt in Southampton County drove the last nail in the abolitionist coffin in Virginia and invoked fears of a race war. This also led to even more restrictive laws for free and enslaved blacks. Lawmakers even discussed expelling Virginia's nearly fifty thousand free blacks but chose instead to pass restrictive laws, including barring blacks from serving as ministers. Virginia officials also claimed the revolt was part of a national abolitionist conspiracy, linking the revolt with William Lloyd Garrison's *Liberator* newspaper debut and the rise of a more radical abolitionism led by northern free blacks.[95]

Undaunted by Virginia's efforts to stymie abolitionism, enslaved African Americans continued using their internal communication network to help daring individuals obtain freedom. The emergence of a larger system with headquarters in Pennsylvania accelerated those efforts, making freedom more obtainable for men and women. This secret association did not achieve any significant success until after the passage of the 1850 Fugitive Slave Act because it enraged enough northerners that they were willing to assist in the escape of slaves either by omission or commission. Fleeing primarily from the cities of Richmond, Norfolk, Petersburg and Portsmouth, fugitives exploited areas with access to rivers and ports, using the waterways as their portals of hope and freedom. Together with ship captains and stewards willing to assist in this effort, often for a fee, these fugitives passed through the stations established by vigilance committees in Philadelphia, New Bedford, Boston and New York. While some opted to change their names, assume aliases and remain in northern cities, the bulk immigrated to Canada. In fact, accounts noted that the majority of fugitives who reached Canada during the 1850s were Virginians, settling in the cities of Toronto, Hamilton and St. Catharines.

The maritime industry in the Greater Tidewater, which extended from Richmond to Hampton Roads, and northern Virginia complicated these forces of freedom that helped the Underground Railroad to flourish. Because its numerous port cities provided countless avenues of escape for African Americans, it quickly became the primary center of departure on the Underground Railroad. Interestingly, men and women—single and

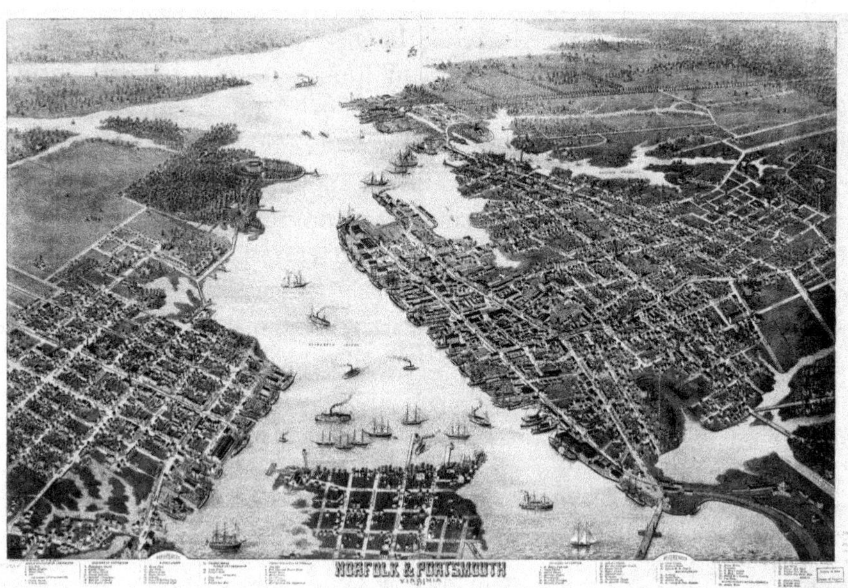

This 1873 C.N. Drie map of the Norfolk and Portsmouth, Virginia harbor highlights the importance of the waterways and the numerous inlets and access points available to freedom seekers. *Library of Congress.*

married—and children escaped aboard the thousands of small vessels and steamships that frequented the waterways along the seaboard, often traveling as families.

So who were these freedom seekers from Virginia? Our knowledge of the numbers, activities and struggles of freedom seekers prior to the 1850s is incomplete because of the lack of a more systematic accounting of runaways that would later be reflected in many of the records kept by William Still, the stationmaster in Philadelphia. It was Still who provided a glimpse into the endeavors of abolitionists and the lives of approximately 763 freedom seekers who acted with the assistance of a loosely organized network while others acted alone.

According to Still, many fugitives lived close to the docks, where friendly conductors, ship captains and steamboat stewards were easily accessed. Some historians have suggested that fear of flight or rebellion in cities resulted in the sale of slaves to the interior or lower South. Certainly, William Still's account highlights that flight by about 30 percent of the fugitives from Virginia was precipitated by fear of being sold away from these port cities. The emotional turmoil that accompanied these escapes, especially when men left their wives, children, mothers, fathers and siblings behind, was captured in his accounts. And unlike the white abolitionists who wrote about the fugitives, Still thought it important to document the lives of these individuals, not simply *how* they escaped.[96]

William Still discussed the lives of 350 freedom seekers from Maryland; 285 from Virginia; 57 from Delaware; 42 from Washington, D.C.; 18 from North Carolina; 6 from Georgia; 2 from South Carolina; and 1 each from Missouri, Louisiana and Kentucky. In Virginia, Still recorded 102 who left from Norfolk, 51 from Richmond, 22 from Petersburg, 20 from Portsmouth, 17 from Alexandria, 14 from Loudon County and small numbers from all over the rest of the state. Specific departure points did not indicate that freedom seekers were from those areas, especially if it was a port city, because Still did not always differentiate between the departure point and where they were from. Moreover, the maritime industry was shifting its locations during these years, centralizing Virginia's operations in Norfolk, so even those departing from Hampton, Williamsburg, Petersburg and Richmond passed through Norfolk on their way to points north.[97]

John Henry Hill from Petersburg realized that he had to escape from slavery. At the age of twenty-five, Hill was married to Rose McCrae, a free black, and a father of two children. He was tired of working on behalf of someone else and getting nothing in return. He knew he had

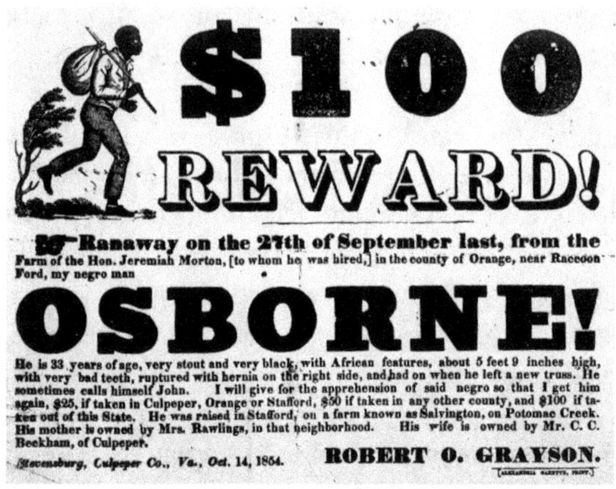

By the early 1850s, freedom seekers sought port areas as their avenues to liberty aboard ships sailing to northern ports. Such was the case of this advertised fugitive who attempted to get to Norfolk with the intent of getting aboard a ship out of Virginia. This 1854 advertisement, posted by the Honorable Jeremiah Morton from Orange County, offered a $100 reward, representing the lengths owners would go to secure the return of their slaves. *Library of Congress.*

a valuable skill as a carpenter because his owner John Mitchell hired him out for $150 a year. But his owner somehow knew he wanted his freedom. In 1853, without warning, Mitchell took Hill to Richmond with the intent of selling him. Once they reached the auction house, Hill knew it was now or never. When he was told to submit to handcuffs, he fought his owner and several others who attempted to subdue him and somehow managed to flee, seeking sanctuary in the kitchen of a merchant near Franklin and Seventh Streets where a friend of his mother's worked. For nine months, Hill was secreted from one hiding place to another. He even wrote a pass for himself so that the watchmen would not arrest him on the streets. Eventually, word reached him that passage had been arranged to rendezvous with John Minkins, the black steward on the *City of Richmond* steamship. After Hill paid $125, a hiding place was secured for him aboard the ship, and he was taken to Philadelphia, where the vigilance committee met him. Eventually, he was forwarded through the network by train to Albany, Rochester and Lewiston, New York. A letter of introduction accompanied him on his journey so that agents would meet him and forward him to his next stop. Hill was eventually placed on a ship and sent to Toronto, Canada.[98]

On December 29, 1853, after four separate letters to William Still, Hill wrote that his family had arrived safely, yet his thoughts still turned to those who were left in slavery. Hill moved his family to Hamilton, where he secured farmland and eventually began a prosperous tobacco business.[99]

During that time, he was interviewed by Samuel Howe, the Boston physician, educator and abolitionist who served as a member of the U.S.

Sanitary Commission and on the American Freedmen's Inquiry Committee during the Civil War. Hill recounted some of his experiences to Howe:

> *I was in slavery until I was about eighteen years old. There were four uncles, myself and mother, and another sister of my uncles. My uncles paid fifteen hundred dollars apiece for themselves. They bought themselves three times. They got cheated out of their freedom in the first two instances, and were put in jail at one time, and were going to be sold down South, right away; but parties who were well acquainted with us, and knew we had made desperate struggles for our freedom, came forward and advanced the money, and took us out of jail, and put us on a footing so that we could go ahead and earn money to pay the debt. We have an uncle in Pittsburg, who has accumulated a good deal of property since he obtained his freedom. My uncles bought me and my mother, as well as themselves. I saw a great deal of slavery; and not only that, but my parents had to undergo a great deal of hardship in their earlier days. I never suffered any particular hardship myself. I had a grandfather who had long been free, and when the boys grew up, he would take them and learn them a trade, and keep them out of the hands of the traders; and when they became men and women, having had his industry instilled into them, they would be able and willing to work.*[100]

John Hill's escape aboard a steamship was not unusual. According to historian Wilbur Siebert, an Underground Railroad station keeper at Valley Falls, Rhode Island, said that slaves in Virginia in the 1850s secured transit on small trading boats coming from Portsmouth and Norfolk either secretly or with the consent of captains. While the majority of fugitives departing aboard ships came from the cities and counties of Hampton Roads, some did not. The area around Norfolk County (the Dismal Swamp) linked regions as far away as Florida and as close as eastern North Carolina through a continuous line of swamps offering a refuge for those seeking liberty and freedom. With an average of 1,000 to 1,500 ships sailing annually into the Hampton Roads harbors throughout the 1850s, it was difficult to monitor activities. Virginia senator James Mason estimated that Virginia lost an average of $100,000 worth of slave property annually. Based on some of the figures published in local Hampton Roads newspapers, this was a rather low estimate, given that the region was among the largest Underground Railroad embarkation points in Virginia.[101]

From the 1820s through the 1850s, reports appeared that created the perception that a clandestine organization was making considerable headway

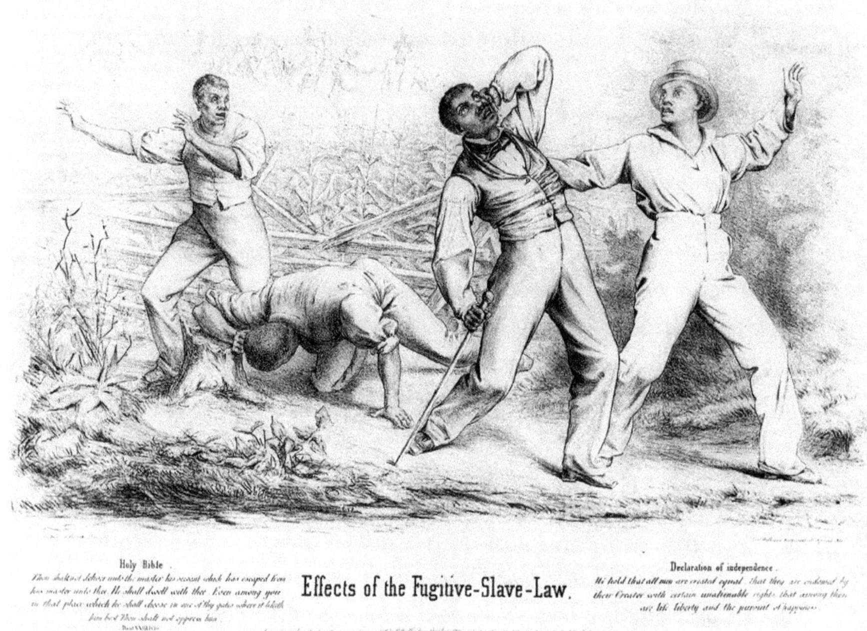

Titled *Effects of the Fugitive-Slave-Law*, this 1850 political cartoon condemning the Fugitive Slave Act was published by abolitionists in New York. The image highlights the violent actions by slave catchers against those accused of being fugitive slaves. It also underscores how states that abolished slavery within their borders would be forced to comply with the return of freedom seekers even when the seizure violates state law. *Library of Congress.*

in undermining slavery in Virginia. In 1827, the *Norfolk and Portsmouth Herald* reported in a special article that steamboats served as agencies of escape for fugitive slaves. According to the *Herald*, steamships from Baltimore and Philadelphia were either the known or unknown carriers of fugitive slaves. To encourage their recovery, in 1836 the state fined and/or imprisoned anyone who assisted fugitives. When slaves who absconded aboard these vessels were recovered, those who assisted them were punished with fines double the value of the slave or were imprisoned.[102]

In February 1834, Norfolk constable and notorious slave hunter John Capheart discovered a runaway aboard the *Patrick Henry*, a luxurious steamship that made frequent visits to the Norfolk and Portsmouth docks. It seems that the male fugitive, belonging to a Mr. Williams of Richmond, claimed that he was "seduced away from home by a gentleman aboard." Presumably, this gentleman was white. In that same year, a number of fugitive slave advertisements suggested that running away was common. In April, fifty dollars was offered by Portsmouth owner John G. Hatton for the return of his twenty-year-old slave Moses, who was described as a stout, dark-complexioned and high-cheek-boned man who left wearing a blue cassinet jacket and trousers.[103] Obviously, his owner suspected that he would attempt to leave the state because he offered one hundred dollars to anyone who secured him beyond state boundaries.[104]

So threatening (and apparently successful) were these efforts that Virginia's urban newspapers effectively lobbied the state legislature to pass an act requiring all ships to be boarded and searched prior to departure and sending bounty hunters to the North to retrieve fugitives. Some newspapers, such as Norfolk's *American Beacon*, sarcastically noted that the apprehension of three runaway slaves in 1855 must have resulted from the Underground Railroad being "out of order." The *Southern Argus* highlighted a "Break Down on the Underground Railroad" when a slaveholder alerted the constable, resulting in the capture of six runaways and a drayman named William Sales, who had arranged transport for them aboard a northern vessel in the Norfolk harbor.[105]

In the state's capital, the perception was that Richmond was the mecca for runaways. In a December 1845 *Richmond Whig* issue, an editorial letter complained that the blacksmith, carpenter and other shops were filled with black skilled workmen, many of whom hired out their own time and thereby made a nuisance of themselves with their liberties. Those who hired out their own time often learned to write or earned extra money that made it possible for them to escape by bribing willing whites.[106]

What concerned many lawmakers in Virginia was the correlation between those who escaped and their freedom of movement because they hired out their own time. Hiring out slaves was a thriving business as the enslaved population grew in antebellum Virginia. Lewis and Robert Hill, for example, were the leading slave-hiring brokers of Richmond in the 1840s and 1850s. What is most interesting about this group was its focus on securing situations for hired out slaves that were not "dangerous or excessively laborious." Some owners wanted the terms to allow for family visitation by those hired out. But while not all brokers operated under such humane strictures, these conditions suggest that slaveholders believed that if slaves were treated well and allowed to visit their families, they would not seek to escape.[107]

Newspaper articles highlighted the extent of the hiring out practices in Virginia and the frequency with which these slaves also escaped. In May 1834, James Thomas of Portsmouth hired out Mat Drewry from owner

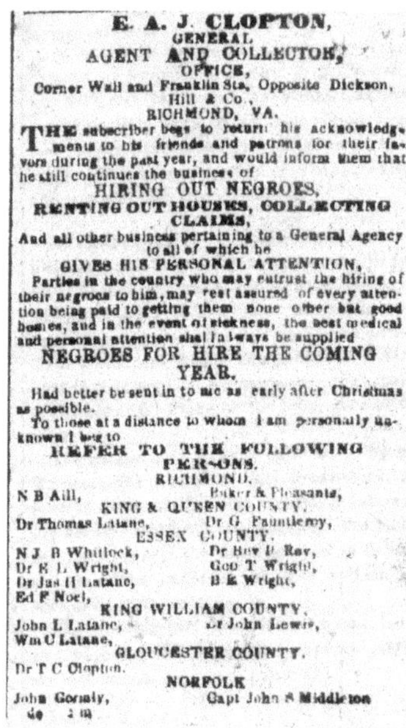

E. A. J. CLOPTON,
GENERAL
AGENT AND COLLECTOR,
OFFICE,
Corner Wall and Franklin Sts, Opposite Dickson, Hill & Co.,
RICHMOND, VA.

THE subscriber begs to return his acknowledgments to his friends and patrons for their favors during the past year, and would inform them that he still continues the business of

HIRING OUT NEGROES,
RENTING OUT HOUSES, COLLECTING CLAIMS,

And all other business pertaining to a General Agency to all of which he

GIVES HIS PERSONAL ATTENTION,

Parties in the country who may entrust the hiring of their negroes to him, may rest assured of every attention being paid to getting them none other but good homes, and in the event of sickness, the best medical and personal attention shall always be supplied

NEGROES FOR HIRE THE COMING YEAR,

Had better be sent in to me as early after Christmas as possible.

To those at a distance to whom I am personally unknown I beg to

REFER TO THE FOLLOWING PERSONS.

RICHMOND.
N B Aill, Baker & Pleasants,
KING & QUEEN COUNTY.
Dr Thomas Latane, Dr G Fauntleroy,
ESSEX COUNTY.
N J B Whitlock, Dr Bev B Roy,
Dr E L Wright, Geo T Wright,
Dr Jas H Latane, B E Wright,
Ed F Noel,
KING WILLIAM COUNTY.
John L Latane, Dr John Lewis,
Wm C Latane,
GLOUCESTER COUNTY.
Dr T C Clopton.
NORFOLK
John Gormly, Capt John S Middleton
de 2 m

This January 15, 1859 *Southern Argus* article highlights the importance of slave hiring in many of Virginia's port cities, such as Norfolk, even though an 1854 Virginia law attempted to restrict hiring out slaves. Resistance was strong from slaveholders, because for many, hiring out their slaves was their primary source of income. *Author's collection.*

William Portlock. Drewry, a light-skinned slave between the age of fourteen and fifteen, wore good clothing when he escaped on May 20, but not before robbing Thomas of twenty-five or thirty dollars in cash. Thomas offered five dollars for Drewry's capture, but to no avail. Numerous other advertisements documented fugitive activities in Hampton Roads, including many from North Carolina whose owners believed their slaves had made their way to the region in order to pass as free people or to secure passage out of the state. One advertisement from Petersburg noted that the owner believed the fugitive "went to Norfolk in a training stable" and would probably try to get a job as a free person.[108] If fugitive slaves were leaving the area, however, they needed assistance. The first concrete evidence of that assistance was in 1845 when Henry Boyer, a free black steward, was arrested in Portsmouth for assisting in the escape of a fugitive aboard the schooner *Cornelia*.[109]

Some industries depended on hired out slaves, such as Richmond's Tredegar Iron Works factory. Its president, Joseph Reid Anderson, hired up to 750 slaves during the Civil War because of labor needs. Anderson also hired slaves as strikebreakers, paying as much as $150 per year with additional monies to slaves if they worked overtime. Frederick Law Olmsted, the noted American landscape architect, journalist and social critic, observed that hiring out slaves made them more independent, which threatened the institution by providing the first step toward freedom.[110] With over one thousand ships coming into these ports annually, maintaining security was impossible. It seemed that Underground Railroad activities in Virginia had reached a pinnacle.

Prior to the 1840s, most slaveholders hunted for fugitive slaves in likely places, such as areas familiar to the enslaved or where their families lived. By the 1850s, a more systematic effort had developed involving train and

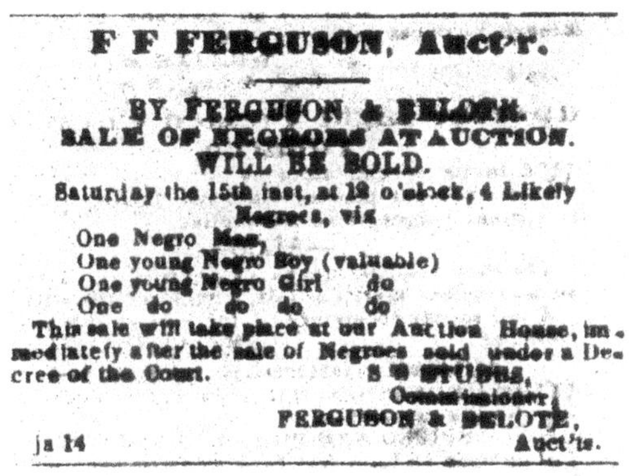

F F FERGUSON, Auct'r.

BY FERGUSON & BELOTE.
SALE OF NEGROES AT AUCTION.
WILL BE SOLD.
Saturday the 15th inst, at 12 o'clock, 4 Likely Negroes, viz
One Negro Man,
One young Negro Boy (valuable)
One young Negro Girl do
One do do do do
This sale will take place at our Auction House, immediately after the sale of Negroes sold under a Decree of the Court. S W STUBBS, Commissioner.
FERGUSON & BELOTE, Auct'rs.
ja 14

Left: This January 15, 1859 *Southern Argus* advertisement illustrates the frequency of slave auctions. *Author's collection.*

Below: This map is a sketch of the road from Fredericksburg to Norfolk in Virginia, circa 1781. What is clearly indicated on the map is the distance between the major cities and towns from Fredericksburg to Norfolk and the prominence of the waterways for those traveling in this region of Virginia. *Library of Congress.*

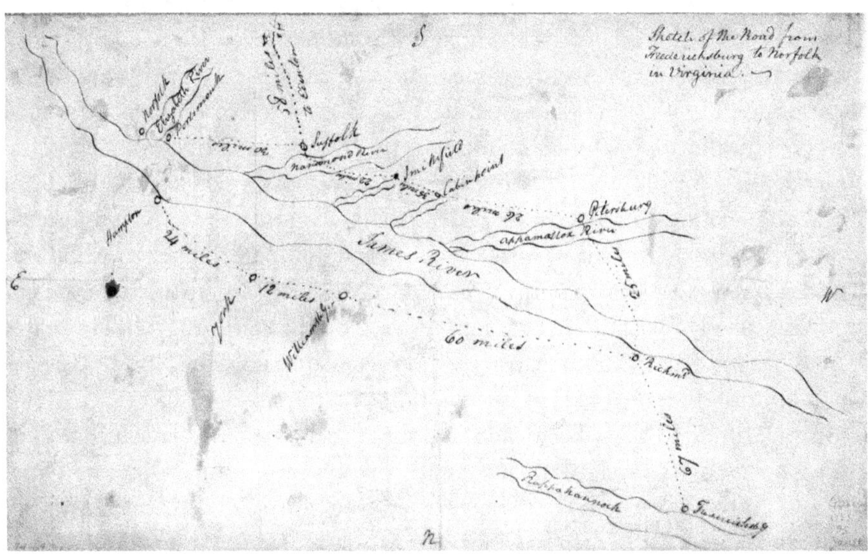

ship personnel as well as constables and mariners whose information was generously rewarded. The result was the arrest and detention of numerous ship captains, stewards and crewmen for assisting runaways. An article in the *American Beacon* argued that between $40,000 and $50,000 worth of slave property left the Hampton Roads port in 1853 alone. In 1854, the *American Beacon* exclaimed that slaves escaped "almost daily," with leaders from both Portsmouth and Norfolk fearing that their cities' losses totaled as much as $500,000. These losses caused lawmakers to step up efforts to deter escapes with increased night watchmen, laws penalizing those who assisted fugitives and severe prison terms. Yet even with these efforts, only a few were convicted and received prison terms. In fact, despite efforts by local and state officials, the Virginia Penitentiary records between 1842 and 1860 included only twenty-seven men who were imprisoned for assisting fugitives in the state.[111]

Escape aboard ships was sometimes a double-edged sword. Because so many took money in exchange for transport to the North, fugitive safety was always at risk. Fannie Nicholson, the former slave of Mrs. Margaret Hodges, the daughter of Portsmouth slaveholder General John Hodges, recounted in a Works Progress Administration narrative that some of the slaves resorted to extreme measures in their attempts to escape, such as being placed in wooden boxes on ships bound for the North. According to Nicholson, some slaves met a watery doom when these boats were boarded by slaveholders, especially at the inspection stations. To avoid imprisonment, some of these captains even dumped overboard boxes containing slaves.[112]

Not surprisingly, fugitive accounts illustrate how the escapes sometimes corresponded with auction schedules. The case of Shadrach Minkins provides another opportunity to observe this intertwined dynamic between the cities of Norfolk and Portsmouth and how slaves, fearing the auction block and working in proximity to the ports, would take advantage and escape. Shadrach Minkins would be the first nationally known runaway arrested under the 1850 Fugitive Slave Act, designed to ensure a captured fugitive's speedy return to his or her owner. Consequently, the Minkins case gained national attention because of the successful efforts by Boston's black abolitionists, who ensured that he would not be returned to slavery.[113]

Born around 1822, Shadrach Minkins, who was called Sherwood during his formative years, was originally owned by Thomas Glenn, a New Kent County native who had been operating the Eagle Tavern (a hotel and eatery) near the Norfolk waterfront at the foot of Market Square and Commerce Street for at least fifteen years in 1830. It was easily accessible to officers stationed at the Gosport Navy Yard. As one of twelve slaves owned by Glenn, who ran the Eagle Tavern (and hotel), Minkins was familiar with whites and blacks from Portsmouth and Norfolk and glaringly cognizant that his situation was tenuous.[114]

Visitors to the tavern occasionally heard the shouts and cries of the city's slave auctions. As an important slave depot situated along the Eastern Seaboard, dealers collected and confined enslaved African Americans in Norfolk's slave pen until a sufficiently large enough number could be transported farther south, where their labors in the field were most needed. Even a white visitor to Norfolk remarked about the horrible conditions in these slave pens. Published in the local newspaper, this visitor in the

1830s remarked, "Here they are kept. With as little food and clothing as is compatible with bare existence: for, regarding them as articles of traffic, they spend no more upon them than will suffice to keep them alive, and in traveling condition."[115]

By 1832, Minkins's fears about being sold came to fruition. His owner died, and like many widows in the area, Glenn's wife hired out her slaves as a way to sustain herself with an annual income. So Minkins went to work for Martha Hutchings, who operated the R.S. Hutchings & Company, a store and warehouse on Newton's Wharf (located at the foot of Market Square), a few steps from Eagle Tavern. The year 1849 would be a turning point for Minkins, who endured three purchases. Finally, Minkins was sold in November to John DeBree for $300. What exactly prompted Minkins to leave Norfolk may never be known, but a reference made by a woman who passed through William Still's station indicated that he was not alone in his escape. Rebecca Jones, a twenty-eight-year-old mulatto who escaped to Boston in 1856 along with her three children, noted that her husband, Henry Lewey, the notorious Underground Railroad conductor Bluebeard, had escaped with Shadrach Minkins six years prior.[116]

Historian David Collinson, who chronicled the life of Minkins, believed that he departed Norfolk aboard either the *Alvaro Lamphir* or the *Vesper*, schooners destined for Boston and New Bedford, respectively. More likely, Minkins headed directly to Boston, hiding in Boston's Sixth Ward, also known as the West End.[117] Reportedly, this neighborhood sheltered so many Hampton Roads residents that fugitives like Mary Millburn wrote to William Still that "I have met with so many of my acquaintances hear, that I all most immagion [*sic*] my self to bee [*sic*] in the old country."[118]

Shortly after arriving in Boston, Shadrach Minkins encountered a white southerner, William H. Parks, a commission merchant who had been employed by Minkins's second owner, Martha Hutchings. Minkins's fears were not realized when, instead of contacting Norfolk's authorities, Parks gave Minkins his first paying job. Sometime later, Minkins found work as a waiter in the Cornhill Coffee House, a restaurant and hotel that "stood in the heart of Boston's business and government district." This was a particularly conspicuous place to work for a fugitive trying to remain anonymous in a city teeming with slave owners and bounty hunters bent on retrieving their slaves.[119]

Unfortunately for Minkins, anonymity was short-lived. Unbeknown to Minkins, Norfolk's constable John Capheart, a veteran in the world of fugitive slaves and seaports, arrived in Boston in February 1851 armed with John DeBree's legal papers, proving his ownership of Shadrach. So intimidating was Capheart that his image and persona were copied by Harriet Beecher Stowe in her book, *Uncle Tom's Cabin*, and by abolitionists for their posters warning citizens of the slave hunters. Eventually, a warrant was issued for Minkins. He was identified despite the efforts of fellow Norfolk fugitive George Latimer, who had been asked to try and keep Minkins safe from being identified by slave hunters. Nevertheless, Minkins was identified and brought to the courthouse; over one hundred people had assembled after receiving the news of his arrest.[120]

The black community, in particular, was determined to prevent his removal from Boston and was prepared to take action against any officials willing to enforce the Fugitive Slave Act. This position differed from New York's, where many black abolitionists struggled against the pro-slavery position of city officials and the milder stance of its white abolitionists. Until the 1850s, when a strong vigilance committee was established by David Ruggles, fugitives were at the mercy of slave hunters, constables, lawyers and others willing to assist slave owners in retrieving their slaves. In fact, there was even a New York Kidnapping Club, composed of local officials who recaptured slaves or captured free blacks and turned them in for a reward. They justified their actions by claiming that freedom was a curse and that blacks were better off in slavery. Fortunately for New Yorkers, the regions outside New York City were more protective. Many fugitives were dispatched in upstate New York, either by train or steamboat, with many continuing on until reaching Canada. Such an attitude did not exist among many in Boston.[121]

During Minkins's arraignment, a group of fifteen black abolitionists forced their way inside the locked courtroom, rescuing him from the federal marshals and rushing him through the streets of Boston. Reportedly, Lewis Hayden, a staunch abolitionist and fugitive slave who vowed that he would never be returned to slavery, and one of his attorneys, black abolitionist Robert Morris, temporarily hid him in the attic of a widow, Elizabeth Riley, whose house was located a few blocks from Hayden's on Southac Place. Lewis Hayden took Minkins by horse-drawn cab to Cambridge, where he stayed at the home of a vigilance committee member, the Reverend Joseph Lovejoy, brother of martyred abolitionist newspaper publisher Elijah Lovejoy. For the next several days, Minkins would be conveyed from home to home until he was taken by carriage across the border into Canada. In the interim, President Millard Fillmore issued a largely symbolic proclamation condemning the rescue and calling on all citizens to obey the law.[122]

Another Virginia fugitive whose efforts to secure his freedom garnered national attention was the 1854 case of Anthony Burns. Like Minkins, he was quickly discovered after arriving in the North. But unlike Minkins, Burns was returned to Virginia amid considerable consternation by those who hoped for this successful escape. Burns escaped from his owner, Charles Suttle, in Alexandria. After reaching Boston, Burns worked at a clothing store owned by Coffin Pitts, an African American trader. However, Boston, like many northern cities with a robust trade with the South, was filled with slave catchers who spied on businesses in the black community. Asa O. Butman was one such slave catcher who watched Burns for a while before arresting him on false charges that he robbed a jewelry store. Suddenly, Burns was subdued by several men and taken bodily to the courthouse, where a U.S. marshal awaited him. And even though Burns did not resist arrest or refute accusations that he was a fugitive slave, the black community was not so willing to capitulate. Leading black abolitionists Robert Morris and Leonard Grimes held a public meeting at Faneuil Hall, where they vowed they would not allow Burns's return to slavery. Federal marshals intervened, and a fight broke out, resulting in officials doubling the guards around Burns. Once Burns was convicted and ordered returned, the Massachusetts Infantry was called in to escort him to the ship for transport to Virginia. But Burns's return would be short; Grimes collected funds from his congregation, the Twelfth Baptist Church, to purchase his freedom. Burns later used his freedom to garner support for the antislavery cause by joining the lecture circuit.[123]

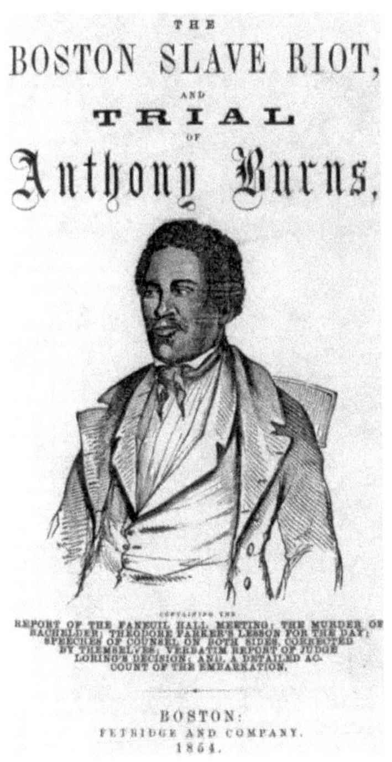
THE
BOSTON SLAVE RIOT,
AND
TRIAL
OF
Anthony Burns,

CONTAINING THE
REPORT OF THE FANEUIL HALL MEETING; THE MURDER OF BACHELDER; THEODORE PARKER'S LESSON FOR THE DAY; SPEECHES OF COUNSEL ON BOTH SIDES, CORRECTED BY THEMSELVES; VERBATIM REPORT OF JUDGE LORING'S DECISION; AND, A DETAILED ACCOUNT OF THE EMBARKATION.

BOSTON:
FETRIDGE AND COMPANY.
1854.

This book cover was published following the case involving Anthony Burns, including his arrest, trial, conviction and return to his owner in Virginia. *Library of Congress.*

Like Burns, fellow Richmond resident Henry Brown, who acquired the nickname Henry "Box" Brown because of the unusual way he escaped, also became a popular figure on the abolitionist lecture circuit. Unlike others who hid in boxes aboard ships, Brown had himself successfully mailed to Philadelphia.[124]

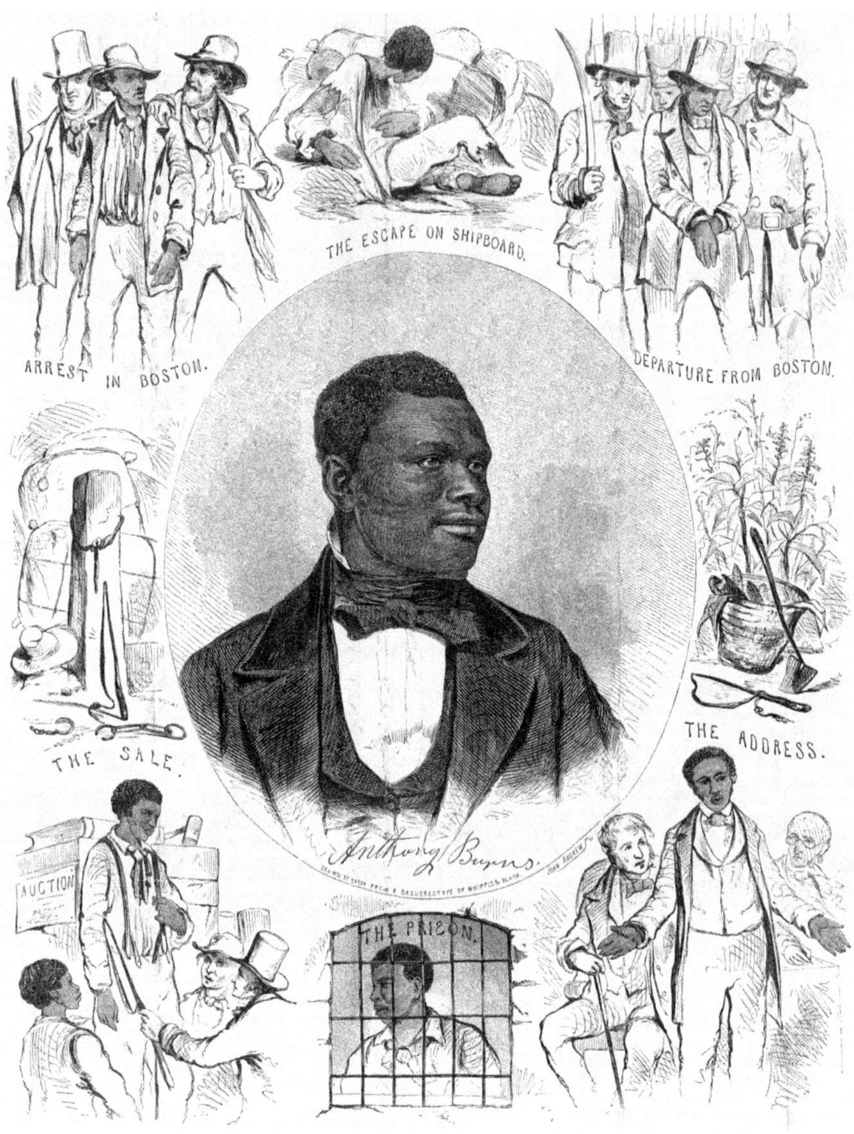

Once black abolitionists purchased Anthony Burns's freedom, he became a popular figure on the antislavery lecture circuit. This broadside was a popular illustration that accompanied his lectures on his travails from his status as a slave, arrest and return to slavery, before eventually gaining his freedom. *Library of Congress.*

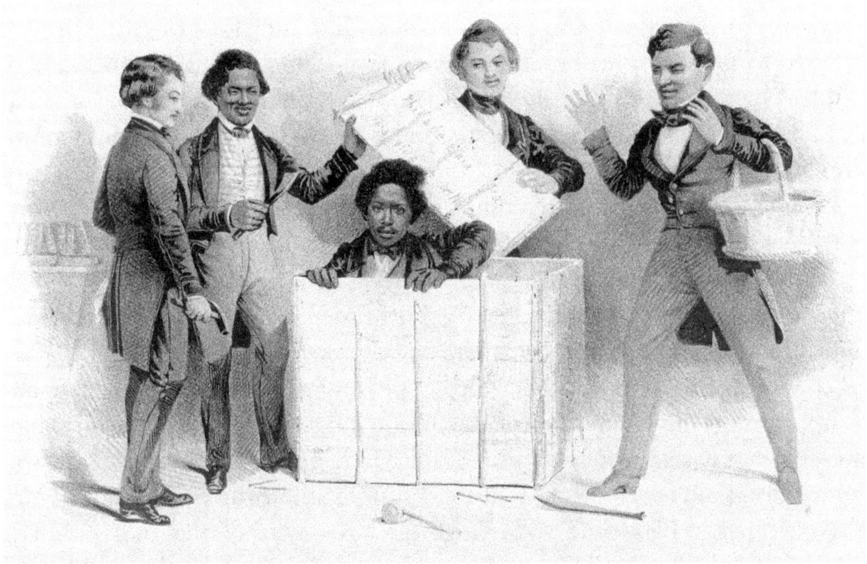

This iconic illustration of Henry "Box" Brown being released by William Still and the Philadelphia Vigilance Committee from the box in which he mailed himself from Richmond to Philadelphia was used to advertise Brown's adventures, struggles and travails. The irony is that the image is not Brown. Instead, Frederick Douglass was substituted because the artist did not know what Brown looked like. *Library of Congress.*

Brown was born about 1815 on the Hermitage plantation in Louisa County, located east of the Blue Ridge Mountains and forty-five miles from Richmond. John Barret, a notable Virginian, owned Brown and his mother and father and six siblings. When Barret died, the fifteen-year-old Brown expected that his owner would free the family because they had faithfully served him. Instead, they were dispersed, along with all forty of Barret's slaves, to the four sons. Brown's new owner, William Barret, owned a tobacco business in Richmond, carrying Brown from his home and family. As William Barret was a member of the Richmond and Manchester Colonization Society, Brown again expected that he would be freed; but the Nat Turner revolt squashed that hope, as many who had previously been sympathetic to abolitionism became slavery advocates.[125]

Brown's wife, Nancy, and their children were owned by Samuel Cottrell, whom Brown described as vile and money hungry. Forcing Brown to provide him with fifty dollars a year and housing costs in exchange for not selling them away placed a tremendous burden on him. Eventually, Cottrell did sell the family, and Brown was left waving goodbye forever to his wife and children. So devastated was he by this loss that after four months, Brown decided to flee from his heartless owner. According to Brown, he pleaded with his owner to purchase his family to avoid sale, reminding Barret that he had served him faithfully. Casting him aside coldly, his owner told him to simply get another wife.[126]

In January 1849, Brown contacted Samuel Smith, a forty-two-year-old shoemaker and Massachusetts transplant. In exchange for money (an estimated forty dollars), Smith agreed to assist Brown in his efforts to escape, but the method was under dispute. A short time later, while praying, Brown recounted how he received the answer about how he should escape. In his 1851 account, Brown said these words, "Go and get a box, and put yourself in it," came to his mind. He quickly had a carpenter construct a box that was commonly sent from Richmond to Philadelphia by the Adams Express. Brown also paid for Smith to visit the Pennsylvania Anti-Slavery Society in Philadelphia on his behalf to arrange for a recipient of the "box." Smith spoke with J. Miller McKim, who agreed to receive the box, along with one hundred dollars that Brown had raised with considerable additional hours of work in the tobacco factory. After an arduous twenty-four-hour journey, Brown was released from his self-imposed prison in the Philadelphia Anti-Slavery office.[127]

Unlike Brown, who took a circuitous journey by train and boat to Philadelphia, others were able to secure a more direct route to the North aboard vessels, sometimes unbeknown to their captains and crews. Most, however, received assistance either from captains and/or stewards on these steamships. William Still noted that key vessels included the *City of Richmond*, the *Pennsylvania* and the *Augusta* steamships, as well as the *Keziah* schooner.

In Norfolk, the *City of Richmond* with Captain Mitchell and the *Pennsylvania* with Captain Teal were Union Pacific Steamship Company vessels that left from Higgins' Wharf every Tuesday and Thursday at noon throughout the 1850s. Another steamship used to secret slaves to the North was the *Augusta*, captained by William C. Smith. This vessel left every Tuesday, Thursday and Saturday at 6:30 a.m. from Wright's Wharf in Norfolk. Moreover, fugitives may have been assisted in their escape by the Norfolk and Western Railroad, whose track ran down Widewater Street and by every major wharf along the waterfront in downtown Norfolk, or by the all-black crews operating the ferries that ran between Norfolk and Portsmouth.[128]

Those who chose to escape by schooner left from vessels docked in the center of commercial shipping activity. In November 1855, Captain Alfred Fountain left for Philadelphia with twenty-two fugitive slaves. His schooner, loaded with wheat, was probably docked at the wharf in Roanoke Square because of the number of hay, wheat and grain dealers. The owner of fugitives Thomas and Frederick Nixon, B.T. Bockover, was a commissioning merchant and grocer at Roanoke Square. After the Nixon brothers boarded Fountain's schooner, a group of city leaders, led by Mayor William Lamb, boarded the ship to search for escaped slaves. Fountain's bravado saved the day when the men came aboard with axes to tear the ship apart. He said, "Now if you want to search…give me the axe, and then point out the spot you want opened and I will open it for you very quick." While uttering these words, he defiantly struck his ship with the axe several times, splinters flying everywhere. Soon, some of the men were convinced that no slaves were on board, and Fountain left Norfolk with all the fugitives in tow, including men, women and children.[129]

One of the freedom seekers who was part of this group assisted by Fountain was thirty-eight-year-old Daniel Carr, who was described by Still as a dark mulatto. Carr had been purchased in Portsmouth for $1,150 by John C. McBole from Plymouth, North Carolina, a steam mill owner. Refusing to go to North Carolina, Carr's first escape effort was unsuccessful; he was stripped naked and flogged severely. During a secret visit to his wife, Hannah, and his three children, Sam, Dan and "baby," he was introduced to Captain Alfred Fountain, who advised him to hide in the Dismal Swamp to raise money for his passage until his ship was ready for departure. Carr took Fountain's advice and hid in the swamp, surrounded by "wild animals and reptiles." Eventually, Fountain came to retrieve him in the swamp and proceeded to Norfolk, where he picked up additional freedom seekers. Unfortunately for Carr, he had to leave his family behind. It is unknown whether Daniel ever reunited with his wife and children. According to the 1861 Canadian census, he was listed living alone as a mulatto in Williamsburg, Dundas, in Canada West.[130]

A year after Fountain's dramatic escape from Norfolk, another schooner left the city under a cloud of suspicion. Fifteen freedom seekers left aboard the schooner owned and captained by William Baylis. Baylis hid the fugitives in a secret compartment in the lower deck of the vessel during two separate inspections. His schooner, the *Keziah*, was suspected of harboring runaways, resulting in a second inspection. After deflecting suspicion by encouraging officials to search as long as they pleased (and by offhandedly referring to the yellow fever that recently raged in the Norfolk area), Baylis paid the inspectors three dollars and they departed. Despite two inspections, city officials were convinced that fugitives were on board, sending a message to

Philadelphia to seize the ship once it arrived. Word got to the captain to go to League Island—a remote island not too far from Philadelphia—instead, where carriages and assistance awaited the freedom seekers.[131]

Aboard this schooner landing on League Island was freedom seeker Rebecca Lewey, wife of the most "dexterous manager" in the Underground Railroad, Henry Lewey. Although Rebecca was a slave, her gentle manner and health suggested that she was not worked severely by her owner. Nevertheless, she was sent northward by her husband. William Still reported that a few months later, Henry and Rebecca were reunited in Canada. Lewey was suspected of being involved with the Underground Railroad and had actually been arrested once. He was released for lack of evidence, however, and later escaped along with Shadrach Minkins.[132]

That same year, while visiting a Richmond oyster house, the captain of the *Keziah* riled a slave owner who had just received a mocking letter from a former slave who had escaped a few months prior and was safely in Canada.

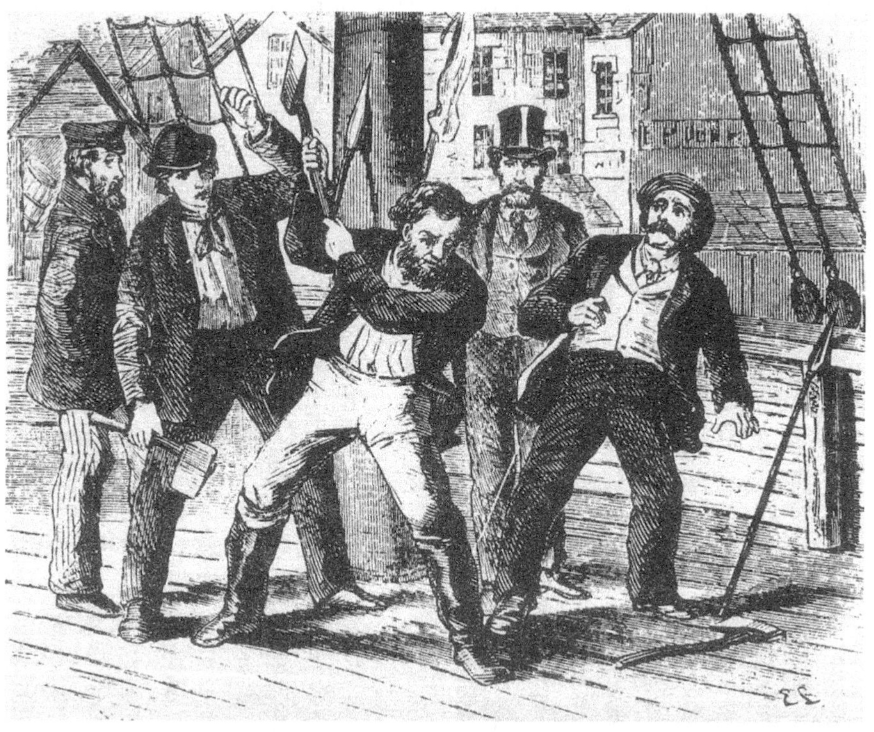

This drawing depicts the daring and quick thinking of Captain Alfred Fountain, who, when challenged by Norfolk leaders convinced he was hiding escaped slaves, successfully left the city with twenty-two fugitives hiding in a secret compartment aboard his schooner. *William Still,* The Underground Railroad, *1872.*

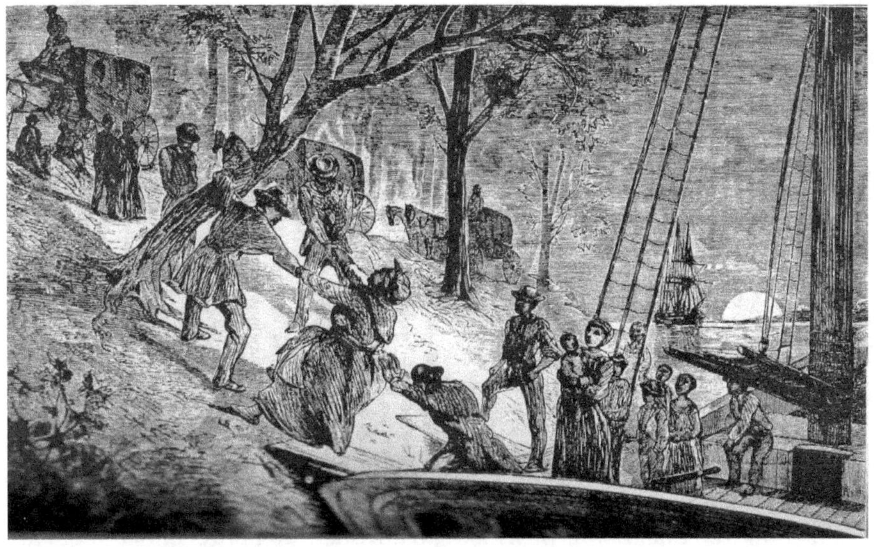

Freedom seekers arriving on League Island being met by abolitionists after successful escape from Hampton Roads, Virginia. *William Still,* The Underground Railroad, *1872.*

Apparently, the slave owner thought Baylis was involved and alerted authorities. On May 31, 1858, the *Keziah* left City Point, Virginia, carrying a cargo of wheat. Norfolk mayor Finlay F. Ferguson contacted officials in Richmond, warning them that Baylis might try to avoid inspection because he was suspected of having runaways on board. His ship was stopped thirty miles below City Point, near Riverport, in Petersburg with five fugitives stowed aboard in sundry places, including one hidden behind a trapdoor in the captain's quarters and another in a special section of the cargo hold.[133]

Baylis was part of a larger network that went from Richmond to Norfolk and involved whites, free blacks and urban slaves. In this incident, he apparently contacted the Railroad conductor in the City Marketplace, who charged each slave $50 in exchange for safe passage to the North. Of course, if they were caught, the money was a small incentive compared to a possible prison sentence of ten years or the $500 paid to anyone turning in a suspected Underground Railroad supporter. Caught with the evidence, Baylis admitted his guilt and was subsequently tried and convicted in the Petersburg Circuit Court. The *Williamsburg Weekly Gazette* declared this as the "most heinous" crime and argued for the death penalty. Instead, the jury sentenced him to forty years. His wife and supporters, including the Wilmington, Delaware mayor, Thomas Young, circulated a petition to commute the sentence. Within two years after being imprisoned, rumors began to circulate about Baylis's death.

Distraught, his wife, Martha, launched an effort to free him. And because of her efforts, including a barrage of letters to Virginia governor William Smith and William Storms, a Cincinnati merchant with connections to Jefferson Davis, Baylis was eventually freed. Baylis was transported along with Union prisoners to his home in Wilmington, Delaware, in March 1865.[134]

The arrests of prominent captains such as Baylis suspected for their involvement in the Underground Railroad may have slowed the numbers who steamed out of Tidewater waterways in the 1850s, but the escapes did not stop. Numerous other freedom seekers continued fleeing with the assistance of conductors who risked life, limb and freedom—sometimes in exchange for money.

Desperate to stop all escapes, in 1856, slaveholders successfully pressured the Virginia General Assembly to pass a comprehensive program that would involve the inspection of all vessels coming into Virginia's ports. A reward of one hundred dollars was provided "to anyone who apprehended fugitives found aboard vessels, a five-to-ten-year imprisonment of free persons found guilty of assisting fugitives, and the payment of five hundred dollars to those who provided information which led to the 'conviction of a free white person engaged in carrying off a slave, or in any manner concerned in helping an escape.'"[135] For instance, Edward Lee was turned in by Portsmouth slaveholders James Murdaugh, William H. Wilson, Joseph Carter and James Hodges. Lee was convicted under Section Twenty-Seven of the 1856 Act because he assisted slaves in April 1858. In July 1858, these men presented evidence of Lee's guilt.[136]

Of course, efforts to stave the tide of those leaving aboard vessels bound for the North did not affect freedom seekers who left on foot or by wagon, horse or train. It also did not impede those who sought the remote refuge of areas like the Dismal Swamp. These individuals chose the life of a maroon, in which life in the swamp provided a seemingly safe haven for runaways; whites avoided the area with its natural dangers, dense vegetation and diseases. At the same time, whites were afraid that the Dismal Swamp allowed maroons to mass in preparation for a revolt.[137]

There were also fugitives who arrived in Pennsylvania without assistance from conductors by pretending to be white or free, traveling on foot at night or hiding on ships from the South. Once in the North, however, the importance of the vigilance committees became critical. Committees in Pennsylvania and Massachusetts forwarded fugitives to more northern states and to Canada. However, those who opted to remain in the United States were assisted in finding housing and jobs and creating new identities. There

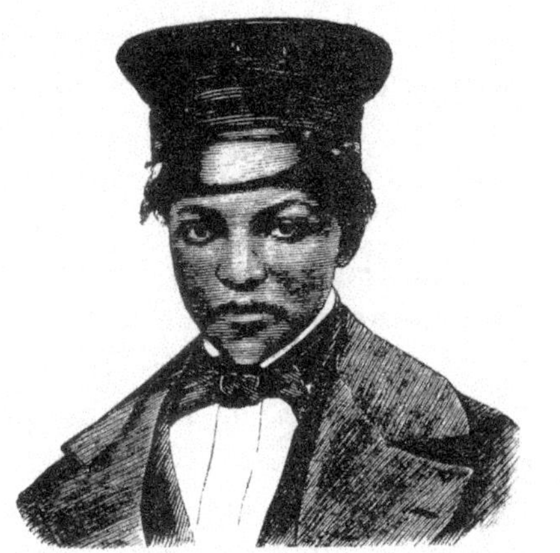

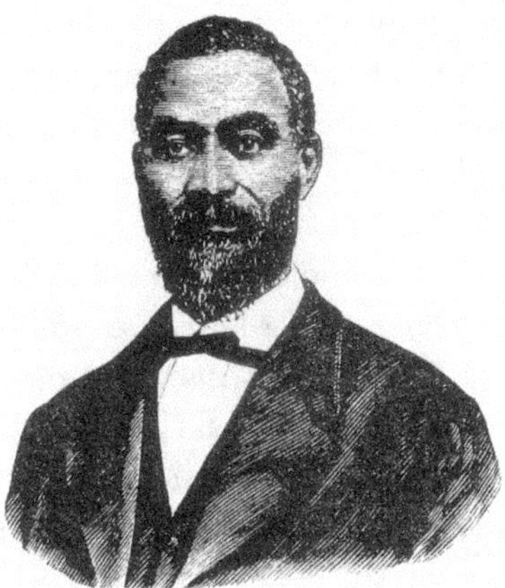

Left: Ann Maria Weems (alias Joe Wright and Ellen Capron) escaped from her owner in Washington, D.C. Weems represented the typical strategy used by many women, such as Clarissa Davis, to escape undetected. By dressing as a man, she avoided questions and attention. *William Still,* The Underground Railroad, *1872.*

Right: In January 1853, John Henry Hill from Petersburg managed to escape from a Richmond slave auction. Hill was a six-foot-tall, twenty-five-year-old literate carpenter who hired out his time. For several years, Hill coordinated with William Still and others to secure the escape of freedom seekers from Petersburg and Richmond, arranging their travel to Canada. *William Still,* The Underground Railroad, *1872.*

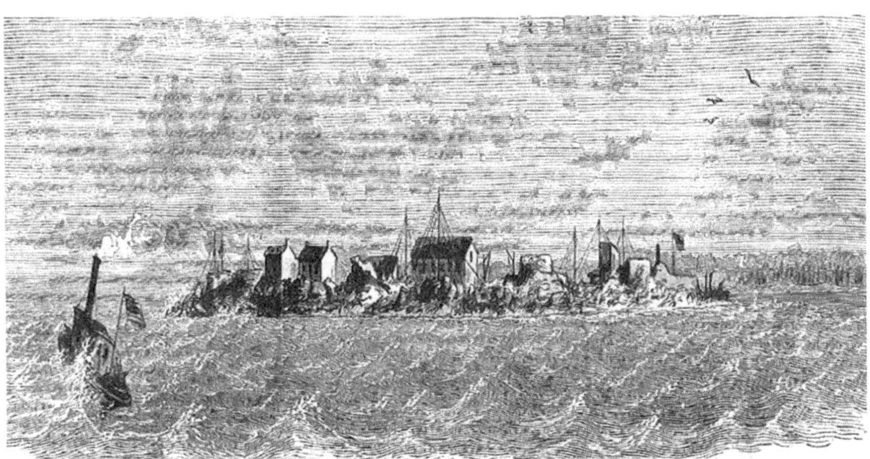

The Rip Raps, reclaimed land positioned in the middle of the waterways called the Hampton Roads, was used as an inspection station for all vessels, especially those with a northern registry, to stop and be scrutinized by state officials. The real purpose of the inspection was to capture freedom seekers hiding aboard any vessels leaving the state. *Harrison B. Wilson Archives, Norfolk State University.*

were also some fugitives who recounted their escape from northern cities after randomly meeting members of a vigilance committee who encouraged them to run away (with their assistance). After the 1850 passage of the Fugitive Slave Act, most abolitionists encouraged all known fugitives to move on to Canada.[138]

Two examples of fugitives who self-emancipated during this period were the Harris and Matterson brothers, who escaped from Martinsburg along with the Grigsby party from Loudon and Fauquier Counties. In 1855, Barnaby Grigsby, Mary Elizabeth, Frank Wanzer and Emily Foster escaped from their owners but found themselves fighting for their lives while near the Cheat River in Maryland. The group was confronted by six white men and one white boy who believed the travelers were fugitive slaves. Wanzer said to them that "no gentleman would interfere with persons riding along civilly." Once the freedom seekers realized that the slave catchers refused to let them continue, they all pulled out their guns declaring that they would not be taken. One of the white men raised his gun at one of the women and threatened that he would shoot. She exclaimed, "Shoot! Shoot!! Shoot!!!" while pulling out a double-barreled pistol. The white men pulled back, seeing they were out-gunned, and allowed the group to flee, with two of the men riding away on horses while the other four drove away in a wagon. The two men on horseback were later captured, according to the *Frederick Examiner*. The others succeeded in settling in Toronto.[139]

These escapes symbolized the lengths to which freedom seekers were determined to go to achieve liberty. In both cases, these fugitives encountered slave hunters who were determined to capture and return them for a reward. Fatalities or captures did occur, with some fugitives failing to escape. Others, however, reached freedom, relaying their accounts to William Still in Philadelphia. Their challenges highlighted how it was more likely for fugitives to encounter slave catchers on land than on water.

Other self-emancipators found safe spaces within Virginia. A few miles from the Norfolk Harbor lay an area that William Byrd II, a prominent Virginia planter and slaveholder, called a "dreadful swamp." By some estimates, the seemingly impenetrable swamp was thirty miles from north to south and ten miles from east to west, while others estimate it was two thousand square miles. Thirty miles west of the Atlantic Ocean between the James River in southeastern Virginia near Norfolk and the Albemarle Sound near Edenton, North Carolina, was the Dismal Swamp, named by eighteenth-century English colonists who saw the swamp "as a vast, dreadful, bleak, and impassable region." Early in its recorded history, the

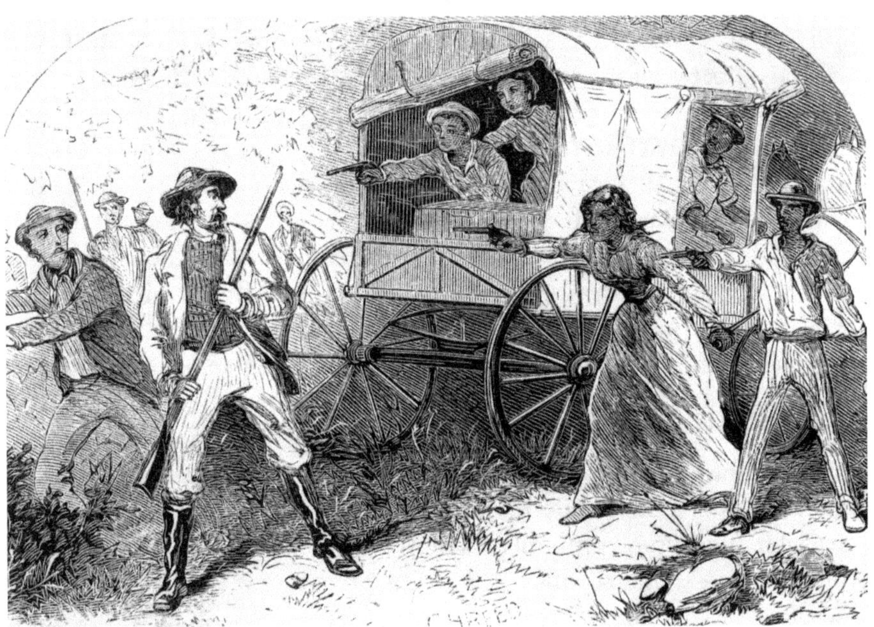

Wesley Harris, alias Robert Jackson, and the Matterson brothers were attacked by slave catchers while being hidden in a barn in Terrytown, Maryland. The men left Martinsburg, Virginia, headed for Gettysburg. *William Still,* The Underground Railroad, *1872.*

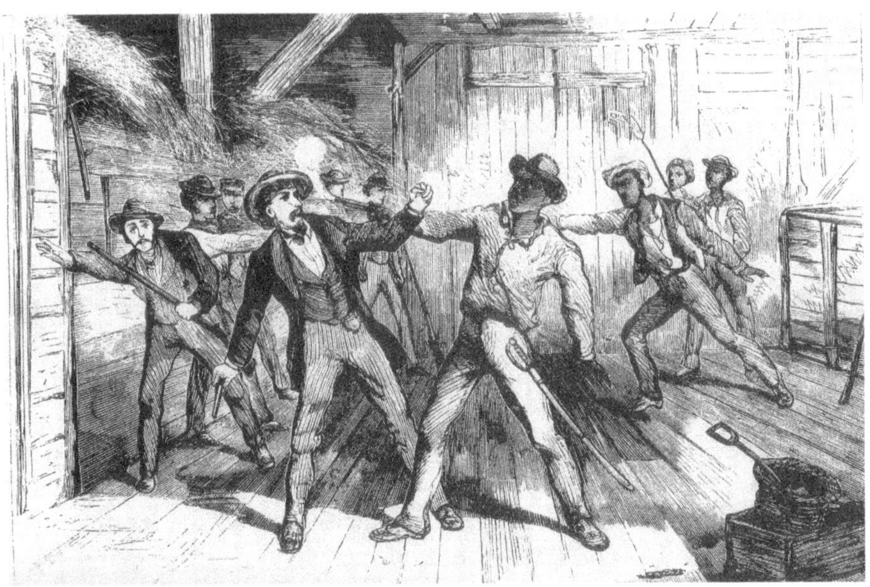

Pictured here are freedom seekers Barnaby Grigby, Mary Elizabeth, Frank Wanzer and Emily Foster defending themselves against slave catchers one hundred miles into their journey from Loudon and Fauquier Counties on Christmas Day, 1855. *William Still,* The Underground Railroad, *1872.*

Dismal Swamp was used as an important refuge for those escaping the many wars waged between the English and native populations. Afterward, many of the swamp's inhabitants were supplanted by freedom-seeking Africans who escaped bondage and formed temporary maroon communities. Only a few successfully maneuvered undetected into the heart of the bog, living off the land and stealing whatever they could to survive.[140]

In 1728, William Byrd II was authorized by the British Crown to settle the Virginia and North Carolina boundary dispute with a survey of the swamp. While conducting the survey, Byrd kept a diary of his adventures, recording sights and sounds of the region and the people he encountered, including a family of fugitive slaves near the Northwest River he described as mulattoes. Expressing concern that the swamp was a refuge for these enslaved runaways, Byrd recommended development of the region to erase the inaccessible areas freedom seekers could use as sanctuaries. Nineteen years later, a group of prominent Virginia speculators formed the Dismal Swamp Land Company with the intent of preparing the area for farming. One of the founders, George Washington, led a crew of men to survey the region, with proposals to use slave labor to drain the water, section off portions and dig ditches. Yet the primary industry remained timbering cypress and Atlantic white cedars, as an economic downturn, combined with internal problems and the start of the American Revolution, brought these ambitions to a sudden halt.[141]

The earliest inhabitants of the Dismal Swamp were indigenous Americans whose presence continued until the 1680s. These first residents of the swamp were Susquehana refugees whose homes had been devastated by war with the English; they were fleeing enslavement. Afterward, they were supplanted by Africans and African Americans who saw the swamp as a place of refuge from slavery and oppression. Early runaway slave advertisements revealed the search by slaveholders of men and women they believed had found refuge within the impassible confines of the Dismal Swamp. Harry was reportedly the slave of Richard Littlepage from Cumberland town; he fled to the swamp because of its proximity to the town where his wife lived. The owner believed that Harry intended to secure passage aboard a ship that would take him out of Virginia. Like Littlepage, many owners believed these fugitives used the swamp as a transit to Norfolk Harbor, where they hoped to gain a pathway to freedom. Others were thought to find freedom within the swamp, such as the 1771 escape of Jack and Venus from Isle of Wight owner Nathaniel Burwell, who believed they had returned to the swamp. The two had worked for

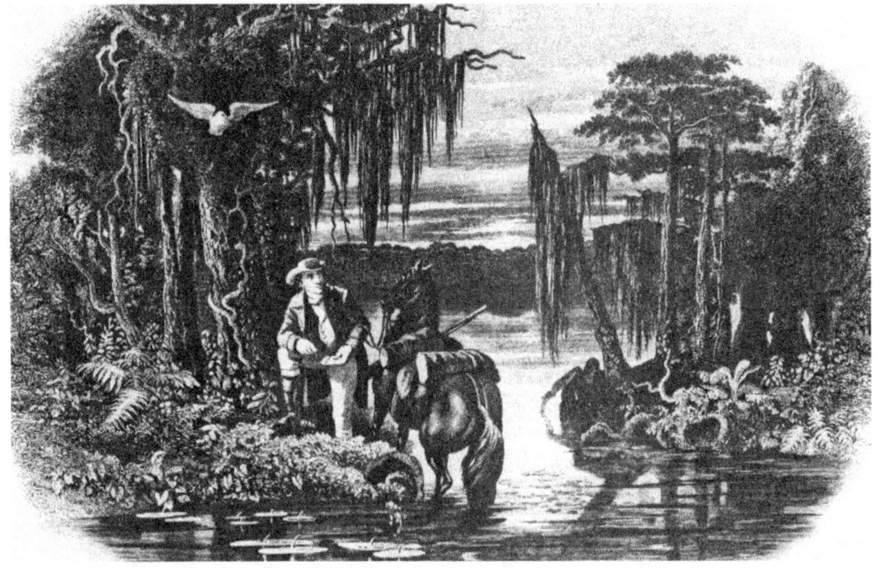

George Washington is depicted here at Lake Drummond in the Dismal Swamp, assessing its value for development. *Portsmouth Public Library*.

George Washington's brother, John, the overseer of the first canal built in the swamp, later known as the Washington Ditch. In fact, fifty-four enslaved men, women and children worked on the Dismal Plantation, located six miles from Suffolk, producing corn, raising livestock and digging the canal. In 1784, reports indicated that some of the blacks residing in the swamp had been there for as long as thirty years.[142]

It was 1793 before the Dismal Swamp Land Company began work on the construction of a series of canals linking the Chesapeake Bay with the Albemarle Sound. The first major canal, or causeway road, opened in 1804. Included in this operation was a narrow canal dug to Lake Drummond, known as Washington's Ditch. Later, the Grand Canal connected the Elizabeth River in Deep Creek, Virginia, to the Pasquatunk River in North Carolina, expanding the global market to this region. By 1805, the Dismal Swamp Canal was officially open for business. Soil from the canals were used to reclaim land for farming on the fringes of the swamp. These developments began transforming the marshy area, bringing in farmers who worked the reclaimed lands and commodity trading that would fill the canals with barges, small ships and lighters. Yet the only industry that succeeded was cedar and cypress trees timbering. These trees were cut into staves, shingles, naval stores and planking and then sent to the

Norfolk port markets for shipment. Eventually, a total of fifty-one miles of canals created a major internal highway, generating revenue for the merchants and producers who could bring their goods quickly and cheaply to market.[143]

Beginning with the Jericho and Washington Ditches, these canals stimulated an increased demand for shingles and timber. For those engaged in constructing those canals, the work was considered "the cruelest, most dangerous, unhealthy, and exhausting labor in the American South."[144] Working in horrific temperatures that ranged from freezing to over 100 degrees, waist-high water, biting insects, venomous snakes and predatory wildlife were typical of the experiences of the enslaved laborers building the canals. A few first-hand accounts portrayed life for African Americans in the Dismal Swamp. Two in particular—Willis Hodges, a free black,

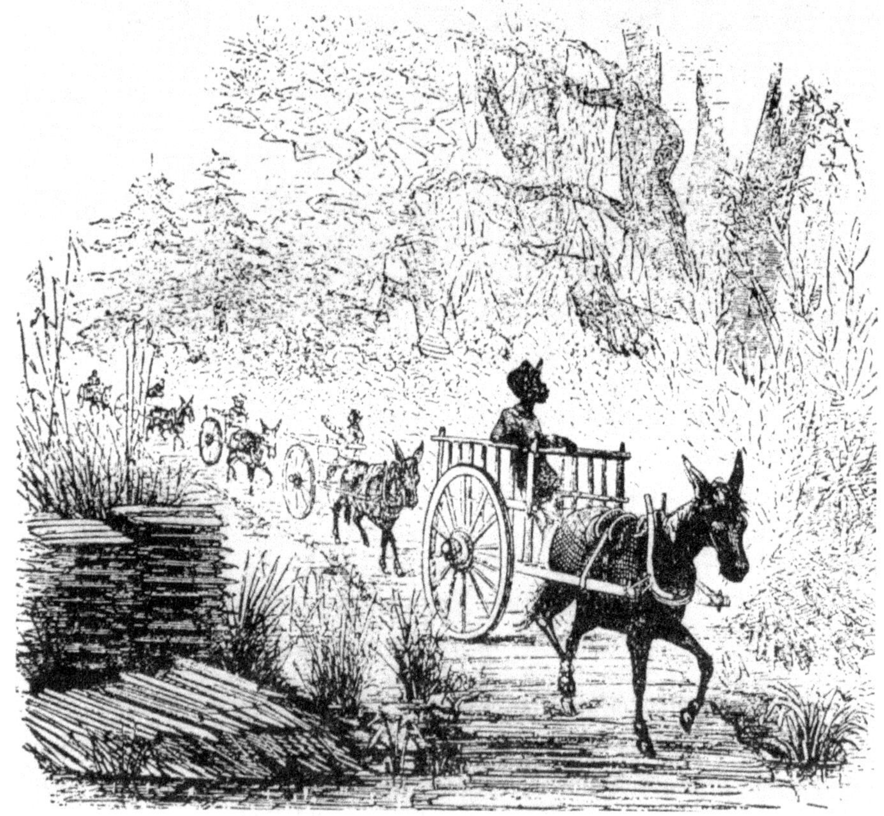

This drawing depicts primarily enslaved blacks working in the Dismal Swamp securing cedar shingles for export and sale. *Portsmouth Public Library*.

and Moses Grandy, an enslaved waterman—wrote accounts of their experiences working on the Dismal Swamp Canal and the fugitives they encountered living on its fringes. Grandy recalled that the ground was so boggy that the men had to work constantly in mud and water. Yet these arduous conditions did not dissuade freedom seekers from making the swamp their sanctuary, so much so that both Virginia and North Carolina were concerned that fugitive slaves passing through the swamps and those living permanently within the swamp as maroons would not be indirectly and secretly employed by those working in the swamp. Consequently, both states required that all enslaved workers register with the county clerks prior to working in the Dismal Swamp. Not surprisingly, this rule was not enforced and offered no deterrence to the ongoing employment of fugitives or maroons in the timbering industry. Throughout the antebellum period, business interests stimulated further canal expansion and reconstruction, widening and deepening channels and creating a navigable passage for larger vessels traveling from Albemarle Sound to Norfolk ports. Despite all intentions, officials knew that the key to these improvements was the employment of enslaved men, both to develop and expand these canals as well as harvest the timber.[145]

The account of Moses Grandy, who gained his freedom in the early 1840s, had some interesting observations. As an enslaved man, he worked as an overseer, supervising and securing cedar shingles, and later as a boat captain, transporting shingles and other supplies from Elizabeth City, North Carolina, to the Norfolk Harbor in the 1820s and 1830s. Grandy confirmed that there was an understanding that a blind eye was turned to the fact that some of the black workers in the Dismal Swamp were maroons who worked with enslaved and free laborers. Grandy also observed in his account that maroons passing through the Dismal Swamp often traveled at night, subsisting on any food they could scavenge, hoping to encounter a passing vessel to take them beyond the borders of slavery.[146]

Evidence as to the presence of generational maroons emerged in two separate events that occurred. In 1845, a great fire ravaged the Dismal Swamp for twelve days, causing severe loss to those in the shingle industry and the maroon communities. A woman who had escaped from her owner twenty-four years prior was forced out of the swamp along with a family of fifteen children, all of whom had been born in the swamp; others had been missing ten, twelve and upward of twenty years. Eleven years later, in 1856, reporter David Hunter Strother published an encounter that he had in the *Harper's New Monthly Magazine*. He ventured into the Dismal Swamp

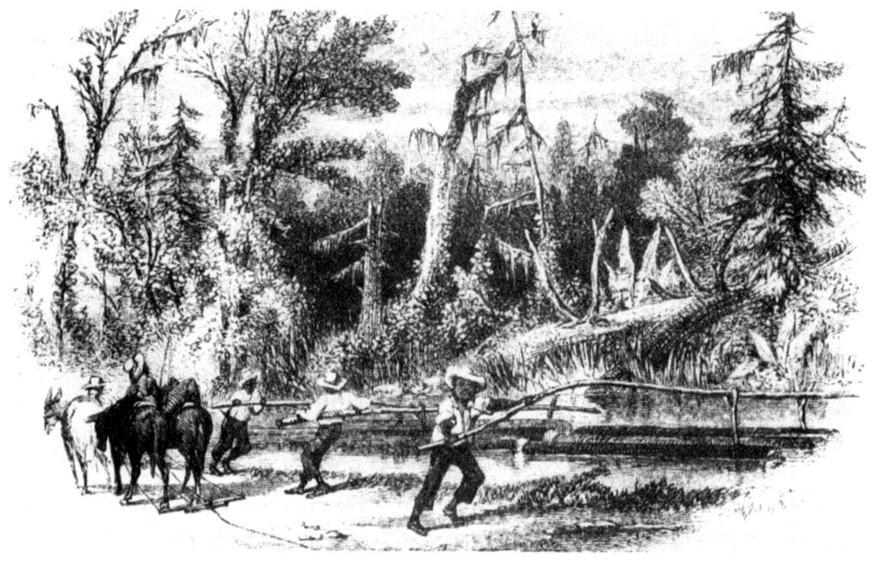

Enslaved black men were often seen working in the Dismal Swamp, moving barges down the canal loaded with logs. *Portsmouth Public Library.*

with the sole purpose of uncovering the maroons who were reported to live in the depths of this impenetrable morass. Strother recounted meeting the sixty-year-old African leader of the maroons, Osman, and the families who generationally lived within the protection of the swamp. After meeting Osman, whose name suggested he was from Nigeria, Strother described him as a formidable and imposing individual with a facial expression that "mingled fear and ferocity" because of a lifetime of "habitual caution and watchfulness."[147]

The *Liberator* published numerous articles about the Dismal Swamp as a hiding place for freedom seekers who would rather endure the harsh environ of the swamp than submit to slavery. The *North Star* called the swamp a "city of refuge" for hundreds of fugitives who sought release from oppression within "the damp and dreary region" of the Dismal Swamp.[148]

Soon, tales of freedom seekers in the Dismal Swamp became a national phenomenon, with Harriet Beecher Stowe and Henry Wadsworth Longfellow penning stories and poems about the imagined and reported experiences of fugitives and maroons. In 1854, Longfellow's poem "A Slave in the Swamp" was republished by many abolitionist newspapers, including Frederick Douglass's:

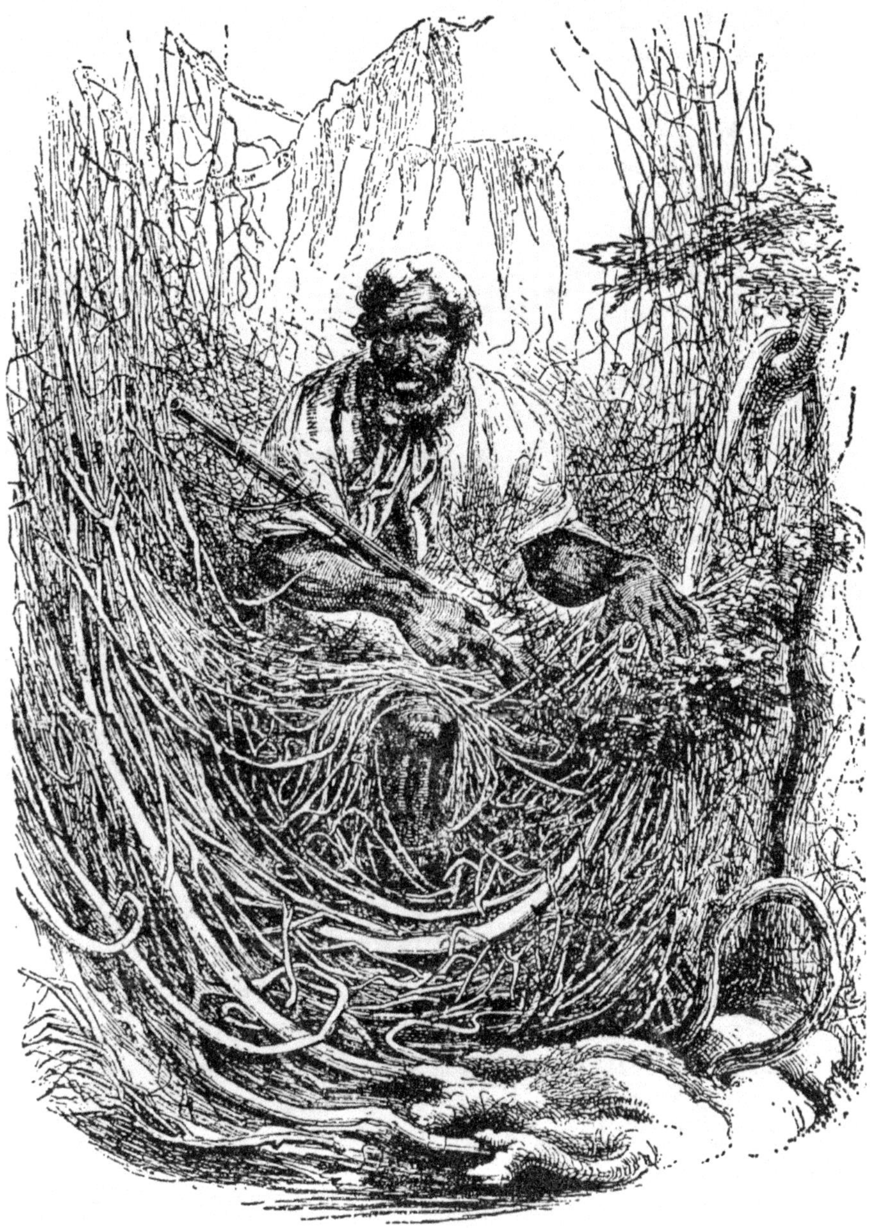

Osman, a maroon leader in the Dismal Swamp whose image was captured by David Hunter Strother in September 1856 and published in the *Harper's New Monthly Magazine*. *William Still,* The Underground Railroad, *1872.*

In dark fens of the Dismal Swamp,
The hunted Negro lay;
He saw the fire of the midnight camp,
And heard at times a horse's tramp
And a bloodhound's distant bay…

Where hardly a human foot could pass,
Or a human heart would dare,
On the quaking turf of the green morass
He crouched in the rank and tangled grass,
Like a wild beast in his lair[149]

These stories became popular among abolitionists because of the experiences some had with those who had concealed themselves in the Dismal Swamp. Such was the experience of Frederick Douglass, who recalled an 1840 meeting with a man recently arrived in New York who had hidden himself in the swamp for quite some time. According to Douglass,

> *He was a large, savage looking man; famine pictured in his face, and clothed with filthy rags;—he was, besides, perfectly black, and scarcely able to make his wants known in English. His state of emanations was frightful and his back was one unhealed gangrene….* [W]*e could merely make out that he was a native African, had been carried forcibly from his own country, and had become a slave on a plantation in the far South; where, hearing to the North Star, and a country where black men might be free, he determined to make his escape….For many days he heard the baying of his master's blood hounds while hiding in the swamps. In an evil hour they found his track—reached him—sprang on him, and lacerated his back with their fangs….An unexpected opportunity offering; he was that very evening passed on to Canada; where in all human probability he is now one of the 40,000 who enjoy, under the scepter of Victoria, that freedom which republican America has denied them.*[150]

Throughout Virginia, African Americans were determined to gain freedom for themselves and their families, if possible. For many who lived in the interior counties, their goal was to travel to more eastern venues where rivers (or safe houses) could be their waterways (or pathways) to freedom. More often than not, unless their labors involved access to ships or they hired out their time, their chances of reaching a non-slaveholding state was slim.

Even with these challenges, thousands managed to successfully achieve their goal of freedom.

There were numerous freedom seekers who fled from the western part of the state. But unlike the rest of the Commonwealth, the whites who inhabited this region migrated to the valley near the Kanawha and Monongahela Rivers to create industries that would employ enslaved laborers. They usually arrived by ship, sailing down the Potomac, Shenandoah, Ohio and Monongahela Rivers to the valley plains between the Alleghany Mountains and the Alleghany Plateau.[151]

The western part of the state had three industries: salt processing, coal mining and iron mongering. The salt industry flourished in this land covered with hardwood trees and 2,500 square miles of salt deposits. Roads were scarce, with only a few major trails—the Shawnee and the Catawba—following the Potomac and Cheat Rivers. At the town of Elkins, the Shawnee Trail split, with one trace running down the Greenbrier River through Lewisburg and another angled southward to the Carolinas. The third split of the Shawnee Trail went westward to the Ohio River. The Catawba Trail went northward through western Pennsylvania and southward toward the Carolinas, Kentucky and Tennessee. Of all of these trails, the most

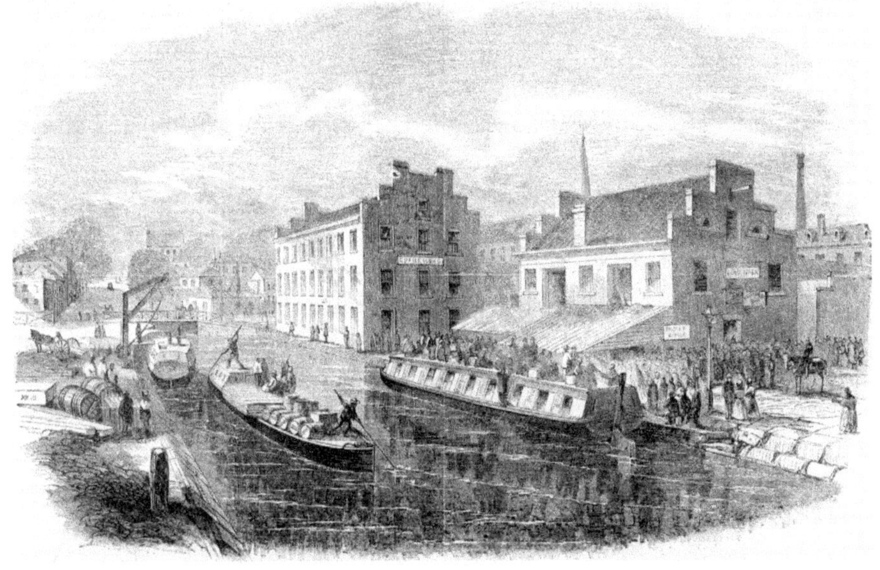

This depiction of barge and schooner traffic on the Kanawha Canal along the James River near Richmond is an indicator of the landscape traversed by freedom seekers in this region of Virginia. *Harrison B. Wilson Archives, Norfolk State University.*

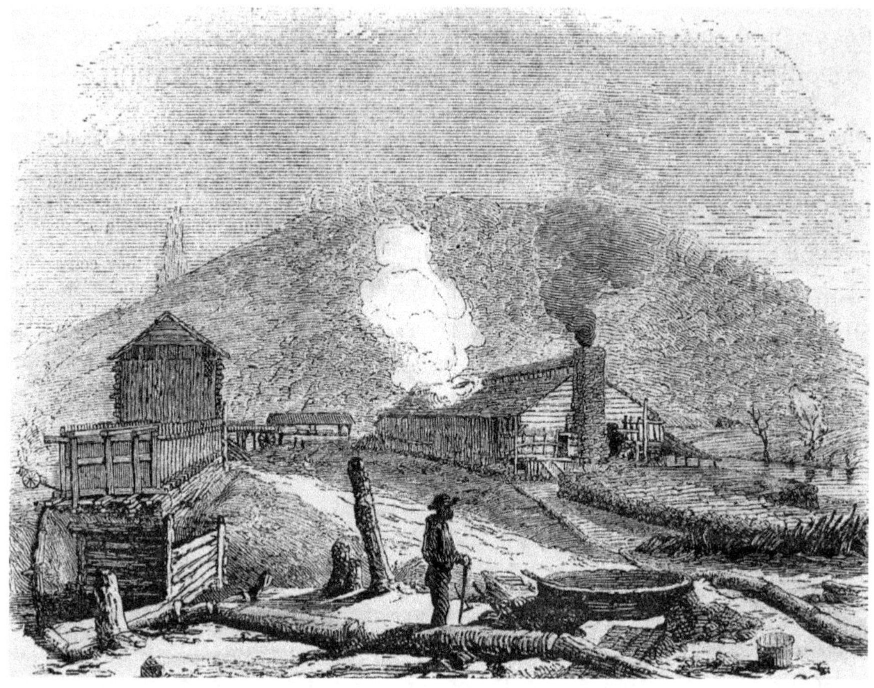

This drawing illustrates the kind of hard work required of enslaved laborers working in the salt works production industry in the western part of the state. *Harrison B. Wilson Archives, Norfolk State University*.

heavily used by freedom seekers was the Catawba Trail, which helped them reach Morgantown and Uniontown, Pennsylvania.[152]

The iron industry in the Monongahela Valley near Morgantown, salt works production in the Kanawha Valley and coalmining in the Alleghany Plateau drew migrants. Indeed, all of these industries relied heavily on a large enslaved workforce that had to be continually replenished because of the harsh working conditions, especially in salt production. So high was the mortality rate in this industry that some owners refused to hire out their workers because it threatened their investment. However, these western counties never had the black population density that existed along the eastern areas of the state. In 1790, for example, there were 55,873 whites, 5,280 blacks and 612 free blacks in the western counties of Virginia.[153]

Despite the low density of the black population, antislavery sentiment was localized to pockets and selected religious groups, including the Quakers and the Baptists who, unlike the Methodists, maintained an antislavery position similar to the national organizations' stance. And while none of the groups openly welcomed blacks as full members, there was support in helping those craving freedom to escape, hiding within the communities of antislavery supporters, especially in Lancaster and West Chester Counties, Pennsylvania and in Ohio. Free blacks helped transform those regions from a strong slaveholding area in the eighteenth century to a benevolent sanctuary for freedom seekers. The main routes in Lancaster ran from Christiana (the main terminal for those coming from Winchester, Virginia, and Frederick, Maryland) through Baltimore along the Susquehanna River, where they met a black conductor who took them farther north. The third route was along the Susquehanna River to the mouth of Octorara Creek near the Maryland border. Using all their resources and their internal communication networks to escape, these freedom seekers were assisted by free blacks in successfully traversing over land and rivers to northern regions.[154]

What is curious about the activities of freedom seekers in the western part of the state is the lack of specific accounts of those who traveled the numerous land routes. Even historian Wilbur Siebert's meticulous documentation of white abolitionists and their safe houses throughout Ohio and Pennsylvania included vague references to specific people. Abolitionists living on the Ohio River later recalled that waterways, such as the Kanawha River, carried boatloads of fugitives to Ohio and Pennsylvania. In fact, freedom seekers used several paths in the most rural areas of the state, including the Northwestern Turnpike that connected Winchester with Point Pleasant, Parkersburg, Moundville, Wheeling and Wellsburg on the Virginia side of the Ohio River. After crossing the Ohio River, freedom seekers could access the Underground Railroad network. Another pathway was the National Road that connected Wheeling with Washington, Morgantown and Uniontown, Pennsylvania. The Monongahela River and its numerous tributaries, such as the Cheat River, provided an entry point into Pennsylvania. The other major river used as an escape route was the Kanawha River, which flowed into the Ohio River. And along these routes, fugitives were able to access the Underground Railroad network in Ohio and Pennsylvania.[155]

The Wheeling-Wellsburg Underground Railroad route included the cities of Washington and West Middleton in Pennsylvania. This path "was so successful that the four counties—Brooke, Hancock, Marshall, and Ohio—lost a large number of slaves to it between 1850 and 1860." In 1850, for example, 247 slaves were registered by owners. Ten years later that number dropped to 149.[156]

Famed white Underground Railroad conductor John Fairfield conducted a complicated operation along the Kanawha River near Charleston, Virginia, in the 1850s. Several free Ohio blacks engaged Fairfield to assist them in retrieving enslaved relatives who were working in the salt works industry. He was accompanied by two free black men who pretended to be Fairfield's slaves. Fairfield hired additional slaves to build two boats along the Kanawha River, supposedly as part of an effort to transport salt to Ohio. After the boats were completed, enslaved men, women and children boarded, guided by skillful boatmen. Afterward, Fairfield pretended that one of his boats was stolen by fugitives, successfully misdirecting unwanted attention. Professing to local whites that he suspected one of his servants, Fairfield continued the ruse of mock outrage following the disappearance of his other boat and ten or twelve additional slaves. Enlisting the aid of a posse of whites, he pretended to track them to the Ohio River, at which point he suggested the party split up and meet at a designated point later. Of course, they never saw Fairfield again or all the freedom seekers he helped reached Canada safely.[157]

By the 1850s, despite the risk of discovery, the majority of freedom seekers opted for the safety of cities such as New Bedford and Boston, Massachusetts, where support was high. In 1850, 29 percent (1,008 people) in New Bedford were reportedly born in the South. Similarly, 15 percent (14,000) lived in New York City and 16.6 percent (1,999) resided in Boston. In New Bedford, estimates ranged from three hundred to seven hundred escaped slaves living there between 1845 and 1864. Indeed, New Bedford's population increased by almost 50 percent when so many escaped slaves found refuge in this important whaling town (forty-second-largest city in America in 1850). From its formation, New Bedford was a diverse and heavily influenced Quaker community. Twelve of America's best-known fugitive narratives were about people who lived in New Bedford, including Frederick Douglass, Harriet Jacobs, John Jacobs, Leonard Black, John Thompson and Virginia natives Henry "Box" Brown, William Grimes and George Teamoh.[158]

Often, the decision to escape resulted from events transpiring in the lives of slaveholders (debt, death, relocation) or slaves (sold away, brutality, opportunity, family). In Virginia's cities where the maritime industry dominated, the Underground Railroad flourished because of the thousands of small vessels and steamships that frequented the waterways. Yet escape was not without risk and occasional capture. Those who attempted or successfully escaped had an advantage over many who were more closely supervised; they either hired out their own time or were allowed relative freedom of movement. Nevertheless, even these advantages were fraught with intrigue and danger; the penalty was often sale to the Lower South rather than simply being returned to their owners. The choices that freedom seekers made were not always easy, simplistic or without considerable sacrifice. And at the core was the inexhaustible focus on love, family and the need to control their own lives.

Selected Freedom Seekers from Virginia, as recorded by William Still

Freedom Seeker	**City/County**	**Destination**	**Mode of Escape**	**Year**
Joseph Viney	Alexandria	Philadelphia	skiff, Robert Lee	1857
Alfred Hubert	Alexandria	Hamilton	skiff, Robert Lee	1857
John Thompson	Alexandria	London, Canada	skiff, Robert Lee	1857
William Robinson	Fauquier Co.	Canada	walked to Philadelphia	1854
James Stewart	Fauquier Co.	Philadelphia	obtained passage	????
Cordelia Loney	Fredericksburg	Canada	vigilance committee	1859
Daniel Davis	Hedgeville	Philadelphia	walked to Greenville, PA	????
Adam Nicholson	Hedgeville	Philadelphia	walked to Greenville, PA	????
Reuben Bowles	Hedgeville	Philadelphia	walked to Greenville, PA	????
Daniel Green	Leesburg	Philadelphia	Fountain's schooner	1856
Emily Foster	Loudon Co.	Toronto	master's horses	1855
Robert Stewart	Loudon Co.	Toronto	vessel	1856
Betsey Smith	Loudon Co.	Toronto	vessel	1856
David Bennett	Loudon Co.	St. Catharines	vessel	1855
Martha Bennett	Loudon Co.	St. Catharines	vessel	1855
George, child Bennett	Loudon Co.	St. Catharines	vessel	1855
Dan Bennett, wife, children	Loudon Co.	Philadelphia	vessel	1855
Hannah Peters	Marshall Hope	Philadelphia	skiff, Robert Lee	1857

Freedom Seeker	**City/County**	**Destination**	**Mode of Escape**	**Year**
Robert Brown	Martinsburg	Philadelphia	horses	1856
Anthony Blow	Norfolk	Philadelphia	*City of Richmond*	1854
Isaac Foreman	Norfolk	Toronto	*City of Richmond*	1853
Emanuel T. White	Norfolk	Syracuse, NY	Richmond steamer	1857
Nancy Little	Norfolk	New Bedford	Fountain's schooner	1855
Phillis Gault	Norfolk	Boston	Fountain's schooner	1855
Alice Jones	Norfolk	New Bedford	Fountain's schooner	1855
William Thomas	Norfolk	St. Catharines	Baylis's schooner	1855
Louisa Bell	Norfolk	St. Catharines	Baylis's schooner	1855
James H. Foreman	Norfolk	Niagara Falls, NY	*Philadelphia* steamer	1855
Albert Brown	Norfolk	Hamilton	stole master's boat	1856
Winnie Patty	Norfolk	Philadelphia	Lambdin's schooner	1855
William Davis	Portsmouth	Canada	*City of Richmond*	1853
Willis Redick	Portsmouth	Canada	*City of Richmond*	1853
Stebney Swan	Portsmouth	Philadelphia	skiff, Robert Lee	1857
John Stinger	Portsmouth	Philadelphia	skiff, Robert Lee	1857
Moses Wines	Portsmouth	Philadelphia	*City of Richmond*	????
John Atkinson	Portsmouth	St. Catharines	Richmond steamer	1854
Charles Thompson	Portsmouth	Canada	Fountain's schooner	1856
Charity Thompson	Portsmouth	Canada	Fountain's schooner	1856
Mary Epps	Petersburg	Canada	Baylis's schooner	1855
John Henry	Petersburg	Philadelphia	*Philadelphia* steamer	1857

Freedom Seeker	**City/County**	**Destination**	**Mode of Escape**	**Year**
Hezekiah Hill	Petersburg	Toronto	*Philadelphia* steamer	1854
Eliza Jones	Petersburg	Hamilton	*Philadelphia* steamer	1855
Harriet Mayo	Petersburg	Canada	Baylis's schooner	1855
Beverly Good	Petersburg	Toronto	*Pennsylvania* steamer	1855
George Walker	Petersburg	Toronto	*Pennsylvania* steamer	1855
Valentine Spires	Petersburg	Philadelphia	Fountain's schooner	1856
Joseph Robinson	Richmond	St. Catharines	Baylis's schooner $100	1855
James Mercer	Richmond	St. Catharines	*Pennsylvania* steamer	1854
Joseph Henry Camp	Richmond	Canada	steamer to Philadelphia	1853
Jack Scott	Richmond	Montreal	skiff, Robert Lee	1857
John Hall	Richmond	Hamilton	Baylis's schooner	1855
Lewis Giles	Richmond	Canada	schooner (paid $25)	1855
Verenea Mercer	Richmond	Toronto	*Pennsylvania* steamer	1855
George Sperryman	Richmond	Philadelphia	Fountain's schooner	1856
Cornelius Scott	Stafford Co.	Philadelphia	traveled as white	1857
Pete Matthews	Temperanceville	Canada	unknown	1855
David Greek	Warrington	Philadelphia	Fountain's schooner	1856
James Burrell	Williamsburg	Toronto, Canada	unknown	1854

4

FREEDOM SEEKERS, CONDUCTORS, SAFE SPACES

Isaac Hopper, an idealistic Quaker and tailor, arrived in Philadelphia from New Jersey the year the 1787 Constitution was written by Congress. Twelve years later, Hopper was elected as a member of the Pennsylvania Abolition Society, the first organization in America with the explicit goal of eliminating slavery. But unlike most of the white abolitionists, Hopper had a personal connection with African Americans, having served as the overseer and teacher in a black school. His passion was educating people about the horrors of slavery and ensuring that blacks were assisted when they were victims of kidnapping or arrested by officials because of mistaken identity.[159]

Investigating these kidnappings and helping liberate blacks who were victims of slave catchers provided Hopper and his associates with opportunities to develop techniques that were later used by Underground Railroad supporters. Hopper borrowed from the highly disciplined and self-contained operations of Quaker society, including a moral opposition to slavery. But unlike the Quakers, who "opposed political engagement and law breaking" and were tainted by a strain of racism, Hopper was inclusive. He established a network of diverse people—black and white—who were committed to using any resources at their disposal, including legal and extralegal remedies, cooperation with local government officials and connections with a diverse religious network. Bringing Evangelicals, Methodists, Baptists, dockworkers, domestics, attorneys, merchants and general laborers into the movement as foot soldiers for the cause allowed Hopper to craft a network that extended far and wide.[160]

One of the earliest opportunities Hopper had in using this network was with Ben Jackson, who worked as a coachman for his owner, Senator Pierce Butler. Jackson came to Hopper for assistance when his owner notified him of his intent to take him to Georgia. Since Jackson was married to a free black woman and had lived in Pennsylvania for longer than six months, he was entitled to freedom, according to state law. Nevertheless, the federal fugitive slave laws forced Hopper to be creative and savvy in identifying legal loopholes. Armed with a legal strategy, Hopper arranged to have an attorney represent Jackson, and a sympathetic constable and judge became involved in the case. In a brilliant maneuver, Hopper asked the judge to move the trial before Jackson's slaveholder arrived so that the case would be dismissed in lieu of the absence of the plaintiff. The judge agreed with his tactic, and Jackson was freed.[161]

Another technique of Hopper's that became an important element in the development of the Underground Railroad was the use of a far-reaching network of friends and associates to pass fugitives from one person to another until that individual reached a safe haven. Later called stationmasters, they provided temporary shelter and assistance when freedom seekers first arrived. Additional assistance sometimes included teaching them basic reading and writing skills and helping them secure a job and a new home if the fugitives decided to remain in Pennsylvania. For others, the stationmaster forwarded these freedom seekers to their next location. Initially, Hopper had them traveling unaccompanied and on foot; but later, they were sent by carriage or on horseback on less traveled roads and at night, sometimes in disguises (women dressing as men, for example). Hopper also connected with ship's captains, arranging travel by water to cities and towns farther north.[162]

In so many ways, Hopper's story represented the transformation of a moderate abolitionist movement into a more aggressive and proactive organization. This movement contributed to the rise and expansion of the Underground Railroad, which guided an estimated 100,000 enslaved people to freedom. Eventually steeped in railroad imagery, Hopper's development of Pennsylvania's Underground Railroad was improvisational at its core and structure. Since that time, the stories that followed illustrated the shifting and individualized nature of America's most secretive organization.

The work of Hopper and others resulted in Philadelphia's rise as the primary terminus for freedom seekers. Initially, runaways arriving in the city were forwarded to the homes of William Still, David Ruggles, the Reverend Jermain Loguen or Frederick Douglass for resettlement or their connections to cities and towns in New Jersey and New York. By the mid-1830s, however,

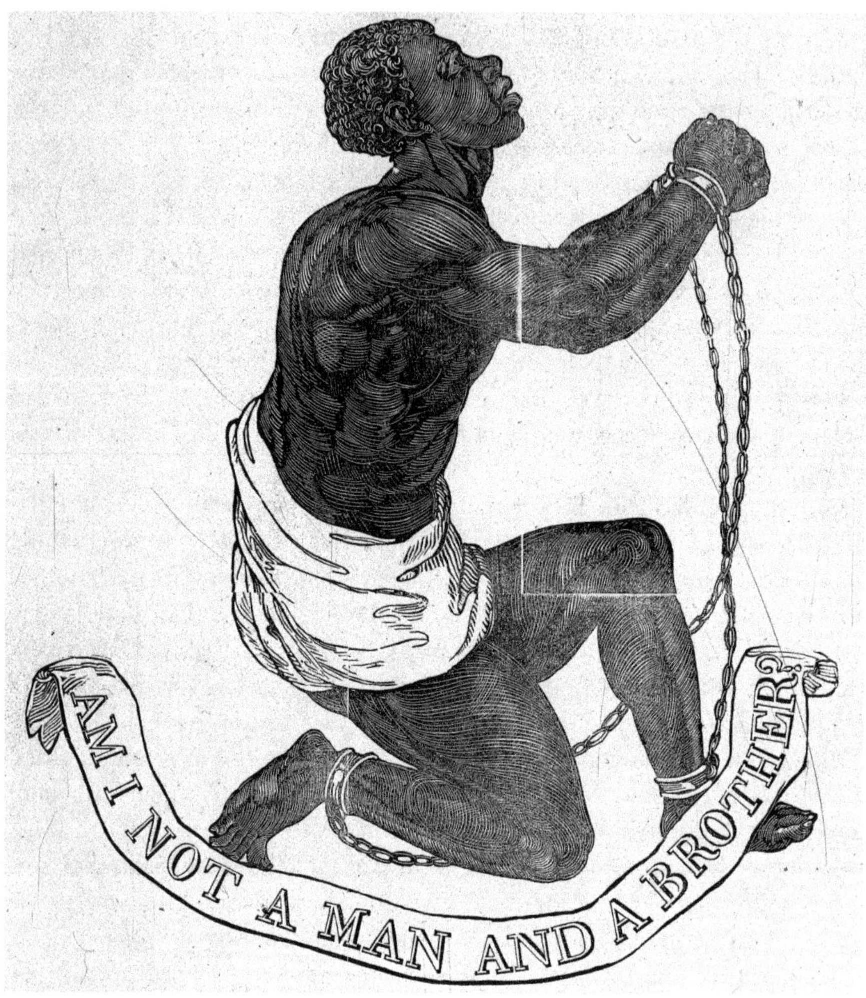

This 1837 broadside, "Am I not a man and a brother?" was nationally circulated by the American Anti-Slavery Society with the publication of John Greenleaf Whittier's antislavery poem, "Our Countrymen in Chains." The image was originally adopted as the seal of the English Society for the Abolition of Slavery in in the 1780s and is indicative of the emphasis on religion and moral rightness as the reason for supporting the abolitionist cause. *Library of Congress.*

fugitives were, in increasing numbers, in danger of being kidnapped by slave catchers because of the monetary incentives provided by slave owners and slaveholding states intent on recovering fugitives. Consequently, a network was established to forward them to specific cities and towns, using the Reading and Pennsylvania Railroads as their primary mode of transportation.[163]

By the 1840s, the region had become a beacon of hope for many freedom seekers. The nation was increasing its once tenuous support of antislavery sentiments, as many northern states resisted efforts by the federal government to expand slavery nationally. Consequently, throughout the first half of the nineteenth century, efforts to assist freedom seekers increased in organization, design and secrecy. Agents on the Underground Railroad used coded language to refer to the fugitives who arrived, referring to them as "passengers."

The strongest organizers of these "networks to freedom" were black church men and women with their collaborative network that spanned across numerous denominations. New York's vigilance committee was one of many organized throughout the North and of critical importance. Free black abolitionists were independent of direct ties with established abolitionist societies, such as New England's Freedom Association, which was formed in 1845. In fact, prior to 1850, many white abolitionists supposed that it was unethical to entice slaves from the South, believing that they should only assist once the fugitives made it to the North. However, the activity of free blacks eventually reversed this sentiment, establishing a blueprint for a fugitive network. In 1848, for example, nationally known freedom seekers William and Ellen Craft described how numerous whites freely approached enslaved blacks, encouraging them to escape, providing clues about local safe houses and speaking openly about their condemnation of slavery. While some of the whites they encountered sympathized with slaveholders, the farther north they traveled, the more egalitarian individuals they encountered. Still other fugitives recounted their escapes from northern cities such as Philadelphia after encountering members of the vigilance committee who encouraged them to run away (with their assistance).[164]

In Pennsylvania, the Reverends Walter Proctor of Mother Bethel, William Douglass, Stephen Gloucester of Central Presbyterian, Daniel Scott of Union Baptist and Charles Gardiner were but a few who forged a network within the black communities in the region. Launching this effort was the 1831 meeting at Mother Bethel AME Church, the first political convention in the city to protest slavery. Following the gathering, antislavery sentiments spread and fugitive slave support was provided by most of the black clergy and their congregations. In turn, they hosted antislavery and fugitive aid meetings, housed fugitives and encouraged ministers to serve as agents in the Underground Railroad.[165]

By 1835, the more militant black and white abolitionists had established the Philadelphia Vigilance Committee to assist fugitives. James

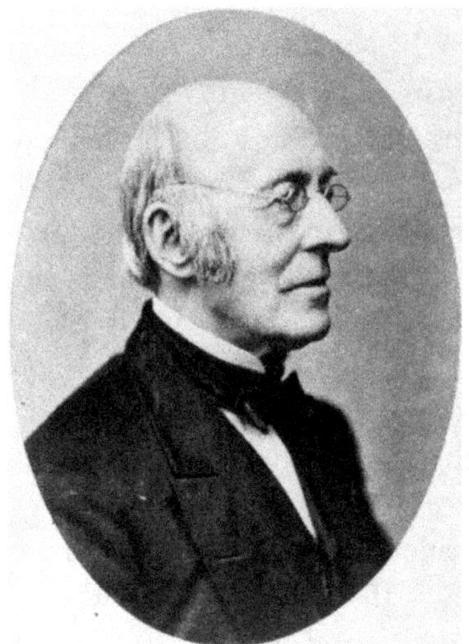

Left: William Lloyd Garrison was a staunch abolitionist whose voice was heard passionately advocating for an end to slavery for over three decades. *Library of Congress.*

Below: This heading used in the *Liberator* newspaper depicts the reasons for William Lloyd Garrison's support of the antislavery cause. In the very first edition, Garrison wrote, "I do not wish to think, or speak, or write, with moderation....I am in earnest—I will not equivocate—I will not excuse—I will not retreat a single inch—AND I WILL BE HEARD." *Harrison B. Wilson Archives, Norfolk State University.*

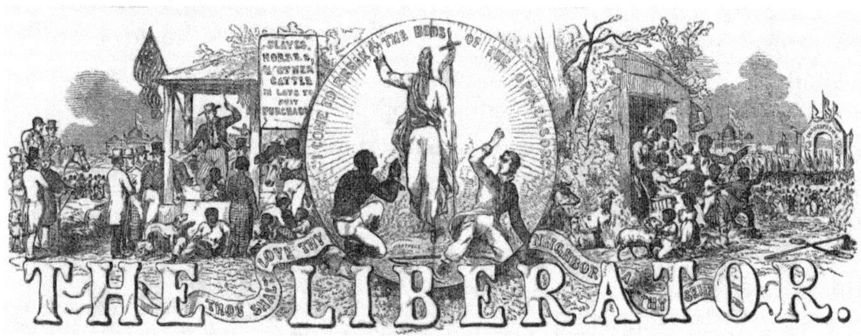

McCrummel was selected president, Jacob White served as secretary and James Needham was the treasurer. Charles Atkins, their authorized agent, immediately went to work soliciting funds to provide food, clothing, shelter, medical assistance and legal representation for the fugitives. After the committee's founding, blacks became officers, including William Still, Robert Purvis, James Gibbons and Charles Reason. This organization was designed to offset what they perceived as weak support from the white abolitionists, although some of the prominent Quakers, such as Abraham Pennock, used the Friends Meeting House in Germantown—located in the northwest section of Philadelphia—as an Underground Railroad station. Because of the strong advocacy of black abolitionists, it was almost twenty years before the Pennsylvania Anti-Slavery Society openly supported freedom seekers who arrived in the region. So powerful was this enclave of abolitionists led by African Americans that Underground Railroad conductor John Fairfield and North Carolina stationmaster Levi Coffin often came to the Philadelphia Vigilance Committee for assistance.[166]

John Fairfield was born into a slaveholding family. And while it is not known why he became a staunch antislavery supporter, these sentiments were present even as a child. Fairfield began his Underground Railroad activities when he journeyed to Ohio with one of his uncle's slaves to help him escape. His uncle sought to have him arrested once Fairfield was suspected. Fleeing back to Ohio, Fairfield began working loosely with Levi Coffin, whose recollections detail life as one of the Underground Railroad's most successful conductors. Fairfield operated throughout Virginia and Kentucky, taking freedom seekers of all ages to Canada. And while some offered him money to take them to freedom, he did not require payment. Instead, accounts suggested that he did it for the "adventure and excitement" as well as for his hatred of slavery.[167]

What made Fairfield so successful were tactics he shared with Harriet Tubman. He had extensive knowledge of the locales where he operated and was a master of disguises. Sometimes, Fairfield pretended to be a slave dealer, conducting slaves across the Ohio River and forwarding them to Canada through the Underground Railroad network. One account tells of a group of armed enslaved men who stole horses from their masters in northwest Kentucky, releasing the horses only after reaching the Ohio River near Mayville, Kentucky. Whenever Fairfield journeyed to the South, he would first scout out the location, find out information about the geography and the slaveholders in the area and make contact with the enslaved populace. For example, Fairfield would sometimes go into an area and secure a room in a boardinghouse or at the house of the slaveholder whose slaves he was about to help escape. He would make other whites feel comfortable about his views by pretending to be a staunch pro-slavery advocate. Fairfield used his Virginia-born credentials to lend credence to his ruse.[168]

So successful was Fairfield that he was able to reunite numerous families in Canada, many of whom employed him in retrieving family and friends still in slavery. According to Levi Coffin, Fairfield was responsible for thousands of people reaching freedom in Canada. His success resulted from daring moves on his part that sometimes included violence. He was always armed with guns and had no reservations about shooting someone who tried to stop him, encouraging freedom seekers to do the same. Not surprisingly, Fairfield was frequently betrayed and arrested. Using his position as a high-ranking Free Mason sometimes got him released, while other times he had to initiate a jail break. However, this kind of risky activity eventually caught up with

Fairfield, who was reportedly killed in 1861 during a slave insurrection in Tennessee, near an ironworks operation on the Cumberland River.[169]

Years later, some of the abolitionists in Philadelphia became even more assertive in their antislavery advocacy, even encouraging enslaved men and women to leave their owners while visiting the city. In 1855, Colonel John Wheeler of North Carolina, U.S. minister to Nicaragua, journeyed to New York from Washington, D.C., by steamship, accompanied by three of his slaves: his wife's servant Jane Johnson and her two sons. While they were passing through Philadelphia, Passmore Williamson was alerted by Underground Railroad agents to come quickly to Bloodgood's Hotel because three people who wanted their liberty were about to board a steamship bound for New York. Williamson quickly ran to the docks and found the woman and her children with their owner. Williamson approached the woman and asked her if she wanted to be free. She indicated that she did, and he told her that because of Pennsylvania's law and the sympathy of many Philadelphia officials, she was entitled to her freedom because she was now in a free state. White passengers aboard the ship were in agreement, with the exception of one man, who, from Williamson's account, was assumed to be an owner based on his statements.[170]

Although Wheeler protested, the woman and her children fled with Williamson. Williamson then delivered them into the hands of operatives to take them to a safe location. The following day, the owner secured a writ of habeas corpus naming Williamson. Apparently, Wheeler used his considerable influence to get famous attorney Daniel Webster and U.S. District Attorney J.C. Vandyke to represent his interests. Locked in jail for four months (July through November, 1855), Williamson became a martyr for abolitionism and a pariah to everyone else. At the same time, six African American men were arrested, charged as accomplices: William Still, James Braddock, William Curtis, John Ballard, James Martin and Isaiah Moore. Despite Wheeler's efforts to secure a conviction and the return of his slaves, the sympathetic environment of Pennsylvania resulted in an acquittal for Williamson and those accused of being his accomplices and the Johnson family's freedom.[171]

The trial of Passmore Williamson highlighted the risks that even those in northern areas took in assisting freedom seekers. His arrest, imprisonment and trial were a warning to all abolitionists that while the northern states might not approve of the institution of slavery, federal law and officials did and were willing to prosecute those who interfered with the return of a slaveholder's human "property." As a result, coded messaging was needed

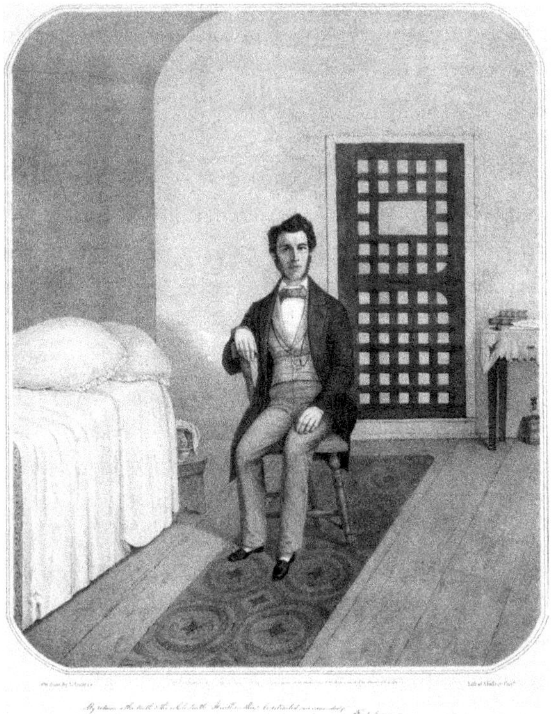

Right: Abolitionist and secretary of the Pennsylvania Abolition Society Passmore Williamson is pictured here in Moyamensing Prison for alleged contempt of court, 1855. *Library of Congress.*

Below: This illustration depicted the rescue of Jane Johnson and her children in 1855 in Philadelphia, with the assistance of Passmore Williams. *William Still,* The Underground Railroad, *1872.*

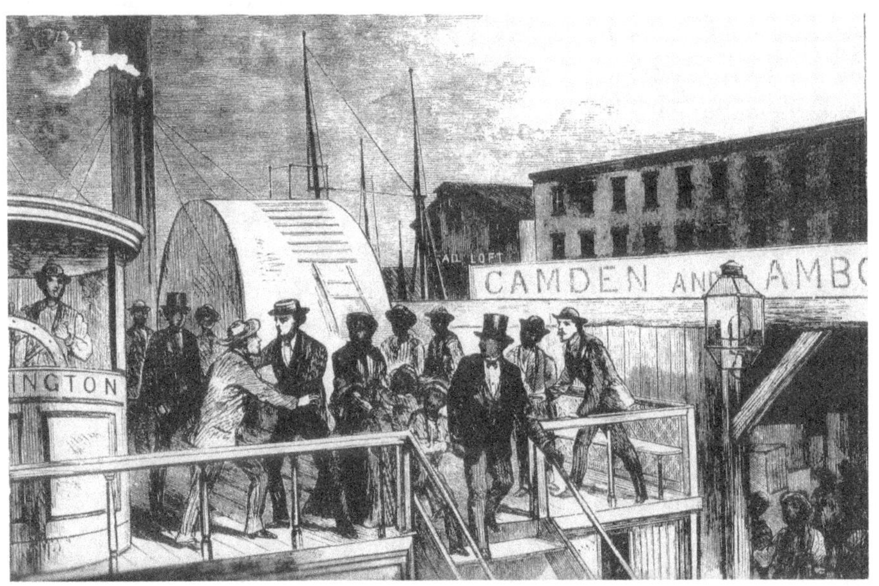

when abolitionists were involved in transferring fugitives from station to station. G.S. Nelson wrote to William Still from Reading, Pennsylvania, on May 27, 1857, saying that he knew that Still was uneasy because "the goods" he was expecting to arrive from Harrisburg by train had not arrived. Nelson said the delay was because the only train from Harrisburg to Reading was so late that it required an overnight stay. The letter reminded Still that two small boxes and two large ones were coming with an additional three more to arrive soon. Clearly, the *boxes* were a reference to the transportation of freedom seekers.[172]

Part of the reason for the increased aggressiveness of abolitionists was the clear and present danger the prospects of being kidnapped into slavery posed to free blacks, especially those living in the southern and Mid-Atlantic states. The lucrative domestic slave trade was accompanied by the growing threat of free black kidnapping by slave hunters. Indeed, kidnapping was rampant in Philadelphia by the 1820s. It forced many to become keenly aware of their own vulnerability as long as the institution of slavery existed in the nation. For that reason, many northern African Americans joined the abolitionist effort to obstruct actions taken by slaveholders when attempting to retrieve fugitive slaves. For example, abolitionist Theodore Parker recalled that when there was an attempt to seize Anthony Burns from officials during his trial, one abolitionist killed a deputy marshal in the courthouse.[173]

New York's free blacks understood the need and were keenly aware of the dangers of kidnapping by the 1830s because of the virulent and growing racism among whites, the history of slavery and the slave trade in the state, the financial connections with southern trading and the constant visits by slaveholding merchants with their slaves to the New York markets. Indeed, slave hunters boldly advertised their services in New York newspapers. Abolitionists revealed that a New York Kidnapping Club existed. This well-known club included prominent Democratic politicians whose positions in law enforcement facilitated the easy seizure and return of African Americans accused of being fugitives without blacks having an opportunity to defend themselves in court. Francis Smith, a fugitive from Virginia, worked as a waiter in New York. When his fiancée tried to purchase his freedom, his owner arranged for his arrest and return to slavery. In another example, a seven-year-old boy, Henry Scott, was snatched from school by a constable and a Virginia slaveholder who claimed he was his slave.[174]

These and many other incidences resulted in New York's African Americans forming the Friends of Human Rights in November 1835. The organization's mission was to ascertain how many and the ways in which these

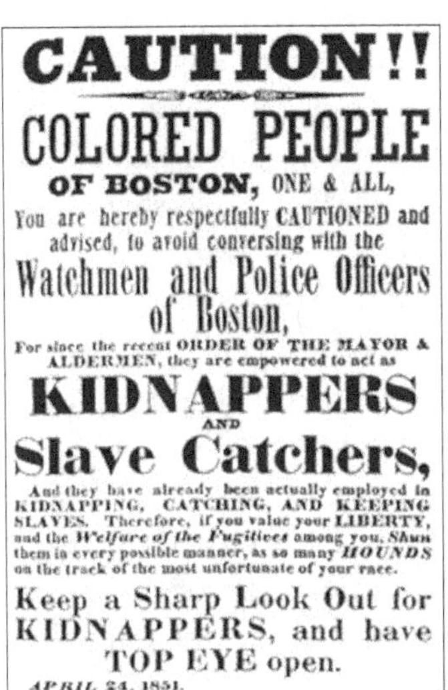

This is a broadside that warned free blacks of the possibility of kidnapping by slave catchers in Boston. *Boston Public Library*.

kidnappings by slaveholders occurred in the city. The outcome of this investigation was the formation of the vigilance committee, with David Ruggles as its secretary. Already well known in the community, Ruggles was a vocal advocate, raising money for fugitives, hiring lawyers, suing ship's captains who participated in the trafficking of slaves and publishing descriptions of kidnapped people. The New York State Vigilance Committee was aided by attorney Horace Dresser in maneuvering through the court system, especially after the passage of the 1850 Fugitive Slave Act. Indeed, in 1841, New York passed a law that gave immediate freedom to any slave brought into the state. Not surprisingly, when the Fugitive Slave Act was passed, the state law conflicted with the federal mandate, requiring creativity on the part of abolitionists. Dresser made headlines between 1851 and 1853 because of the thirty-eight cases he undertook representing freedom seekers.[175]

Abolitionist Robert Purvis, who kept records of fugitives who were assisted by the Philadelphia Vigilance Committee, said that "an average of one a day" went northward, with a total of nine thousand being assisted from 1835 to 1860. So it was that vigilance committees in Pennsylvania, New York and Massachusetts forwarded fugitives to more northern states and Canada. Those who opted to remain in the United States were assisted in finding housing and jobs and creating new identities.[176]

To combat the growing demand for basic assistance to freedom seekers and the pressure coming from the surging populations in northern black enclaves, abolitionists created a more structured organization in the 1830s as a way of helping fugitives once they reached the North. Within a decade, these radical abolitionists believed that more active efforts were needed. The result was the formation of networks of conductors, ship captains and sympathizers in the South with contacts in the North. By the 1840s, people such as Lucretia Goodson of Portsmouth, James and Keziah Fuller of Norfolk and Nancy Atkinson of Southampton County had reached freedom with the assistance of abolitionists. And while slaveholders throughout

Virginia published warnings to "all masters of vessels against conveying off the said negro at the peril of the law," the escapes did not abate. Some of the earliest fugitives who established themselves in northern cities were on the vanguard as emerging radical abolitionists, working tirelessly to help fellow freedom seekers. These included Lewis Hayden of Boston, who was regarded as hospitable toward fugitive slaves, in part because he was one. Living on Beacon Hill, Hayden constantly had freedom seekers in his home. And just around the corner from Hayden was Leonard Grimes, pastor of Boston's Fugitive Slave Church, which later moved to New Bedford, Massachusetts.[177]

Historian Gary Collinson noted that of the four hundred fugitives recorded by the Philadelphia Vigilance Committee from 1842 forward, over one hundred came from the Norfolk region, primarily because so many left aboard ships. This was one of many indicators of the importance of one of Virginia's major port cities as a pathway to freedom. Moreover, based on the records, many of Virginia's conductors were often slaves themselves, while stationmasters tended to be northern free blacks, white Quakers or white evangelical Protestants. Wilbur Siebert identified only a few Underground Railroad operatives in Virginia. Of those, Bryant Joseph operated in Brock, while Joshua Steele and Dick Naler, an African American, operated in Wheeling, Virginia. Eliza Bains in Portsmouth also sent countless freedom seekers to Boston and New Bedford by ship. Some of the small trading vessels willing to transport fugitives from the Norfolk Harbor in the 1850s were Captain Amos Hopkins's *Florence*, the *Sally Ann* and the *Cameo*. While these specific vessels were caught with fugitives aboard, many more successfully escaped with their secret passengers unharmed.[178]

Prior to Philadelphia's prominence as the center for abolitionist activity were actions in Boston. Home to the *Liberator* newspaper and the self-emancipating activities of the Fugitive Slave Church, Boston's self-emancipators established themselves as formidable forces. As early as the 1760s, Boston was a hub for runaway slaves, such as Crispus Attucks from Massachusetts, Peter Randolph from Virginia and Lewis Hayden from Kentucky. While some arrived on foot, many others typically came as stowaways aboard vessels transporting people and goods between southern and northern ports. By the 1840s, Boston had become the primary destination for fugitives because of its port activities and the black and white abolitionist communities who actively sought to thwart any efforts by slaveholders to retrieve their slaves. Indeed, through the 1840s, no area received more fugitive slaves than Boston.[179]

Between 1831 and 1865, when the Boston population increased significantly with white immigrants from Europe, the black community stabilized with strong churches and community organizations. Yet because of the long-standing presence and activity of freedom seekers in the community, chief among their efforts was to help fugitives who came into the city in search of liberty. Consequently, religious institutions like the African Meeting House became critical venues in meeting these goals and organizing efforts. For example, in 1832, the African Meeting House hosted the inaugural meeting of the New England Anti-Slavery Society, and its members were the strongest supporters of the newly minted *Liberator*, written and published by white abolitionist William Lloyd Garrison. Boston rapidly became the hub of a national antislavery movement and a beacon for freedom seekers, including George and Rebecca Latimer, who escaped from Norfolk, Virginia, in 1842.[180]

Needless to say, it was Boston that acted as the backdrop for national fugitive slave cases. These cases would, in turn, serve as pivotal junctures for the defense and assault on slavery. Because most of the northern states had abolished slavery by edict beginning in the late 1790s, the New England region became a haven for fugitives seeking freedom. It was in the North that slavery opponents made systematic assaults not only on the institution of slavery but also on the rights of slaveholders to retrieve their "property."

The most noted case and the first to receive national attention, resulting in the fugitive becoming a national cause célèbre, was the 1842 trial of twenty-one-year-old George Latimer. Latimer and his wife, Rebecca, were the parents of famous inventor and draftsman Lewis Latimer. George was originally the slave of his uncle, Portsmouth resident Edward Latimer, while twenty-one-year-old Rebecca was owned by Mary Sayer.[181] According to his first autobiographical sketch, published in the *Latimer Journal and North Star*, a newspaper founded to support his cause, George was the son of Margaret Olmsted Mitchell, a slave, and Samuel Mitchell Latimer, a white stone mason who worked in the Gosport Navy Yard in Portsmouth. Apparently, Samuel Latimer was the younger brother of and apprentice to Edward Latimer, George Latimer's original owner. After several different owners, George Latimer became the property of James B. Gray, who owned a steam sawmill that was located on South Duke Street near the west end of Upper Washington Street in Norfolk. Interestingly, this area was next to an inlet on the Elizabeth River where a few warehouses were located and some schooners and other small vessels were able to navigate.[182]

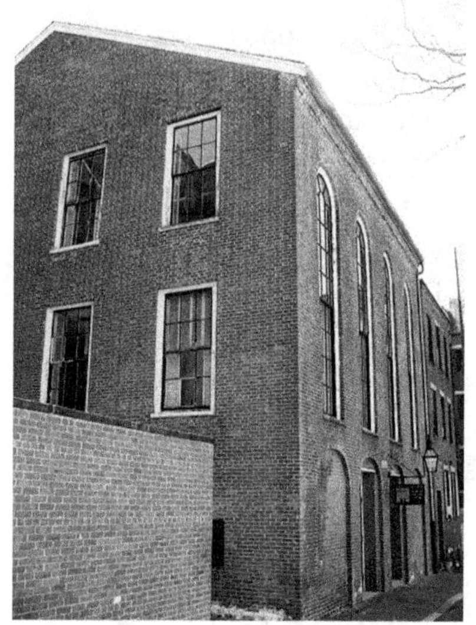

The African Meeting House in Boston was an important site for abolitionist activities. The Meeting House, also known as the First African Baptist Church, First Independent Baptist Church and the Belknap Street Church, was built in 1806. *Boston Public Library.*

Like many enslaved African Americans, George Latimer attempted to escape more than once. Success evaded him until October 4, 1842, when he and his wife, Rebecca, boarded a steamship in the Hampton Roads Harbor. The ship took them on a three-day journey to Boston, where they found sanctuary by hiding with "colored persons living on Joy Street."[183] The day after reaching Boston, however, Latimer was spotted by William R. Carpenter, a former employee of James Gray, who immediately recognized Latimer and then contacted Gray about him. In the meantime, Gray offered a reward for Latimer's return, as did Mary Sayer, Rebecca's owner, in the *American Beacon* newspaper on October 15. Both Latimers were described in the runaway slave advertisement as mulattos and as husband and wife. Immediately after receiving Carpenter's correspondence, Gray went in pursuit of Latimer, arriving in Boston on October 18. Upon his arrival, Gray notified the police that Latimer should be arrested and charged with larceny, claiming that Latimer had stolen goods from his Norfolk store. After Latimer was apprehended, he was placed in the Leverett Street jail, whereupon Gray initiated the extradition process.[184]

Word of his incarceration spread quickly through abolitionist circles, most notably in the black community, resulting in the assemblage at Faneuil Hall of nearly three hundred people, mostly black men, dedicated to preventing Gray from taking Latimer to Norfolk until authorized by the courts. Latimer's warrantless arrest and imprisonment without any written charges resulted in demonstrations in Boston and concurrent abolitionist meetings throughout the state. Apparently, the citizens of Boston were so enraged by the temerity of a slaveholder to remove one of their own that they forced Gray to seek out the assistance of the local authorities. These protests were bolstered by civil action taken by Latimer's attorneys, leading to his eventual release until a November 21 trial date. John Quincy

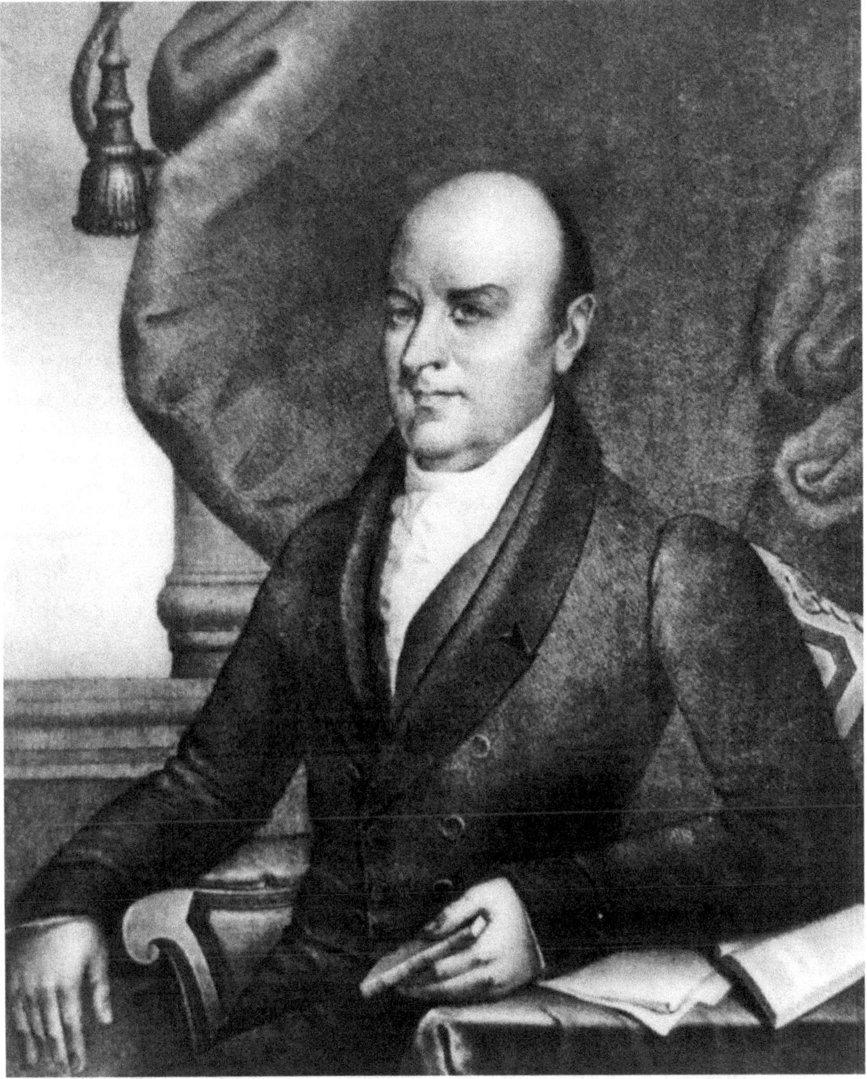

This official portrait of John Quincy Adams, sixth president of the United States, was painted sometime between 1834 and 1840 by G. Stuart. Adams would gain notice once again when he agreed to represent George Latimer during his famous trial in 1842. *Library of Congress.*

Adams, a Massachusetts congressional representative, received a petition signed by sixty-five thousand citizens and addressed to the state legislature demanding Latimer's freedom. Reportedly, Adams said that the fugitive was the son of "a very respectable gentleman of Norfolk, Virginia, a member of one of the most distinguished and respectable families in that state."[185] In the interim, his legal counsel began offering money and pressuring Gray to free Latimer. Fearing that he would lose his slave because the sheriff notified him that he would no longer house fugitive slaves in his jail, Gray reluctantly accepted $400 in payment for the release and freedom of his slave and waived his claims as a slaveholder.[186]

As for Latimer, he was cleared of larceny charges and officially freed on November 21, 1842. Fearing that Gray might be undeterred in his efforts to return him to slavery, Latimer and his wife continued residing in Underground retreats until 1860, in which he was listed in the census as a resident of Charlestown, Massachusetts, a laborer. Sometime after the war, Latimer and his family moved farther north to the town of Lynn, where he resided until his death on May 28, 1896. Like George and Rebecca Latimer, many freedom seekers arrived in northern cities and towns by ship.

Certain captains became known to the underground community as sympathetic to fugitives or at least agreeable to transporting them for a price.[187] In the 1850s, William Still identified the *City of Richmond*, the *Jamestown*, the *Pennsylvania* and the *Augusta* steamships and the *Keziah* and the *Francis French* schooners as the primary vessels aiding Virginia runaways. In the western part of the state, fugitives journeyed by land, crossing the Appalachian, Catoctin, Bull Run, Short Hill and Blue Ridge Mountains and the Ohio River to Ohio and Pennsylvania.

Historian Kathryn Grover noted in her work *The Fugitives Gibraltar* that New Bedford merchants frequently traded in Virginia. Some of those were Quakers with strong antislavery leanings, such as Weston Howland and John Parker, owners of the sloop *Regulator*. Principally transporting flour between Alexandria and New Bedford, the *Regulator* was associated with assisting runaways from Richmond to Washington, D.C. Similarly, the sloop *Mercury*, owned by Samuel Chadwick, reportedly transported fugitives along with goods between various urban ports in Virginia to New Bedford throughout the first half of the nineteenth century. Beginning in 1850, Virginia-born residents emerged as the majority of those freedom seekers living in New Bedford.[188]

Fugitive accounts were replete with harrowing tales of uncomfortable or dangerous trips to the North aboard one of these steamships. Aside from the dangers of travel were the risks involved in trusting unfamiliar persons. Although stewards and cooks were among the most active conductors throughout this period, primarily because these positions were held by free blacks, there were a number who pretended to work as conductors only to

Fellow-Citizens of Massachusetts!

READ
AND
CONSIDER

Last Saturday, the Kidnapper's Counsel, (Seth J. Thomas and Edward G. Parker!) drew up a paper stating "that the person named ANTHONY BYRNES, now and here claimed as a Slave, will be sold by his alleged master for a sum certain, to wit: TWELVE HUNDRED DOLLARS." Saturday night, the money was tendered by Rev. Mr. Grimes and Hamilton Willis, Esq. The Kidnapper's counsel, with Messrs. Grimes and Willis, went to the Office of Commissioner Loring. He drew up papers for the man's release. They all went to the Marshal's Office, to execute the documents, where they met Hallett and the Marshal, who PURPOSELY DELAYED operations until after 12 o'clock, when the deed could not be legally done. The Counsel and the Commissioner agreed to meet Mr. Grimes at 8 o'clock, Monday morning, execute the documents, and release the man. THIS (Monday) MORNING, at 8 o'clock, they were waited on, at the Marshal's Office, by Mr. Grimes. The Kidnapper refused to take the money when tendered to him;

REFUSED TO SELL THE MAN AT ANY PRICE!
And now declares that he will take
HIS SLAVE BACK *TO VIRGINIA!*
MONDAY MORNING, MAY 29, 1854.

Left: This 1854 broadside, titled "Fellow citizens of Massachusetts! Read and consider," was designed to bring attention to the kidnapping and eventual arrest of Anthony Burns in Boston. *Boston Public Library*.

Below: Citizens were called to rally in front of the statehouse in Boston at four o'clock to support abolitionist activities related to the Thomas Sims case. A large crowd gathered to hear Wendell Phillips proclaiming the importance of supporting antislavery measures in Boston. Many of the elite, whose wealth depended on slavery and the slave trade, were opposed to the gathering. *Harrison B. Wilson Archives, Norfolk State University*.

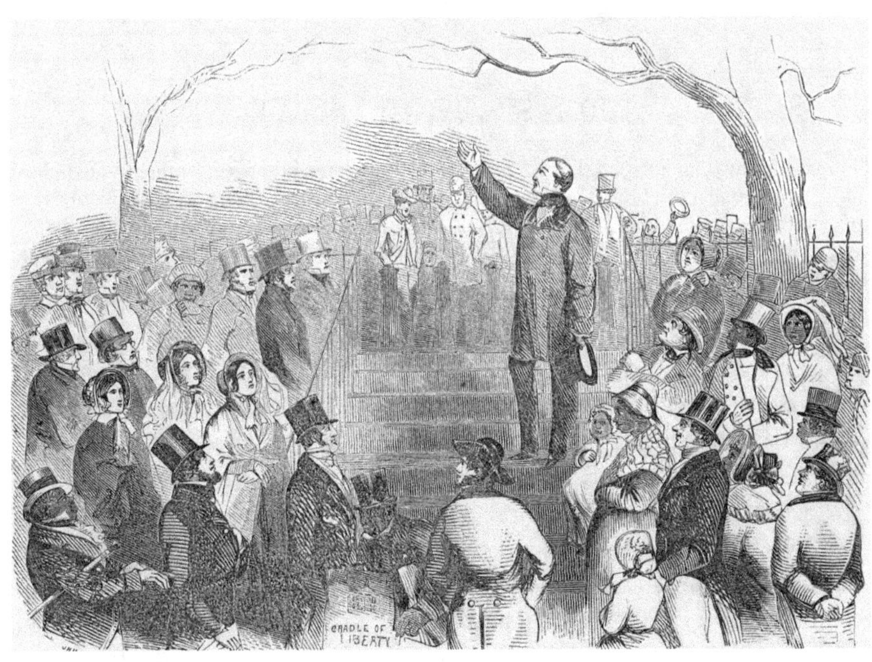

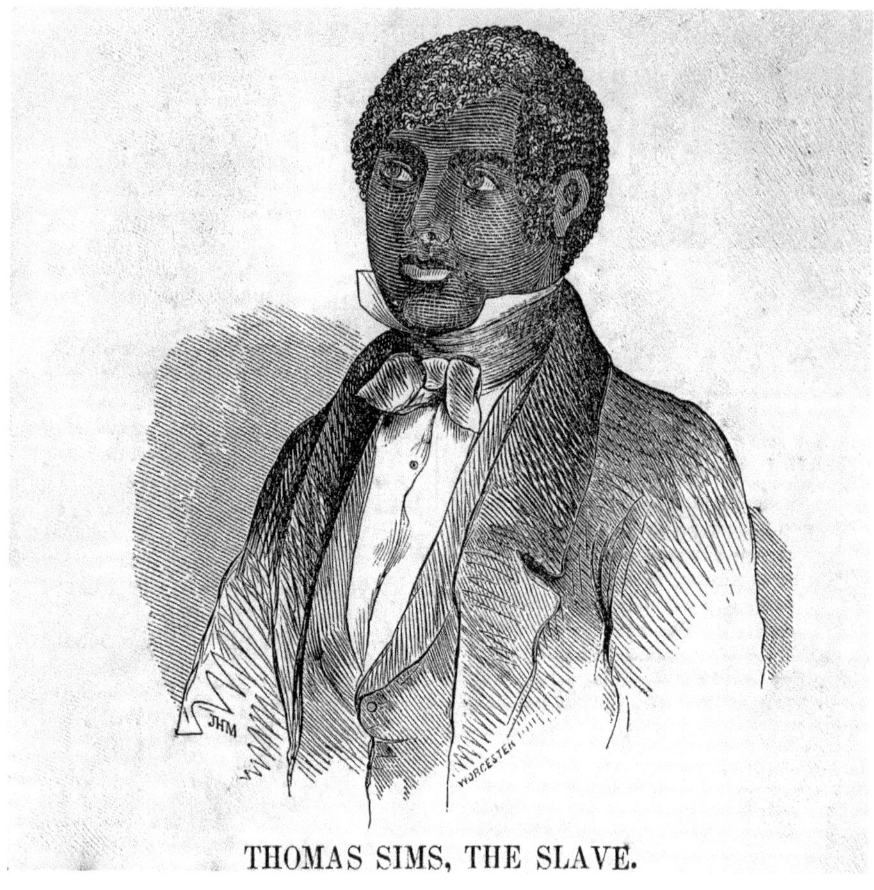

Thomas Sims was an escaped slave who left his wife, children and aged mother in Georgia. His cause became a celebrated case by abolitionists in Boston who wanted to highlight the unfairness of the 1850 Fugitive Slave Act and the need for likeminded ethnical people to support resisting returning these individuals to slavery. Published in *Gleason's Pictorial Drawing Room Companion*, 1851. *Harrison B. Wilson Archives, Norfolk State University.*

get the reward for turning their conspirators in. Those who did work in the network also risked their freedom or their lives.[189]

Those who arrived by ship from Virginia typically disembarked in Philadelphia, Boston and New Bedford. From there, vigilance committees provided train tickets to all those willing to begin a new life in Canada, via New York, Hartford and New Haven Railroads. But fugitives who escaped to southeastern Pennsylvania were not all sent first to Philadelphia. Frequently, they were passed on to the New York Vigilance Committee, with which the Philadelphia committee had close ties. At other times, they were sent northwestward, the final destination being entry into western Canada and the state of Ontario. Caution had to be used at all times because of the Fugitive Slave Act and the very real possibility of recapture for the fugitives or imprisonment for those caught assisting them. There were also fugitives who arrived in Pennsylvania without assistance from conductors by pretending to be white or free, by traveling on foot at night, or by hiding on ships that had sailed from the South.[190]

Many freedom seekers managed to find new lives in northern cities or Canada West with the assistance of conductors. In 1856, Anthony and Albert Brown stole their master's oyster boat from somewhere along Tanner's Creek (presently known as the Lafayette River) in Hampton Roads and managed to escape to Philadelphia with the assistance of Henry Lewey. Later, the Browns settled in the Canada West town of Hamilton along with other fugitives from their region.[191]

Of all the suspected operators of the Underground Railroad referred to in Still's work, William D. Bagnall, a white Norfolk resident, stood out as the most interesting. Employed as a bookkeeper for the Virginia Bank, Bagnall

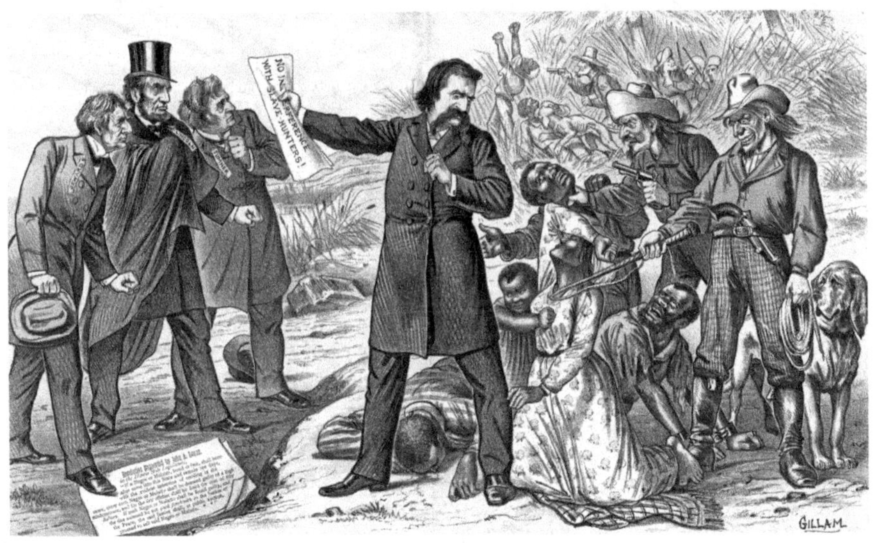

This 1859 picture by Bernhard Gillam illustrates the conflict between slaveholding and non-slaveholding states. Illinois state representative John A. Logan (*center*) was an ardent Democratic Party supporter of states' rights and staunchly advocated the enforcement of the 1850 Fugitive Slave Act and the repressive Illinois Negro Exclusion Bill in 1853. Logan is pictured holding a paper that states, "No Interference with Slave-Hunters!" while looking at two slave hunters arresting a fugitive slave family. Also depicted are Abraham Lincoln, William H. Seward and Charles Sumner watching the arrest angrily but restrained by federal law. *Library of Congress.*

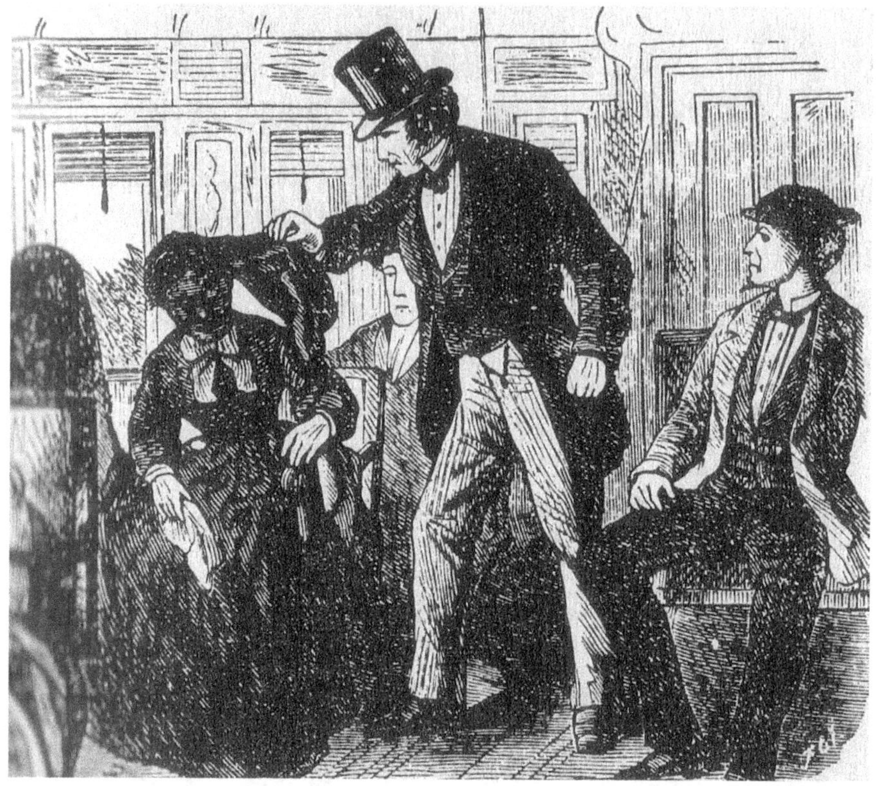

An abolitionist assists two enslaved women—Charlotte and Harriet—who were in disguise escape from their owner while aboard a train from Baltimore to Philadelphia. *William Still,* The Underground Railroad, *1872.*

was a slaveholder who was attributed with helping five fugitives—Clarissa Davis, Tom Page, Isaac Forman, Rebecca Jones and Sam Nixon—escape. He also kept them informed about their families' activities. According to fugitive Clarissa Davis, whom he assisted in 1854, however, Bagnall may have been sympathetic because his wife was a slave. Although the forty-seven-year-old was listed in the 1850 census as married to Elizabeth, thirty-four, who was not designated as black, it is possible that the census taker, who typically assigned race based on observation alone, might have mistaken a very light-skinned African American as white.[192]

White schooner or small vessel captains were also well-known conductors who transported freedom seekers to various locations. Some of the known captains included Robert Lee, Edward Lee, Henry Lee, William Baylis, John Dade, James Carter, William Lambdin, Alfred Fountain, Henry Lovey

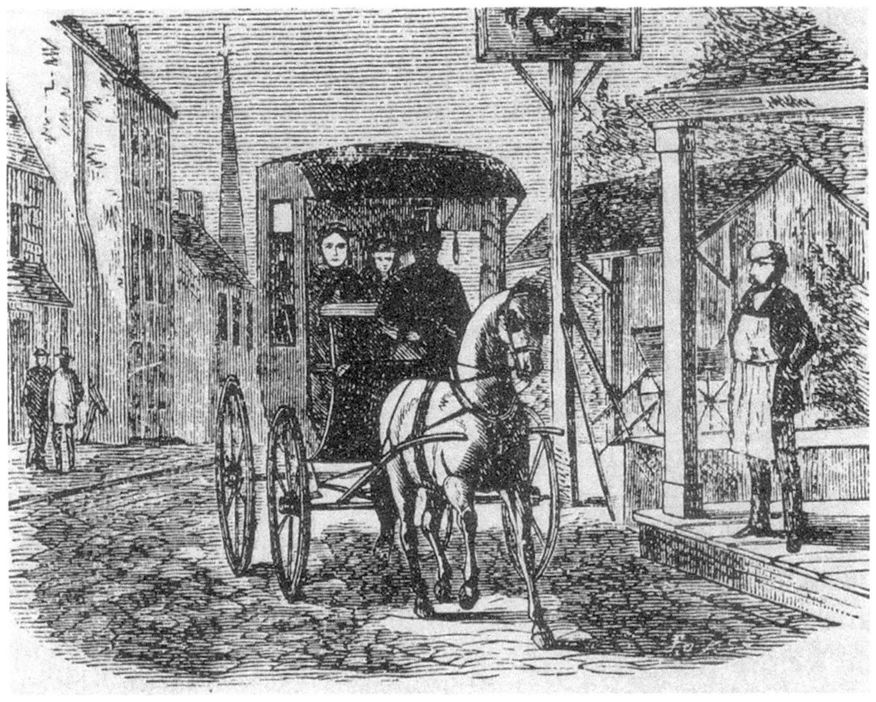

This illustration depicts the escape of a white woman with black coachman and a child from Leesburg, Virginia. Because a black coachman was not unusual, even accompanied by a white woman, the party thought they were safe. *William Still,* The Underground Railroad, *1872.*

and John Thomas. Baylis, Fountain, Lambdin and Lee were the most active schooner and skiff captains who were identified. They transported perhaps hundreds of fugitives to Philadelphia, Boston and New Bedford. What is important to note is that all of these captains either accepted money from the fugitives or charged a fee for transit. Moreover, court records indicated that three out of the four were caught and imprisoned for their activities. In Lancaster and Chester Counties in Pennsylvania, white abolitionist Robert Loney ferried fugitives across the river to Columbia, while white Quaker Daniel Gibbons forwarded men to Jeremiah Moore at Christiana. For all of these conductors and agents, risk was a constant. For instance, Edward Lee was turned in by Portsmouth slaveholders James Murdaugh, William H. Wilson, Joseph Carter and James Hodges. Lee was convicted because he assisted slaves in April 1858; in July, these men presented evidence of Lee's guilt, and he was sentenced to serve several years in the Virginia Penitentiary.[193]

One of the individuals under suspicion following Henry "Box" Brown's escape was Samuel A. Smith, a white shoemaker. When Smith helped two other slaves escape by boxing them up, he was betrayed. Once he was arrested and investigated, officials convicted him of helping Brown and two other slaves escape. The courts sentenced him to eight years in the Virginia Penitentiary in 1849. While incarcerated, Smith was bound with heavy chains for five months, not allowed to call any witnesses in his defense and stabbed five times by a paid assassin for helping slaves escape. Amazingly, Smith survived, and after he was released seven years later, the black citizens of Philadelphia welcomed him to the city, regarding him as a devout hero to the cause of freedom.[194]

One final group identified as frequently aiding runaways were free blacks. Traditionally viewed by slaveholders as a dangerous group, free blacks provided safe havens for fugitives, offered food and clothing and worked as boatmen or stewards (schooners and steamships) throughout the ports. By the 1850s, flight had become more common, as the communication network between southern conductors and northern stationmasters and agents became more refined. Free blacks, such as John Minkins (the steward aboard the *City of Richmond*), Henry Lewey, Eliza Bain and Sam Nixon were among the most noted. And some, like Henry Lewey, a Norfolk slave who used the nom de plume Bluebeard to hide his identity, did his secret work with a lot of panache until he escaped in 1856 after rumors circulated that he was an Underground Railroad agent.[195]

Perhaps no single free black conductor received more attribution by William Still than John Minkins, a steward on the *City of Richmond*. Listed in the 1850 census as an omnibus driver, an occupation that would have familiarized him with passenger ships, mariners, taverns, hotels and the city at large, Minkins found himself out of work in the early 1850s after Norfolk restricted omnibus driving as a white-only occupation. Fugitive accounts between the corridors of Richmond/Petersburg and Norfolk/Portsmouth indicated that John Minkins took a job as a steward aboard steamships operating between Hampton Roads and Philadelphia sometime around 1853. By 1860, Minkins was listed in the fugitive slave fund records as the captain of the schooner *Marcy Pricilla*.[196]

No records survive to explain why John Minkins, who worked as a steward aboard the *City of Richmond* and the *Pennsylvania*, covertly operated as an Underground Railroad conductor, along with cooks Lot Mundy (Monday) and William Thompson, who were employed on schooners such as the *Francis French*.[197] John Minkins and William Bagnall coordinated their efforts in helping Norfolk resident Isaac Forman to freedom. Forman used his mobility to escape in December 1853 aboard the *City of Richmond*, along with fellow fugitives William Davis and Willis Redick. Foreman was a twenty-three-year-old "dark mulatto" and the property of Mrs. Saunders, a widow who hired him out as a steward aboard the steamship *Augusta* for $120 annually. Forman, whose wife lived in Richmond, did not tell his wife prior to his departure, fearing that she would convince him to stay. Yet regret was the rule, as illustrated by Forman's letters to William Still once he settled into Toronto, working at Russell's hotel. Apparently he remained "very gloomy and his heart is almost breaking about his wife." In his second letter, he said, "My soul is vexed, my troubles are inexpressible. I often feel as if I were willing to die. I must see my wife in short, if not, I will die. What would I not give no tongue can utter. Just to gaze on her sweet lips one moment I would be willing to die the next. I am determined to see her some time or other." It is unknown whether Forman was ever reunited with his wife.[198]

Such was also the case for thirty-two-year-old fellow escapee Willis Redick who, like Forman, was assisted by John Minkins. Redick was a slave for hire at one hundred dollars per year by his owner, Portsmouth merchant S.J. Wilson. Redick left his wife of five months, Lydia, without consulting her. He was forced to leave for fear that his owner was planning to sell him, and if he and his wife had children, he would have no means to protect them. He said, "Slavery existed expressly for the purpose of crushing souls and breaking tender hearts." Similarly, William Davis, a thirty-one-year-old mulatto owned by Joseph Reynolds, a Portsmouth businessman who hired him out for twelve dollars a month, left out of fear of being sold away. In doing so, Davis regrettably left his wife, Catharine, daughter Louisa and seven-month-old son. They were placed in the slave jail by their owner, who feared Davis would decamp with them as well.[199]

Many other fugitives from Richmond to the Hampton Roads area escaped with the assistance of John Minkins: Portsmouth natives Moses Wines, Clarissa Davis, Harrison Bell and Harriet Ann Bell and Norfolk native William Henry Atkins.[200] As a slave who hired out his time, performing a number of odd jobs in and around the docks, Moses Wines knew about the steamships and schooners that came in and out of the area every week. Although he was not mistreated by his owner, Abigail Wheeler, he lived in constant fear that he would be sold. He related to William Still that he resented handing over his hard-earned money to Wheeler. As a member of the African Society Methodist Church, Wines came into contact with many unnamed others who escaped or who were secretly involved with the Underground Railroad. He, like Clarissa Davis, escaped aboard a ship with the assistance, no doubt, of John Minkins.[201]

However, this kind of activity was not without considerable risk. Freedom seeker James Gilliam from Richmond mentioned in a letter to William Still that he heard Minkins had been arrested for "rascality" and placed in jail. While Gilliam was happy to hear that Minkins was released because of insufficient evidence, his concern was that the steward's commitment to helping fugitives like himself was very risky.[202]

Aside from John Minkins, William Still mentioned steward and cook Lott Mundy (a free black), whose cover was blown after he was accused of assisting Thomas and Martin in escaping aboard the schooner *Danville* in July 1856. This ship was in the Richmond harbor bound for New York. The crew discovered the two runaways and implicated Mundy, who was sentenced to ten years, serving until the Civil War period. Other blacks caught helping freedom seekers included Richmond slave Jacob Dill, who was whipped for harboring a runaway in his Broad Street cellar. Another account mentioned that a free black woman, Mary Stark from Chesterfield County, was sentenced for harboring a runaway slave from Norfolk for several months. Just across the James River in Petersburg was an active enslaved conductor known only as Ham and Eggs who was responsible for sending numerous freedom seekers on ships departing Virginia.[203]

Eliza Bains, the probable slave of George M. Bain, the pastor of the African Methodist Society Church, worked at the Crawford House, a Portsmouth boardinghouse that catered to those in the maritime industry. She was credited with helping to secret a number of enslaved African Americans to northern cities by boat. In the summer of 1855, she became a victim of the yellow fever epidemic that devastated the population in Hampton Roads. This was a tremendous blow to the secret network, but Henry Lewey continued his work through 1856, when, according to his wife, Rebecca, he secured passage to Canada. One brief reference in a letter to Still from Anthony and Albert Brown, brothers who escaped from Norfolk in 1855, reported that Lewey did indeed make his escape successfully.[204]

Samuel Nixon, like William Bagnall, was described by William Still as having unfettered access to almost every neighborhood in Hampton Roads. As the apprentice of his owner, Norfolk dentist Dr. Charles. F. Martin, Nixon made evening house calls and worked as his bookkeeper. Consequently, Nixon's unconstrained movement and ability to read made him a dangerous ally of Underground Railroad activities indeed.

Eventually, Nixon had to leave Norfolk, as did Lewey, because suspicions arose about his secret activities.[205]

An 1851 incident involving the USS *Susquehanna* resulted in a near riot when Norfolk watchmen attempted to arrest a free black sailor, but his shipmates came to his rescue. The precipitant of this incident was a public discussion about adopting a law prohibiting the boycotting of boats employing black sailors. After the *Susquehanna* incident, ships with black crewmen were more closely watched. In the 1858 case of William Thompson, a free black cook aboard the *Francis French* schooner bound for New York, he was arrested for assisting a slave from Smithfield escape. The captain and crew were arrested when the vessel was searched and the runaway discovered. Following the discovery and arrest, Thompson confessed, taking full responsibility, claiming he was duped by the fugitive's brother, Ned, who told him that the nineteen-year-old fugitive had been brutalized by his owner. Unlike many of the white ship captains who often charged a fee for passage to northern areas, free blacks working aboard ships assisted fugitives freely. Perhaps it was this obvious sympathy that led Virginia authorities to adopt extreme measures to reduce contact between free blacks and enslaved African Americans.[206]

The Virginia General Assembly reacted to these and other cases in 1856 by passing an act mandating severe punishment for free blacks and whites assisting runaways. For example, in May 1858, Norfolk residents caught the *Francis French* schooner with a runaway on board. The captain and crew were tried and convicted. The Norfolk City Council also demanded that Willett Mott, another northern ship captain, leave the harbor within twenty-four hours or face a tar and feathering. Mott's commercial associate, William Dandenberg, was branded a traitor. In October 1854, Peter, an African American living in Petersburg, was accused of harboring runaways and taken before the mayor's court.[207]

Other men, like Paul J. Ballas and Washington Ashby from Virginia, were arrested and sent to the state penitentiary for "slave stealing." This was the common explanation given for those arrested for assisting fugitives to escape. Interestingly, Ashby had just gotten out of prison after serving ten years for the same offense in Northampton County. He was subsequently arrested again in Richmond.[208]

In 1856, Virginia's legislature passed a comprehensive program that would involve the inspection of all vessels coming into port, the reward of $100 to anyone who apprehended fugitives found aboard vessels, a five-to-ten-year imprisonment of free persons found guilty of assisting fugitives and the payment of $500 to those who provided information leading to the "conviction of a free white person engaged in carrying off a slave, or in any manner concerned in helping an escape."[209]

An article in the *American Beacon* suggested that between $40,000 and $50,000 worth of slave property left the Hampton Roads port in 1853 alone. In 1854, the *American Beacon* exclaimed that slaves escaped "almost daily," with leaders from both Portsmouth and Norfolk fearing that their cities' losses totaled as much as $500,000. These losses caused lawmakers to step up efforts to deter escapes with increased night watchmen, laws penalizing those who assisted fugitives and severe prison terms. There were also numerous ship captains, stewards and crewmen who were arrested or detained for assisting runaways, but only a few received prison terms.[210]

The state penitentiary, located at the western terminus of Byrd Street, northwest of Gamble's Hill in Richmond was, for some, a death sentence. Despite arresting and imprisoning twenty-seven men in the state penitentiary between 1842 and 1860 for helping enslaved people escape, only a few were actually captured. Virginia toughened the penalties by 1860 and increased the sentence to twenty years.[211]

Those who escaped to points north and Canada transformed those areas to some degree. William Still's *The Underground Railroad* and Benjamin Drew's *The Refugee: A North Side View of Slavery* recount Underground Railroad activities in both the United States and Canada, tracing the descendants of fugitives to provide a revealing analysis of the African diaspora in North America. Countless men and women, according to William Still's account, freely served as conductors, agents and stationmasters, believing they had a moral and ethical responsibility to defend and protect those seeking freedom with all resources at their disposal.

1860 Virginia State Penitentiary Records for those Imprisoned for Assisting Fugitive Slaves

P.R. Smith (black, shoemaker, 1842)
H. Charous (mulatto, wheelwright, 1844)
B. Jackson (black, wheelwright, 1844)
Cato Ricketts (black, wheelwright, 1847)
John A. Blevins (white, shoemaker, 1848)
S. Brooks (white, blacksmith, 1848)
A. Ewing (white, carpenter, 1848)
H. Morrisett (white, wheelwright, 1849)

Abby Ann Dixon (black, seamstress, 1849)
Samuel A. Smith (white, shoemaker, 1849)
J. William Wingfield (white, carpenter, 1849)
Thomas Blackson (?, shoemaker, 1850)
Washington Asbury (white, blacksmith, 1854)
Lot. Monday [Munday] (black, cook, 1856)
James Smith (black, blacksmith, 1856)
*William H. Lamden (white, shoemaker, 1856)
W. Reynolds (mulatto, laborer, 1856)
John McKinney (white, blacksmith, 1857)
Thomas J. Dunn (white, carpenter, 1857)
A. Cottingham (white, sailor, 1858)
*William B. Baylis (white, sailor, 1858)
Paul Dallas (white, shoemaker, 1858)
W. H. Thompson (black, blacksmith, 1858)
Jackson Ottuger (white, blacksmith, 1858)
Armistead McGuire (white, stonemason, 1859)
Ab. Nelson (white, blacksmith, 1859)

** Ship captains captured with fugitives aboard vessel*

Courtesy 1860 U.S. Census, County of Henrico, City of Richmond

5

FROM VIRGINIA TO THE NORTH AND VIRGINIA TO CANADA

Henry "Box" Brown's sufferings were mild compared to the experiences of William Henry Gilliam, James Mercer and John Clayton. A steamship's black steward (probably John Minkins) hid them in a small compartment next to the boiler, where for days they endured excruciating heat, breathing in coal dust that burned the nose and throat each time they took a breath. So suffocating was the compartment that every few minutes each man took turns crawling to a small aperture where they were able to take a few deep breaths of fresh air. Finally, on February 26, 1854, the men arrived in Philadelphia from Richmond with hearts full of excitement at their first taste of liberty.[212]

Freedom was especially sweet for Gilliam, a baker by trade who had been hired out to drive a bread wagon by his owner. He had tried to escape many times before and somehow managed to escape the usual form of punishment: being sold down South. Instead, his "readiness of speech and general natural ability" worked to his advantage with his owner, a widow who received $135 annually for his work. Moreover, Gilliam was literate, giving him an advantage over most enslaved people.[213]

Three months after their escape, they settled into new homes in St. Catharines, in Ontario, Canada. Gilliam wrote a letter to his mother, Marena Mercer, and his owner, Louisa E. White, expressing hope that White would show kindness to his mother. The response from his owner was filled with both sadness at his departure—entreating him to return with a promise of good treatment—and outrage because she felt her good treatment was rewarded with betrayal. After receiving the response, delivered to him by the Philadelphia Vigilance Committee, Gilliam wrote again to William Still indicating that he had little compassion for his owner because he served her for twenty-five years and two months. He also informed Still that he and others from his group had left St. Catharines and moved to Toronto—even though most had not secured jobs—because the opportunities were greater in a larger city. He concluded by asking Still to get word to his mother that he loved and missed her and wanted her to send him news of what was happening in Richmond. He also hoped that Still could help him get his mother out of slavery, but no information survived indicating whether his wish was fulfilled.[214]

William Gilliam's story, and that of his compatriots, was not unusual for those who were successful in their quest to escape from slavery in Virginia. In fact, Virginia's Underground Railroad, more perhaps that any other in the United States, succeeded in sending hundreds if not thousands of runaways to areas as far away as Canada West. As early as 1815, blacks negotiated the journey from the South across the Western Reserve in Ohio. One of the earliest white settlers in this area who assisted freedom seekers on their way to Canada was Owen Brown, father to abolitionist John Brown. Once blacks began seeking refuge in Canada, word spread quickly about the nation through "vague rumors." Josiah Henson and Harriet Tubman helped to disseminate the promise of Canadian liberty with such success that by 1860, an estimated five hundred freedom seekers journeyed annually to America's neighbor to the north.[215]

The Reverends Calvin Fairbank, Charles Torrey and Dr. Alexander Ross assisted black abolitionists in spreading word about Canada to potential freedom seekers in America. Traveling in slave states, Ross journeyed through cities and towns disseminating information about Canada and the routes by which that country could be reached. Moreover, as the Underground Railroad network became more sophisticated, letters from freedom seekers to their loved ones in the South also spread word. Ross remarked in a later memoir that when he visited cities such as Richmond (Virginia), Nashville (Tennessee), Columbus and Vicksburg (Mississippi), Augusta (Georgia), Charleston (South Carolina) and Huntsville (Alabama), he encountered enslaved people who had already heard about the prospects available to freedom seekers in Canada.[216]

Ross shared information about Canada while holding clandestine meetings with potential freedom seekers, even connecting them with Underground

Railroad conductors in their localities. In Richmond, for example, Ross recalled the following:

> *On my arrival in Richmond, I went to a house of a gentleman to whom I had been directed and I was known in the North to be a friend of freedom....I invited a number of the most intelligent, active and reliable slaves to meet me at the house of a colored preacher, on a Sunday evening. On the night appointed for this meeting, forty-two slaves came to hear what prospect there was for an escape from bondage....I explained to them my... purpose in visiting the slave states, the various routes from Virginia to Ohio and Pennsylvania, and the names of friends in border towns who would help them on to Canada. I requested them to circulate this information discreetly among all upon whom they could rely.*[217]

At the appointed time, nine "stout, intelligent young men" arrived, determined to achieve freedom. Ross continued:

> *To each I gave a few dollars in money, a pocket compass, knife, pistol, and as much cold meat and bread as each could carry with ease. I again explained the route....I never met more apt students than these poor fellows....They were to travel only by night, resting in some secure spot during the day. Their route was to be through Pennsylvania, to Erie on Lake Erie, and from thence to Canada.*[218]

Ross later discovered that all the freedom seekers arrived in Canada, and in 1863, the men enlisted in the United States Colored Troops (USCT) during the Civil War.[219] Clearly, the work of many abolitionists guaranteed that Canada would become an important player in the fight for liberty. The road to Canada, however, would not be easy or absent of challenges.

At the end of the American Revolution, Thomas Jefferson argued that the British took three thousand black slaves to Canada. The British responded to his protests, saying that "every slave like every horse, which escaped or strayed from within the American lines, and came into the possession of the British army, became by the laws and rights of war, British property." With this statement began the construction of a contested boundary that people of African descent used to gain social, political and legal freedom in North America. While the Revolution unintentionally initiated a movement contesting this northern political boundary of states free of

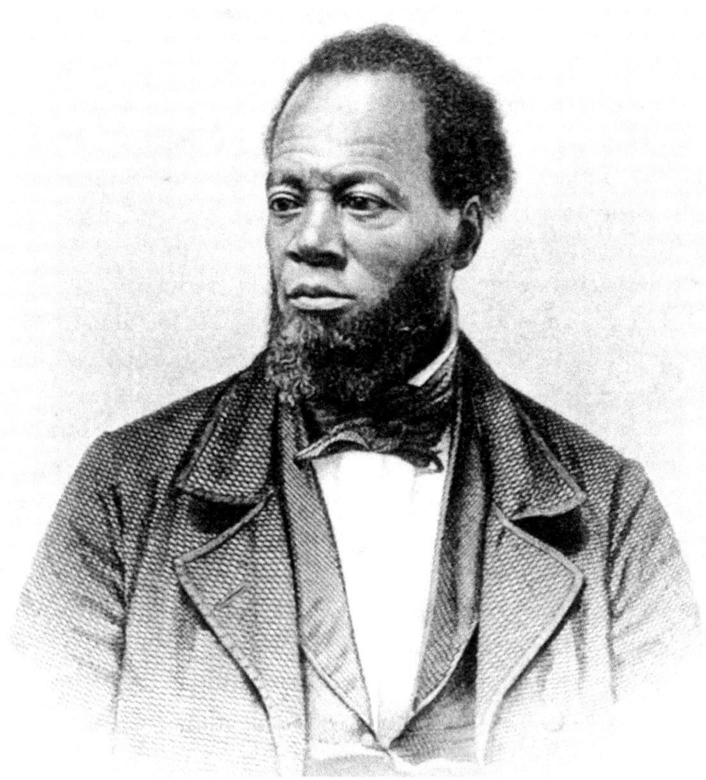

Born to enslaved parents in Prince William County, Virginia, Austin Steward was eight years old when his owner, Captain William Helm, sold the plantation and moved all the enslaved people to his new estate in New York State. Steward was hired out as a laborer and eventually escaped to Canandaigua, New York, around 1813. In 1857, Steward published an account in *Twenty-Two Years a Slave, and Forty Years a Freeman; Embracing a Correspondence of Several Years, While President of Wilberforce Colony*. *Library of Congress*.

slavery, it also resulted in a boundary that was fluid in terms of identity (of blacks as legally free) and association.[220]

Africans and those of African descent brought to the Americas as forced laborers saw this period as a "protracted struggle for inclusion." People began crossing boundaries designed to solidify the system of slavery at a time when Enlightenment ideas of freedom were gaining support. Complicating the physical boundaries between the newly formed United States of America and the English colony to its north was the passage of the 1787 Northwest Ordinance, which forbade slavery and the transportation of slaves into the Northwest Territory (Great Lakes region). This law made the Detroit River a fluid boundary between the free American territory and the British territory that allowed slavery. The result was a bizarre situation in which enslaved blacks in Canada crossed the Detroit River to to the free territories in the United States while enslaved Americans crossed the river to self-emancipate in Canada. Four years later, the Canadian Constitutional Act established two colonies—Upper (Canada West) and Lower Canada—and independent rule, opening the door for changes to slavery laws.[221]

This new constitution set into motion a shift in how and why enslaved African Americans sought refuge in Canada. Attorney General John White of Upper Canada, under the direction of Lieutenant Governor John Simcoe, introduced a 1793 bill to the House of Assembly that would gradually abolish slavery. The Simcoe bill, although conflicting with the Imperial Act of 1790, asserted that "no Negro or other person who shall come or be brought into this Province…shall be subject to the condition of a slaver or to burden involuntary service for life." In other words, once black fugitives reached Canada, they immediately had a free status. According to historian Jason Silverman in his seminal work, *Unwelcome Guests: Canada West's Response to American Fugitive Slaves*, enslaved blacks had been treated relatively benignly by white Canadians, with only a few receiving brutal treatment or punishment. Prior to Simcoe's efforts, slaves in Canadian society were restricted to a socially, economically and politically subservient status, resulting in some choosing emigration to distant Sierra Leone.[222]

Following the emergence of this "Back to Africa" movement in Sierra Leone, a small but growing antislavery effort, led by Simcoe, was initiated to eventually erase the discriminating association of slavery with Canada's black populace. Simcoe encouraged blacks who entered Upper Canada to settle in mainstream communities instead of in the established segregated black townships and neighborhoods. He believed that by integrating into the broader society, free blacks would shed the inferior stigma that relegated them to the lower rungs. Simcoe's plans, however, were met with resistance by some and support from others.[223]

By 1829, the Executive Council of Lower Canada had officially abolished legal slavery. The immediate result of the 1829 decree was the establishment of numerous black communities in Upper Canada composed of American fugitives and free blacks who joined pre-established settlements of free blacks. Most who came to Upper Canada in the early nineteenth century crossed the Niagara and Detroit Rivers aboard ships on the Great Lakes. By 1819, communities had developed at Amherstburg, LaSalle and Sandwich, with African Canadians and African Americans coordinating their efforts to resettle black refugees into the various communities in the region. Prominent black activists and abolitionists championed international immigration. These included Mary Ann Shadd and Martin Delany. Both Shadd and Delany immigrated to Chatham in Canada West and founded businesses. So popular and successful was Chatham that it was nicknamed "the colored man's Paris." And perhaps more than any other place in Canada West, Chatham represented this blended culture that emerged.[224]

According to *A Fluid Frontier*, by Karolyn Frost and Veta Tucker, this region of Canada bordering the Detroit River was a "complex and often conflicted borderland, an often amorphous district where the peoples on either side of the divide shared common cultural traits and political aspirations, but also a tangible, concrete border that, when traversed by people of African descent in search of freedom, offered a more than reasonable chance they would achieve their goal."[225] Captain Chapman, whose ship plied the waters between Lake Erie and Canada, remembered an instance when fugitives aboard his ship asked if they were in Canada. When he responded in the affirmative, Chapman recalled, "They seemed to be transformed; a new light shone in their eyes, their tongues were loosed, they laughed and cried, prayed and sang praises, fell upon the ground and kissed it, hugged and kissed each other, crying, 'Bress de Lord! Oh! I'se free before I die.'"[226]

In the first twenty years of the nineteenth century, Fort Malden in Amherstburg was where freedom seekers initially arrived once reaching Canada. Located fourteen miles south of Detroit, this area quickly acquired a substantial black population. Afterward, a regular ferry service transported people from Detroit to Windsor. Soon, black communities grew in Detroit and in the many Canadian towns and settlements along the river. The region also saw a number of resettlement organizations emerge, including the Refugee Home Society, founded by Kentucky-born newspaper publisher and fugitive slave Henry Bibb.[227]

The areas of Amherstburg, Colchester, Windsor (just across the lake from Detroit), Welland, St. Catharines (across the Niagara River), Chatham, Dresden and London (paralleling Lake Erie) were favored locales, along with Toronto, Oro and Queen's Bush. Before 1830, settlement patterns were uneven, disorganized and small. Most came from the Upper South, especially Virginia, introducing tobacco as the favored product to cultivate as early as 1819. In fact, for a short time in the 1820s, tobacco production helped make Amherstburg a thriving community until the bottom fell out of the tobacco trade.[228]

Abolitionist, journalist and Boston educator Benjamin Drew traveled through Canada West in the 1850s, recording over one hundred firsthand accounts illustrating the conditions of fugitives in Canada. One of the people he included in his book, *A North-Side View of Slavery*, was a man who arrived in 1824. Virginia fugitive James Adams said that he grew up near the mouth of the Big Kanawha River. Adams was seventeen years old when he escaped with one of his cousins, Benjamin Harris, because he noticed how poorly slaves were generally treated and he wanted to avoid that for his life. He and Harris reached Ohio and were hidden by sympathetic friends and, after numerous close calls and dangers, connected with the network of ministers and others who were part of the Underground Railroad. Once in Cleveland, they were put on Captain William Baylis's schooner headed for Buffalo, New York. During their travels, they were alerted that a one-hundred-dollar reward each was posted for their return. Nevertheless, the duo finally reach Canada and settled in St. Catharines.[229]

What Adams and Harris found when they arrived was essentially a wilderness. Eleven years later, in 1835, conditions in Canada West were still considered very poor. J.W. Loguen recounted his arrival in Hamilton as "penniless, ragged, lonely, homeless, helpless, hungry and forlorn." He said, "Hamilton was a cold wilderness for the fugitive when I came there." By 1838, however, a mission in Upper Canada had been established to help with the establishment of schools and other assistance. Soon, the mission began coordinating efforts with northern U.S. friends. In 1844, for example, Levi Coffin and William Beard traveled to Canada West to assess the needs and experiences of freedom seekers. Many others also went, including John Brown and the Reverend Samuel May.[230]

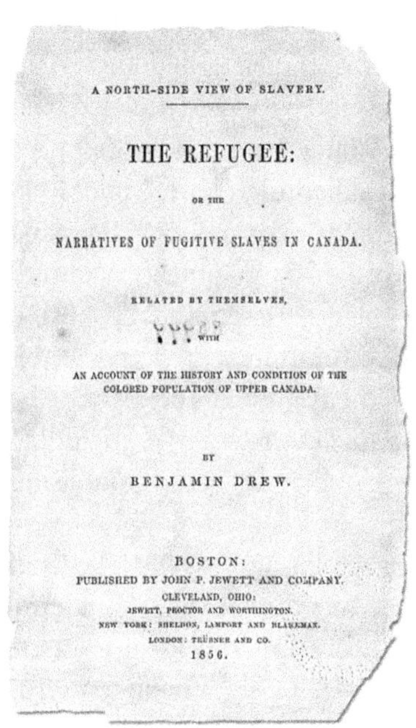

A NORTH-SIDE VIEW OF SLAVERY.

THE REFUGEE:

OR THE

NARRATIVES OF FUGITIVE SLAVES IN CANADA.

RELATED BY THEMSELVES,

WITH

AN ACCOUNT OF THE HISTORY AND CONDITION OF THE COLORED POPULATION OF UPPER CANADA.

BY

BENJAMIN DREW.

BOSTON:
PUBLISHED BY JOHN P. JEWETT AND COMPANY.
CLEVELAND, OHIO:
JEWETT, PROCTOR AND WORTHINGTON.
NEW YORK: SHELDON, LAMPORT AND BLAKEMAN.
LONDON: TRÜBNER AND CO.
1856.

This is the title page of Benjamin Drew's 1856 book, *A North-Side View of Slavery: The Refugee: or the Narratives of the Fugitive Slaves in Canada*. This monumental account is one of the few that provides insight about the lives of freedom seekers in Canada. *Archives of Ontario.*

According to Drew's accounts, fugitives referred to themselves as refugees. This attitude suggests an awareness that these individuals saw themselves as taking shelter from enslavement in Canada, articulating a clear national identity as

Americans. While parallels can be drawn with the experiences of political exiles and illegal immigrants coming into North America and Europe since the 1960s, these immigrants typically entered a society ill-prepared to receive them, especially as the population increased in size throughout the 1850s. It was because of the uneven, inconsistent and perhaps half-hearted assistance provided by Canadian officials and abolitionists and the conflicted feelings about their presence by white Canadians that historians have accurately characterized African American fugitives in Canada as unwelcome guests.

Drew's study of these black fugitives in Canada highlighted the social alienation faced by many, especially those in segregated towns or communities. Unfortunately, while Drew devoted countless pages to recording and analyzing perceptions of white Canadians toward the African American immigrant population, he gave almost no attention to the attitudes of these African Americans to Canadian society. There were only a few interviewed who noted that while the harsh Canadian winters presented a challenge of adaptation, returning to a nation that legally deprived them of their humanity was not an option. Accounts verified the assertion that those who fled to the safety of Canada regarded themselves as refugees and expatriates rather than immigrants seeking Canadian citizenship. But how "blackness" shaped the communities that would be established by these fugitives and their perspectives on how they felt as refugees have not received any attention until fairly recently and only then in a peripheral manner.

Levi Coffin and J.W. Loguen visited Amherstburg and Isaac Rice's missionary building, where a school for black children was conducted for children of fugitives in November 1844. Rice had been a Presbyterian minister in Ohio, and he wanted to help the freedom seekers, who often had nothing but the clothes on their backs. Coffin and Loguen also visited Hiram Wilson's British and American Manual Labor Institute for black children and the Wilberforce Colony, where they encountered some of the freedom seekers who had passed through Coffin's station and stayed in his home ten to fifteen years earlier. He was delighted to see they were thriving in their new homes.[231]

After assessing conditions during these early decades of refugee resettlement, Coffin and Loguen identified the localities in most need as they planned fundraising efforts. They did notice that land in Canada West was "easily obtained," and many blacks acquired it. Government land was divided into fifty-acre lots for sale at two dollars per acre, but it would take years to pay for it. The Elgin Association was formed in 1848–49 to settle new arrivals on Crown or clergy land. The native peoples also welcomed the

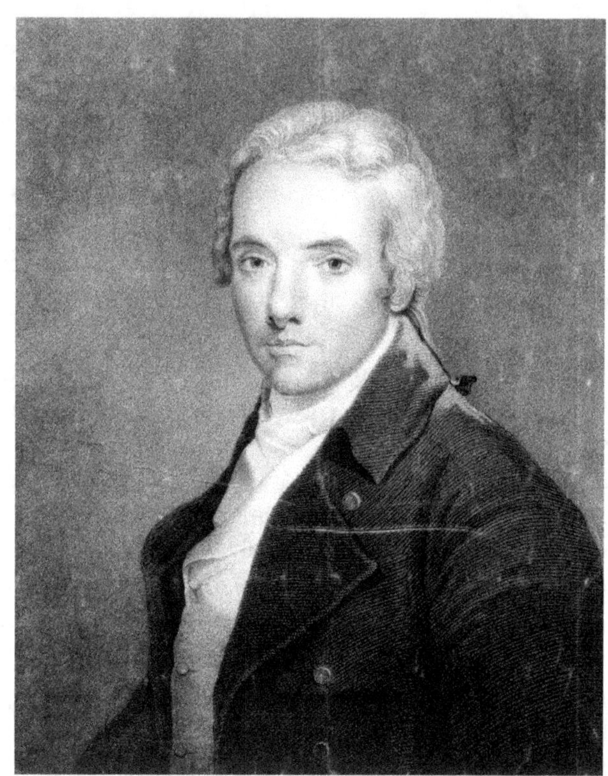

Right: This circa 1884 portrait of William Wilberforce, Esq., MP, by R.A. Russell captures the essence of the famous English abolitionist. A deeply religious man, Wilberforce's service as a member of the British Parliament focused on social reform, the abolition of Britain's participation in the transatlantic slave trade and eventually slavery itself throughout the British Empire. *Library of Congress.*

Below: This map of the southwestern counties of Canada West highlights the locations and principal stations of the free black populations in 1855. *Archives of Ontario.*

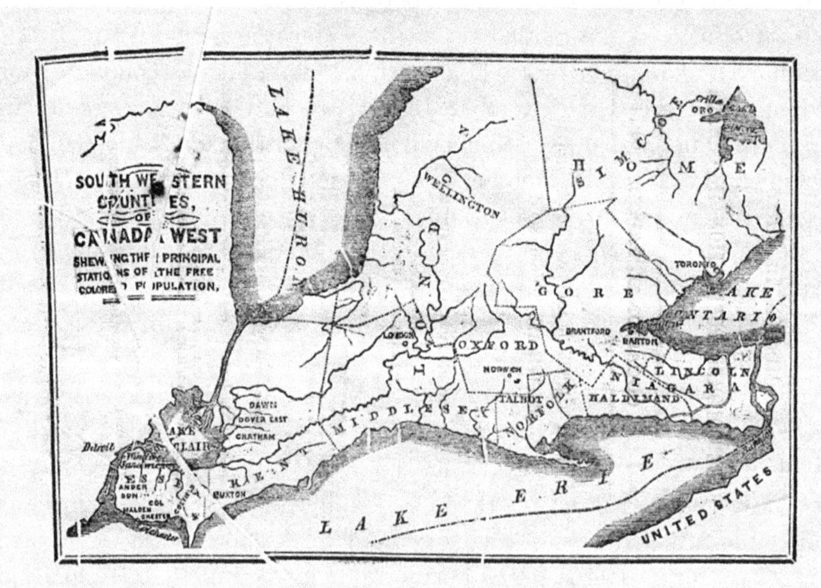

fugitives, who sometimes adopted the culture of their benefactors, located between Lake Ontario and Lake Erie.[232]

In the 1830s, many of the freedom seekers arrived in Essex County, Ontario, before traveling inland. In 1851, for example, the black population in Essex was 11.2 percent (1,871) of the total population. Ten years later, that number increased to 2,381, although its overall percentage (9.5 percent) had declined because of European immigration. Most settled near the waterways in cities such as New Canaan, Maidstone, Harrow, Colchester, Gosfield, Amherstburg, Fort Malden and Anderdon.[233]

Amherstburg, Oro and Wilberforce were favorite locations of American fugitives and free blacks in the 1820s through the 1840s. This migration trend continued, with an increase occurring in the 1850s after enforcement of the Fugitive Slave Act began. Most significantly, the majority of those who were successful in making it to Canada came from states in the Upper South in general and port areas in particular. This was certainly true of Virginia's fugitives.[234]

Amherstburg, founded in 1796 as the site of the original Fort Malden, was located at the narrowest crossing of the Detroit River. Some freedom seekers arrived by swimming or sailing across the river. Since its beginning, blacks had been part of the town as the slaves of white Loyalists following the American Revolution. Among the most noted residents was Josiah Henson, the famous abolitionist and model for Uncle Tom in Harriet Beecher Stowe's *Uncle Tom's Cabin*. Once slavery ended in Canada West, black residents were important to the town's growth and prosperity as innkeepers, shoemakers, millers, carpenters and government representatives on the local school board. So threatening was this town to slavery that slaveholders perpetrated myths about the region, telling slaves such as William Johnson who left Hopkins County, Virginia, that the Detroit River was impassable, exaggerating its width. By 1848, the town had become the regional headquarters of the American Missionary Association (AMA) for Canada, illustrating the fluid boundary for many of these progressive organizations.[235]

In 1840, James Dougall, a Scottish immigrant, established an integrated private school in Amherstburg because the public schools prohibited black children from attending. Unfortunately, six years later, the school closed because of inadequate resources. Undeterred, the black community pooled its resources to establish a school with the assistance of the Common Schools Act. These and other activities resulted in the growth of the town's black residents. According to the 1850–51 census, 205 blacks were listed as residents of Amherstburg; the Regular Missionary Baptist Association indicated there were 600 in 1853. By 1859, 800 freedom seekers (15.5 percent) were living in the town. And while organizations like the Freedmen's Inquiry Commission described the black inhabitants as poor and in desperate need, perhaps to encourage more donations, many of its black residents enjoyed prosperity.[236]

Another community in Essex, Malden, already had 100 blacks living in the town at its founding in 1828. Known for tobacco production, like its neighbors Colchester, Anderdon and Maidstone, the town was very small. In fact, twenty-two years after its founding, the black population had only increased to 279. Given the immigration of freedom seekers from tobacco-producing American states such as Virginia and Kentucky, accounts suggest that black farmers' expertise stimulated production that led to these towns becoming Canada's primary producers of tobacco.[237]

While the towns throughout Essex County were separate entities, the black communities were not. Instead, they were connected through their complex religious associations. The Baptist Association was formed in Amherstburg in 1838, reflecting early black transnationalism; within four years, the congregation was holding joint meetings with Detroit, Michigan's Second Baptist Church. So strong was this association that it established other Baptist churches throughout the county. At the same time, the Methodist and the African Methodist Episcopal churches established a network of churches throughout the region as well. This also led to the formation of self-help and mutual aid societies based in churches. One important group was the True Band Society, with fourteen chapters throughout the county.[238]

What made these communities a challenge for most of the newly arrived freedom seekers was their isolated nature and limited resources. For some, these challenges caused them to move to Toronto, even though they would have to face more prejudice from white Canadians. After the 1840s, the migration of fugitives into areas around St. Catharines became evident.[239]

St. Catharines was made popular when Harriet Tubman chose it as her home in 1851. Hiram Wilson, an Underground Railroad agent in St. Catharines, reported to William Still that Elias Jasper and Lucy Bell arrived safely. Wilson commented that they were about to cross the river to Toronto in the hope of better opportunities, even though he doubted they would succeed. He also reminded Still of the tremendous needs of freedom seekers arriving almost daily. The numbers apparently overwhelmed the meager resources Wilson and other abolitionists had in resettling and assisting those yearning for freedom north of America.[240]

By the 1840s, a more structured organization had formed through contacts made between regional vigilance committees in northern states

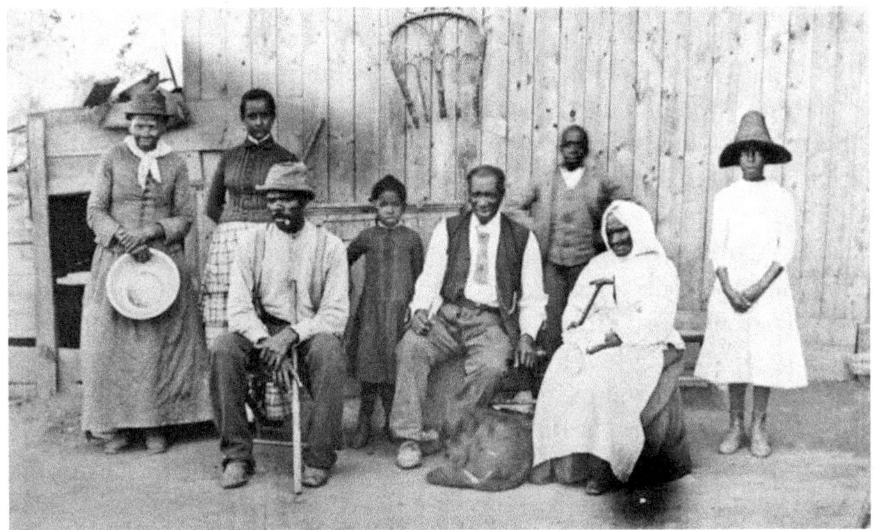

This famous image of Harriet Tubman and her family while living in St. Catharines, Canada, provides an important view of the world of freedom seekers living in a country that provided sanctuary from slavery. *From left to right*: Harriet Tubman, Gertie Davis (Tubman's adopted daughter), Nelson David (Tubman's second husband), Lee Cheney, "Pop" Alexander, Walter Green, Sarah Parker ("Blind Auntie") and Dora Stewart (granddaughter of Tubman's brother, John Stewart). *New York Public Library.*

and Canada. Abolitionists created a network so that once freedom seekers reach the waterway border between the United States and Canada, small vessels would be available to take them into Canada West. Soon, this would be where the largest numbers crossed into Canada by way of the "lake ports between Oswego, New York and Detroit," by train or by steamship.[241] Some of those arriving from Virginia included Norfolk natives Richard Bohm, James M. Williams and John Atkinson. Williams said, "Slavery is horrible! Horrible! Horrible!" Bohm commented, "Slavery is the worst kind of robbery." For Atkinson, slavery was "like trying to get religion, and not seeing the way to escape condemnation."[242] Frederick County man Dan Josiah Lockhart, who escaped in 1847 while his owner was in Philadelphia, said farewell to his wife and children, got some meat and bread, took his master's saddlebags and left. After crossing the Potomac River on a ferry boat, he was confronted with questions about his status but was dressed well enough that many whites assumed he was free. Not until he reached Pittsburg and secured a job did he send a letter to his wife assuring her of his love. However, his owner intercepted the letter, tracking him down with a bill of sale and two constables. He was sent to one of the local boardinghouses under a false pretense so that he could be arrested. After a scuffle, Lockhart's friends intervened and helped him to a house not far away. Eventually, Lockhart was forwarded to Canada, where he started a new life. Other immigrants to St. Catharines included William George, who left from Harpers Ferry in 1851; Henry Banks, who escaped with Isaac Williams from Ayler's slave pen in Richmond; Christopher Nicholson from Fredericksburg; and David West, who arrived in 1854 from King and Queen County.[243]

Amherstburg and Colchester were areas where almost six hundred blacks were recorded as living in 1827. Sandwich, on the other hand, attracted black immigrants from Detroit. Generally, blacks entering Canada independently without assistance were fairly well acknowledged, but the response to the arrival of black fugitives varied from region to region, with some facing prejudice and discrimination while others were well received. Voices of protest among white Canadians accompanied the increase of black immigrants, especially by the 1840s and 1850s. Some were even distinctly unwelcoming in many areas of the province. Historian Robin Winks identified five major developments that changed the way white Canadians viewed black immigrants in the mid-nineteenth century.[244]

Not surprisingly, border and national identities became an issue, as blacks began moving between these nations even in the decades before the most active period of the Underground Railroad, when the majority of freedom seekers sought relief from slavery. In particular, many freedom seekers coming from the United States regarded themselves as American refugees, thus creating an identity that was at odds with their borders. Adjusting to this identity required resourcefulness and proactive efforts, assisted by the formation of numerous self-help organizations. And as they sought to protect themselves, their families and their communities from the subtle yet pervasive racial discrimination in Canada by building up their communities with schools, businesses and support groups, as the Reverend Samuel Ringgold Ward maintained, "Canadian Negro hate" was still very common.[245]

Quite understandably, this movement by freedom seekers across the borders into Canada was problematic for slaveholders, who were painfully aware that word had spread among the enslaved populations that freedom lay to the north. In 1821, while Maryland petitioned Congress to redress grievances against Pennsylvania abolitionists for the loss of slaves, Kentucky congressman Henry Clay demanded that Congress open negotiations with Canada for the return of fugitives slaves. After he was rebuffed by his colleagues, five years later, he found a more sympathetic ear in President John Quincy Adams. As the secretary of state, Clay again attempted to secure the return of fugitives using the pretext that he needed to renegotiate formal treaty relations. In 1827, Clay was assured that Canada would never comply with the request to allow the seizure of people considered citizens of Canada.[246] Indeed, Clay was convinced:

> [Slaves] *escape, principally from Virginia and Kentucky to Upper Canada, whither they are pursued by those who are lawfully entitled to their labor: and, as there is no existing regulation by which they can be surrendered, the attempt to recapture them leads to disagreeable collisions.*[247]

After diplomatic efforts to return fugitives failed, owners, intent on recapturing their slaves, sent slave hunters to invade the province. While there were some recorded incidences of kidnapping, most of the attempts were accompanied by accusations that the fugitives had committed a crime. This tactic was a common one used frequently in the northern states. John DeBree unsuccessfully used this tactic in his attempt to secure extradition for his slave through the courts. Parliament attempted to resolve this issue with an 1833 act designed to provide for the extradition to foreign countries of "fugitive offenders," but the black and white abolitionist communities rallied with resistance and legal challenges. Eventually, Upper Canada's officials relented and continued providing sanctuary to freedom seekers with little cooperation with requests by slaveholders for extradition. This allowed the migration trend to continue for the next thirty years, with an increase occurring in the 1850s after the enforcement of the Fugitive Slave Act began. Most significantly, the majority of those who were successful in making it to Canada came from states in the Upper South in general and port areas in particular.[248]

In 1853, for example, both William Davis and Willis Redick, who escaped aboard the *City of Richmond*, migrated to Canada after a short stay in Philadelphia. A year later, John Atkinson migrated to St. Catharines. The year 1856 was monumental for many fugitives from Portsmouth and Norfolk who managed to escape aboard Captain Alfred Fountain's schooner. Included among those nine escapees were Portsmouth natives Nathaniel Bowser, Charles and Charity Thompson and Thomas Cooper. According to a letter to William Still from Thomas Garret in Wilmington, Delaware, all nine were sent by steamboat to Elijah Pennypacker in Schuylkill, Pennsylvania.

Afterward, the four Hampton Roads fugitives settled in Canada. Records revealed that Cooper returned to Philadelphia and worked as a waiter after the Civil War.[249]

When the most successful Underground Railroad conductor, John Fairfield, arrived in Canada West on his many frequent visits, he always brought freedom seekers with him and usually stopped in Windsor. Laura Haviland, a mission teacher, recalled that on one occasion, when Fairfield arrived with twenty-seven fugitives, the group was received and a reception and dinner was given in Fairfield's honor by local black church members in appreciation of his work.[250] Haviland recalled that the event was like a jubilee, with one elderly woman exclaiming, "This pays me for all the dangers I have faced in bringing this company just to see those friends meet."[251]

Fitch Reed recalled seeing Fairfield bring twenty-eight freedom seekers to Canada in 1853. According to Reed, this group arrived with rounds of ammunition because they were all determined they would not be returned to slavery. Over two hundred abolitionists met the group outside of Detroit. They procured enough boats for the entire group to cross the Detroit River into Canada, and Reed remember the fugitives singing, "I'm on my way to Canada, where colored men are free," as they crossed the river in boats. Reed reiterated how daring and determined Fairfield was, echoing the sentiments of Underground Railroad conductor Levi Coffin. In addition to Fairfield's success in leading so many fugitives to Canada, he also was credited with liberating all of his father's and uncle's slaves.[252]

So how were escaped slaves viewed by Canadians, particularly those in western Canada, and how did they view themselves? Letters, diaries and other accounts almost without exception reflected the great hope that Canada represented to the freedom-starved fugitives. Virginia's Underground Railroad, more than any other in the United States, succeeded in sending hundreds if not thousands of runaways to areas as far away as Hamilton, Ontario. Even before the 1850s, the most active period of the Underground Railroad, enslaved Virginians made their way to Canada.

Boston abolitionist Samuel Howe's 1864 study of freedom seekers in Upper Canada observed that Canadian census records consistently undercounted the black population. For example, in 1850, records stated that there were 500 blacks in Hamilton, with three black churches. However, according to the secretary of the board of school trustees, there were 934 blacks in living in Hamilton. Similarly, the St. Catharines town clerk said that 7,007 blacks resided in the town, even though the census recorded 6,284. Even in the small town of London, the mayor stated there were 75 blacks at a time when the census recorded there were only 36. The Anti-Slavery Society of Toronto estimated there were as many as 30,000 blacks in Canada West.[253]

By 1850, Canada West and Nova Scotia had established segregated school systems that provided a veneer of equality while simultaneously slowing assimilation.[254] However, one issue not discussed by historian Robin Winks that had a tremendous impact on race relations was miscegenation. William Still noted that "with reference to marrying, that of the great number of fugitives in Canada, the male sex was largely in preponderance over the female, and many of them were single young men. This class found themselves very acceptable to Irish girls, and frequently legal alliances were the result. And it is more than likely, that there are white women in Canada to-day, who are married to some poor slave woman's fugitive husband."[255] Samuel Howe observed that most of the blacks who came from the United States tended to already be of mixed blood.[256] Whether this was a factor in race mixing is unknown.

Nowhere did this integration appear more frequently than the city of Toronto, a place teeming with diverse immigrants, especially those from Virginia. In fact, many of Portsmouth's fugitives eventually found their way to the city. According to one 1856 letter from several fugitives who escaped aboard Captain Fountain's schooner addressed to William Still, "Toronto is a very extensive place. We have plenty of pork, beef and mutton. There are five market houses and many churches. Female wages is 62 1/2 cents per day, men's wages is $1 and york shilling. We are now boarding at Mr. George Blunt's, on Centre street, two doors from Elm, back of Lawyer's Hall, and when you write to us, direct your letter to the care of Mr. George Blunt, &c. (Signed), James Monroe, Peter Heines, Henry James Morris, and Matthew Bodams."[257]

At the beginning of the 1850s, Toronto was a city of forty-seven thousand, one thousand of whom were black, living in the northwest section of the city with houses similar to those in St. Catharines but without the garden space. But unlike some of the areas in Canada West, most of Toronto's black citizenry owned their own houses, and their children attended integrated schools. The community of industrious blacks had two Methodist churches and one Baptist church. James Sumler and Elijah Jenkins were both Toronto residents from Norfolk who arrived in the 1850s, while others such as Charles Peyton Lucas came from Loudon County. Sumler arrived with his family after witnessing the sale of his brother to the Deep South, hoping that he would find a free and nondiscriminatory environment.[258]

While some settled in the downtown area of Toronto, others lived on the outskirts in Ward 3, in the township of York, which had the second-highest black population in Canada. The Wanzers and the Grigsbys, who made a dramatic escape from Virginia in 1855, settled in a one-story frame house on a half-acre in the York Township. Both families worshipped at the Wesleyan Methodist Church and lived the remainder of their lives in Canada. And while the Grigsbys did not have children, the Wanzers did, although none of them survived to adulthood. Despite the success of many freedom seekers, low access to healthcare resulted in a high infant and child mortality rate. For the Wanzers, their son George died of tuberculosis at the age of one and half. Frank died of whooping cough at the age of four months, Nathaniel died after eleven days of teething and Mary died at age fourteen of an abscess.[259]

It was not surprising that many freedom seekers would make their way eventually to Toronto. While newly arrived persons tended to settle in the rural communities, where farmland was plentiful and self-governance was possible, the lure of an urban environment and more job opportunities ensured that Toronto was the primary destination for most. By 1865, two thousand blacks had settled in Toronto alone, with the majority fugitives and free blacks who left America in search of freedom.[260]

African Torontonians established some of the earliest self-help organizations in the city, including the Society for the Protection of Refugees, the Ladies Colored Fugitive Association, the Ladies Freedman's Aid Society and the Queen Victoria Benevolent Society. All were founded by black church women who created these organizations to help freedom seekers settle into the city, find jobs, make burial arrangements and support educational endeavors. Moreover, the leading black church in Toronto, First Baptist, was at the forefront of black abolitionist activities.[261]

Canadian census records noted that 80 percent of the southern-born blacks living in Canada in 1861 were from Virginia, Kentucky and Maryland. Of course, the reality of life in Canada, with its harsher winters and racial prejudices, differed from the expectations of many refugees. The alternative of submitting to America's slave system was much less appealing, and these challenges may explain why many returned to the United States at the conclusion of the Civil War.

Returning to a familiar environment surrounded by family and friends was preferable to remaining in what many considered, even after ten or more years, as a foreign land. Former Norfolk resident and fugitive slave Isaac Foreman, who escaped in December 1853 aboard the *City of Richmond* along with William Davis and Willis Redick, resided in Toronto during his years of exile. Foreman was described by William Still as a twenty-three-year-old dark mulatto who had been the slave of Mary Saunders, a sixty-year-old widow. Using the services of steward John Minkins to secure passage to Philadelphia, Foreman regretfully arrived without his wife (Ann) and three children (Benjamin, John and Alfred), all of whom were still owned by his original owner, Colonel Cunnagan. What was interesting about Foreman was his past association with Captain Drayton of the *Pearl.* Apparently, Drayton was captured with seventy fugitives who were headed for Canada. Cunnagan had hired out Foreman to work on Drayton's ship. Although exonerated, the foundation for Foreman's decision to escape may have been laid during that period. In any case, Foreman immigrated to Toronto and lived in Russell's hotel, which was one of several places used by Underground Railroad agents for fugitive resettlement. While there, Foreman wrote several letters to William Still in 1854, requesting information and assistance in helping his wife and children escape. So desperate was Foreman to secure the escape of his family that he wrote: "My soul was vexed, my troubles are inexpressible. I often feel as if I were willing to die. I must see my wife in short, if not, I will die." Curiously, he also requested that William Bagnall communicate with his extended family, including his mother, brother and sister-in-law, illustrating once again how connected Bagnall was with the black community.[262] Unfortunately, no records have been found that relate what became of Foreman or whether he was eventually reunited with his family.

Another account of a successful fugitive who fled to Canada West was thirty-two-year-old James Washington Sumler, alias James Moore, who was owned by a merchant named Smith and encouraged to escape because of his poor treatment. For many years, Sumler was punished for any infractions with flogging, paddling and other forms of torture. Sumler recalled that "[o]n one occasion, about two months before I was secreted, [Smith] had five of the slaves (some of them women) tied across a barrel, lashed with the cow-hide and then cobbed [beaten with a flat instrument]—this was a common practice." Just prior to his departure aboard the *City of Richmond* in early 1855, Sumler saw his wife's two-year-old child given as a gift to Smith's niece after his owner fell into debt and sold most of his slaves. No doubt this prompted his escape with the assistance of friends in Norfolk. However, Sumler's ship had to return to Norfolk because of ice that blocked the Philadelphia port. Again, friends hid him for eight months, during which an agent hired by his owner advertised a $200 reward for his return. Once he arrived in Philadelphia, like many freedom seekers during this period, he was forwarded to operatives in Canada West on March 3, 1855.[263]

The *Provincial Freeman* (1854–57), a weekly newspaper originally published in Toronto by Mary Shadd Carey, was a font of information for many of Hampton Roads' residents. Clarissa Davis noted in an 1855 letter to William Still that she read about the devastation caused by the yellow fever epidemic. According to a May 15, 1854 letter to Still, Gilliam noted that he saw a May 10 article in the *Provincial Freeman* about himself and John Minkins, who went on trial for assisting fugitives. Gilliam also discussed how he remained in contact with fellow Richmond fugitives James Mercer and John Clayton, companions in the hot berth where Minkins hid them while aboard the steamship. Fortunately for Minkins, he was released because of a lack of evidence.[264]

These fragments of information contained in letters written by fugitives about their experiences in Canada underscore how little is known about the lives of these men and women who braved the unknown to travel to a new country. Most historians examining the Canadian experiences of African American fugitives failed to address whether those black immigrants ever developed a clear self-identify apart from their debasement as fugitive slaves or the social discrimination that separated them from general society. Letters written to William Still and other abolitionists with whom they communicated provided only marginal clues about the fugitives' recognition of race apart from discrimination or enslavement. They came to Canada seeking freedom from slavery rather than freedom from social, political or economic oppression. Instead, their letters reflected an almost singular objective, highlighting the primacy of their need to secure freedom and security through the acquisition of a home and employment and their gratefulness for benefactors. Noteworthy were the correspondences that thanked abolitionists for their assistance and requested help securing the rescue of family members, conveying clothing from their former homes to Canada and receiving information about events on the home front. What was clear from the surviving documents about these immigrants was that given the opportunity, most wanted to return to the United States after the legal cessation of slavery. In fact, the majority maintained an American identity. To many, they were merely American citizens in exile.

In St. Catharines, a number of accounts survived from those who fled Hampton Roads in search of freedom beyond the boundaries of America. One man, a Mr. Bohm from Norfolk, recalled that slavery was "the worst kind of robbery." Norfolkian James M. Williams exclaimed, "Slavery is horrible! horrible! horrible!" John Atkinson said, "I escaped from Norfolk, Va. A man who has been in slavery knows, and no one else can know, the yearnings to be free, and the fear of making the attempt. It is like trying to get religion, and not seeing the way to escape condemnation."[265]

Others landed in Canadian communities with a better support system, such as Hamilton. A number of people mentioned Richard Bohm, a fugitive from Norfolk, as important in assisting them with resettlement.[266] In 1855, Anthony and Albert Brown stole their master's oyster boat. Owned by oystermen John and Henry Holland, the Brown brothers planned their escape seemingly without the knowledge of their wives, Ellen and Alexenia, respectively. The Brown brothers claimed that although they suffered brutal treatment from their owners, oystering familiarized them with the boating and the local waterways. They were also members of a black church in Norfolk, suggesting they had some degree of mobility. Miraculously, the brothers managed to escape to Philadelphia with the assistance of Henry Lewey, arriving safely despite the navigational guess work. Like many of their fellow fugitives, these two men were forwarded to Hamilton, Canada, by the Reverend J.W. Loguen, who lived in Syracuse, New York.[267]

An interesting point was included in the Brown brothers' letter to William Still almost a year later on March 7, 1856. The brothers noted that while they desperately missed their wives, they were not lonely because of the numerous acquaintances who had similarly found their way to Hamilton. What this strongly suggests was that networks of fugitives from Virginia were escaping and relocating together. In fact, most of the refugees initially lived in the Anglo American Hotel and the City Hotel. Three months later, Anthony Brown recorded that his wife had successfully escaped and was being sent by William Still to Hamilton to reunite with him.[268]

After his arrival in Hamilton, John Henry Hill from Petersburg regularly corresponded with William Still. In a September 15, 1856 letter, Hill informed Still that Mary Weaver arrived safely and was married. Hill also said that Willis Johnson needed assistance in escaping from his cruel master and hoped arrangements could be made. He also asked that Still write to his uncle in Petersburg, sending the letter via his captain friend. In the letter, Hill detailed specific directions in coded language about how his uncle could escape by ship once he journeyed from Richmond to Petersburg. It seems that he wanted Still to make sure that Ham and Eggs, a slave conductor from Petersburg, would assist his uncle in getting aboard a freedom seeker–friendly ship.[269]

What is important about Hill's experiences were the letters he wrote to William Still documenting his first experiences in Toronto. He observed that the city was "Beautiful and Prosperous" and noted that there were many wooden cottages, with some made of brick and stone. He also wanted Still to know that blacks were able to earn "bread and money enough to make us comfitable [*sic*]. But I say give me freedom, and the United States may have all her money and her Luxtures [*sic*], yes give Liberty or Death."[270]

Hill also discussed his experiences in Hamilton with missionary Samuel Howe, who was completing a report for the Freemen's Commission. Describing his activities, Hill noted the following:

> *We are manufacturers of tobacco, and there are merchants here who have agreed to take all we can manufacture, and to encourage us all they possibly can. I came from the South in September, 1853, and my family followed in December. My wife had to get a voucher for her freedom, before she could come on. Sometimes they put obstructions in the way of free people coming away, if they are so disposed.*[271]

Settling in Hamilton meant that Hill would become a tobacco farmer. With plenty of land and determination, Hill established a thriving business. Soon, he took on three business partners, and together they hired a building and manufactured tobacco with between twenty and fifty employees.[272] Yet he clearly longed to return to America once slavery had ended. In the interim decade, Hill prospered.

Not all fugitives fled to Ontario Province. Shadrach Minkins, who was assisted in his flight from Boston when on trial for being a fugitive in 1851, settled in Montreal and in the neighborhood where a few other fugitives resided, including Charles Williams from Washington, D.C., and John Scott from Richmond. Like many freedom seekers, Minkins found success and a new home, eventually marrying a young Irish woman named Mary in 1853, working as a waiter in the Montreal House hotel at Commissioners Street and Custom House Square and then later opening his own restaurant on Notre Dame Street, the West End Lunch. And while his restaurant did not succeed, he found prosperity in an occupation that was typically dominated by blacks: barbering. Such was the case in Montreal as well; almost 25 percent of Montreal's blacks worked in the barbering and hairdressing industry. Unlike in other areas of Canada where black abolitionists organized, forming the Anti-Slavery Society of Canada in Toronto, those fugitives in Montreal seemed remote, uninformed and uninvolved. Not until November

1859, after John Brown's raid, did the fugitives of Montreal rally in prayer for Brown and his men. Otherwise, life for Minkins and the other fugitives in Montreal appeared relatively calm, with isolated incidents of overt racism. Only once while Minkins resided in Montreal was he threatened by a white southerner attempting to retrieve runaway slaves. That incident occurred in January 1855, when Frederick, Maryland policeman John H. Pope attempted to bribe the Montreal police chief into assisting him in luring fugitives to the Canadian-American border.[273]

What is most striking, however, was Minkins's emigration to Montreal as opposed to a more southern Canadian region with a more familiar and hospitable climate. Moreover, his decision to live in Canada for the remainder of his life, unlike that of many former fugitives after the Civil War's end, was more likely influenced by his marriage to an Irish woman. Regardless of these variations, Minkins's odyssey forecasted the migrations of those who would follow his treacherous journey northward in search of freedom. Until a comprehensive study is done examining the dynamics involved in determining who returned to the United States and who remained in Canada in the post–Civil War world, one can only speculate that familial and spatial connections affected who remained and who returned.

Integration and assimilation quickly became issues for these American refugees fleeing to Canada. Identity constructs did not really apply to American fugitives because of their unique circumstances coming into Canada. By the 1870s, slavery had been absent in Canada for seventy years, while American slavery was over a mere five years prior. Free blacks in America had decades to develop their identities, with the oppression of slavery reinforcing their sense of unity. However, that identity was based primarily on their shared marginalization from society as opposed to their recognition of a unifying heritage. Attempts had been made in the late eighteenth century to identify with Africa. Unfortunately, this early Black Nationalist movement was hindered by the concurrent emergence of a virulent scientific racist and pro-slavery justification that dominated Western society. Furthermore, nationally publicized slave conspiracies and revolts in the 1820s and 1830s provided lawmakers with widespread public support for the infringement on the rights of free blacks, in the North and South, including the prohibition of education for free blacks in the South following Nat Turner's rebellion and the federal government's struggle to address the freedmen's immediate needs and of colonization to Liberia. For fugitives unfamiliar with liberty, striving toward self-identity was a leap beyond their immediate needs, concerns and priorities.

Unfortunately for race relations, slavery laid the groundwork for present and future race relations because blacks were seen first as slaves. While the status of blacks would improve, eventually, the cultural underpinnings of their relationship with white Canadians were founded on slavery and thereby influenced their perception during these years. Nevertheless, the accessibility, convenience and decided antislavery position of Upper Canada encouraged the migration of blacks, free and enslaved, to regions just across the border. The geographic accessibility was important for cash-strapped fugitives, for those who wanted to pursue farming because the soil was similar to the United States and for those who considered themselves refugees as opposed to immigrants. The manner of their establishment as racial and cultural segregated areas, however, created a crucible of white Canadian paranoia. Yielding to fears born from slaveholding, whites believed that blacks congregated in one location would foment a conspiracy against them. Moreover, the failure of some communities, such as Wilberforce, provided fodder for those opponents who were against black immigrants. This gave whites ammunition to criticize blacks and these segregated communities based on their economic failings and their inability to assimilate. However, by the 1860s and 1870s, these communities developed into thriving towns with numerous skilled workers, entrepreneurs and professionals.[274]

When substantial numbers of black immigrants began arriving in the 1820s and 1830s, they were immediately met with hostility from the white population. In response, these early groups founded black enclaves in Upper Canada that would serve as a barrier to white racism. White fear of growing and concentrated black communities increased open prejudice along with efforts to stymie large-scale resettlement by free blacks. However, when many blacks promoted resettlement on the African continent during the National Colored Convention in the 1830s, it lessened fears among some of the white Canadians. The social and political environment promoted ambivalence, especially among freedom seekers, about whether to remain in Canada as citizens or to immigrate to Sierra Leone or Liberia in the hopes of finding true liberty. For white Canadians, ongoing prejudice and discrimination ensured that they would continue viewing freedom seekers as transient or unwanted permanent members of society. Added to this biased treatment was the arrival of Irish immigrants in the 1840s, giving a new excuse to reduce opportunities for blacks seeking employment. This discrimination prompted many to move to larger cities or to black neighborhoods in the larger towns, where the environment was more welcoming.[275]

Poor treatment from white Canadians did not deter the resolute freedom seekers, whose antislavery activities increased beginning in the 1830s, with Toronto serving as a hub. Henry Bibb, a fugitive from Kentucky, founded and edited the first black-owned newspaper in Canada: *Voice of the Fugitive*. Founded in 1851 and published in Sandwich, near Windsor, the newspaper called for full civil rights in Canada and an end to slavery everywhere in the world. That same year, the Anti-Slavery Society of Canada was established in Toronto by prominent groups of black and white abolitionists and led by freedom seekers. To debut their efforts, the North American Convention of Coloured People, chaired by Henry Bibb and attended by fifty-three delegates, promoted the safety of Canada, concluding that despite challenges, Canada and Jamaica were the best places in North America for blacks and black freedom.[276]

Not surprisingly, a number of black Canadians eagerly enlisted in the U.S. military beginning in 1863 to defeat slavery and to expand the safe spaces that people of African descent could live in and thrive. Enlisting primarily in Michigan, African Canadians were important in the 102nd United States Colored Troops (USCT), the 54th Massachusetts and the 55th Massachusetts Infantry. *Provincial Freedman* publisher Mary Ann Shadd Cary even moved the newspaper to Detroit during the war to ensure her connection to the war effort and to use her international voice to recruit black men into the military.[277]

The Underground Railroad's work ended only with the abolition of slavery in 1865, and the experiences of those who escaped (or attempted to do so) cannot be overdramatized in terms of risk to themselves, their families and those who assisted them. What many freedom seekers aspired toward was survival, resettlement and a nurturing environment, even if that meant relocating to a foreign land and segregated communities. This may have explained why many, in spite of efforts made by white abolitionists to the contrary, opted to settle in black communities like Elgin and Oro and in segregated sections of St. Catharines, Hamilton and Amherstburg, as opposed to integrating themselves into the larger community. Drew's study showcased how racist attitudes of white Canadians expanded and hardened as the nineteenth century progressed. It is little wonder that many of the émigrés opted to seclude themselves into the nurturing environment of the black community.

What is often ignored within the pantheon of famous fugitives and colossal myths about the Underground Railroad is that the effort to escape slavery in America unintentionally spurred a second African diaspora out of the South and into many sections of the North and Canada. The racial and physical violence that many would endure in their new environments, which were not always sanctuaries of freedom, constituted an ongoing saga about the struggles of Africans in America, their enduring spirit and the external fight against discrimination, marginalization and dehumanization and their internal struggle to persevere despite the loss of family and community.

6

FREEDOM SEEKERS AND THE CIVIL WAR

On the night of May 23, 1861, three enslaved men—Shepard Mallory, Frank Baker and James Townsend—threw caution to the wind and set out on a small boat across the dangerous waterway called the Hampton Roads. Desperate to stay close to their families in Hampton, the men decided that it was now or never. In the middle of the night, the men crept away from their encampment, stole a boat and rowed toward Fort Monroe—held by the Union army—and hopefully freedom.[278]

Despite the danger, they journeyed across the Hampton Roads, a deep channel where all the major waterways in Virginia intersected with the mouth of the Chesapeake Bay. Twenty-five miles from the fort was the Atlantic Ocean. Any high swell could have overturned the boat and drowned the men. Yet they were undaunted in their quest to reach Hampton, despite these dangers. Once they arrived on shore, the men began looking for Union forces. Finally, in the wee hours of the morning of May 24, the men encountered a Union reconnaissance expedition. Letting the soldiers know their intent, the three men were interrogated and then taken to Major General Benjamin Butler for further examination later that morning.[279]

Frank Baker was the oldest of the three men. Born around 1819 in North Carolina, he was forty-three years old and married to Mary Baker; they had two sons (Henry and Dempsy) and two daughters (Easter and Frances). James Townsend was about thirty-six when he escaped in 1861 (birth year was recorded as around 1825). A resident of Hampton in Elizabeth City County, he later married Maria Townsend, and together they had two children, John and Press. The youngest was Shepard Mallory, who was only twenty years old at the time of their departure (born about 1841). It is unclear whether he was married yet to Fanny, but clearly the three men were an important part of the Hampton community. One account mentioned that the enslaved men's owner, Colonel C.L. Mallory of Hampton, planned to ship out all the enslaved men to Florida, while other accounts claim that the strategy was to move them to the forces consolidating in North Carolina. Either way, the intent was to take them far from home and their families.[280]

When Mallory, Baker and Townsend were taken before the recently arrived commander of Fort Monroe, Major General Butler, they explained that their owner had made preparations to withdraw his forces from the area and take all the enslaved laborers to continue building fortifications. This meant that the men would be forced to leave their families. The official response should have been for Butler to refuse sanctuary to the escaping slaves, as had other Union generals in occupied regions throughout the South. The Fugitive Slave Clause and the Fugitive Slave Act of 1850 compelled Butler to return all runaway slaves to their proven owner. However, this was war, and the men explained that the enemies of the United States were using them to help them fight the war. While Lincoln refused to formulate a policy regarding escaped slaves for fear of antagonizing the border states, Butler caught hold of the argument provided to him by the freedom seekers. He decided that seizure and confiscation of these able-bodied slaves for military purposes would be beneficial to the fort, inoffensive to the border states and a blow to the Confederacy without violating the Constitution or federal law.[281]

What Butler may not have realized at the time was that his actions would set in motion the eventual end of American slavery. His explanation about declaring the three men "contrabands of war" paved the way for the 1861 and 1862 Confiscation Acts, which officially authorized the Union seizure of "rebel property," slaves who were employed in Confederate military service. The acts also liberated enslaved people who fled Confederate territories. Moreover, this decision opened the door for President Abraham Lincoln to issue the Emancipation Proclamation in 1863 and guide the nation toward adopting the Thirteenth Amendment, officially ending American slavery. But before any of these laws and proclamations were issued, the realities of war and the ongoing efforts by enslaved people to obtain freedom defined the landscape of the nation, especially in Virginia. Viewing the actions of freedom seekers during the Civil War in Virginia—especially as they related to their wartime state as contrabands of war—

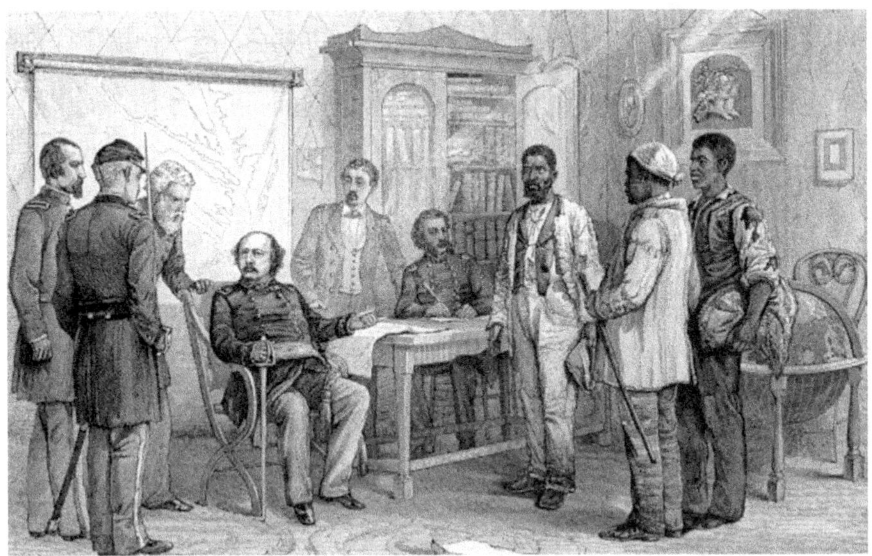

This *Harper's Weekly* illustration depicts this important meeting between Shepard Mallory, Frank Baker, James Townsend and General Benjamin Butler on May 24, 1861, that resulted in the contraband declaration. *Harrison B. Wilson Archives, Norfolk State University.*

should be viewed through the lens of power and projection of power. This overarching theme allows for an understanding of how freedom seekers bridged the divide between slavery and freedom and their role in transforming the nation's legacy and memory.[282]

In April 1861, it was very much business as usual in Hampton Roads despite the ongoing Civil War. Local papers advertised the sale of slaves and complained about the laxity on the part of some masters who allowed too much mobility for their slaves in a time of war. Joel Collins in Hampton received a summons in 1861 "to show cause why he should not be fined for permitting his slaves to go at large." Free blacks also had to proceed cautiously. When arrested for infractions, they were often "hired out," as was the case for Norfolk resident Elizabeth Cuffee in 1861 "for her jail fees."[283]

At the same time these mundane activities were proceeding, the Confederates made plans to "dig in" in the Hampton Roads area—but so did the federal government. The Union had made it clear that Fort Monroe would be held at all costs. A week after the fall of Fort Sumter, the Federal navy burned and evacuated the Norfolk Navy Yard and shored up defenses at Fort Monroe. Six weeks later, its strength increased from four hundred to twelve thousand men. But the Confederacy's occupation of Norfolk gave it a major shipyard and thousands of heavy guns, making the Union decision to abandon the navy yard regrettable. Confederate brigadier general Walter Gwynn, who commanded the Confederate defenses around Norfolk, also erected batteries at Sewell's Point, both to protect Norfolk and control Hampton Roads.[284]

In response, President Abraham Lincoln made it clear to his commanders that in order to establish a blockade of the North Carolina and Virginia coastlines, he would have to control all of Hampton Roads. Interestingly, on May 11, 1861, several Confederate officers from Norfolk arrived at Fort Monroe under a flag of truce in order to retrieve several enslaved men who had escaped from their owners. Interestingly, the commander of the fort was not sympathetic to the plight of the runaways and immediately arrested the slaves and turned them over to the officers.[285]

On May 23, 1861, President Lincoln sent General Benjamin Butler to Fort Monroe in hopes of keeping the controversial officer out of trouble in this "out of the way" post. The president was soon to discover the error of this assumption. Prior to his arrival, Butler discovered that the Confederates were constructing batteries at Sewells Point and Pig Point in an effort to command the Nansemond River. To counter these moves, Butler was determined to extend Union control into Hampton and Newport News. One day after his arrival, Butler sent a detachment of Union soldiers to capture Hampton.[286]

Because of the overwhelming numbers of U.S. military reinforcements at Fort Monroe, Colonel Benjamin Ewell, commander of the Peninsula Confederate forces, abandoned any attempts to defend Hampton against Union encroachments. Instead, Ewell concentrated on building up defenses on the opposite shores of Hampton Roads, leaving Hampton's whites with the decision to accept federal occupation or flee with the Confederate troops. Even with this decision, the blacks conscripted by the Confederates to build fortifications saw that they had a different choice: leave with the whites or take a chance and make their way to Union troops at Fort Monroe in the hopes of securing sanctuary and perhaps freedom.[287]

But the Confederates did not want to leave any structures standing that could be used by the Union officials. So prior to their departure, they burned parts of the village rather than see it occupied, making numerous blacks homeless. To avoid capture by departing Confederates, many blacks hid in the nearby woods and fields, contemplating whether to risk fleeing to Union lines that may or may not provide them sanctuary.

Since the Confederates were already using African Americans as laborers, Butler saw the return of slaves to their masters as hurting the

Union war effort. So when their owner, Colonel Charles Mallory, sent his envoy, John Cary, to meet with Butler outside of Fort Monroe and demand the return of Mallory's slaves under the 1850 Fugitive Slave Act, Butler refused and declared them confiscated slaves. Further, Butler made it clear that he would "continue to receive and protect all negroes…who come to see [him]." After writing to his supervisors about his actions on May 31, 1861, Secretary of War Edwin Stanton approved the independent actions of Butler, thereby establishing a policy that affected the course of relationships between African Americans and the federal government. Not until August 10, 1861, was the term *contrabands of war* used by Acting Master William Budd of the gunboat USS *Resolute* to refer to freedom seekers who fled to Union lines for sanctuary.[288]

But this was not just a humanitarian gesture. Butler planned to employ all able-bodied African American men to help Union troops in exchange for food and supplies. For enslaved people, Butler's goal did not matter. They had another plan, and their power was in their numbers. Word quickly spread, and thousands of fugitive slaves fled to Fort Monroe—with many coming from as far away as Richmond and North Carolina.

Butler's position differed from that of another commander who had a similar experience the same day Butler agreed to provide sanctuary to Mallory, Baker and Townsend. Colonel Ephraim Ellsworth in Alexandria,

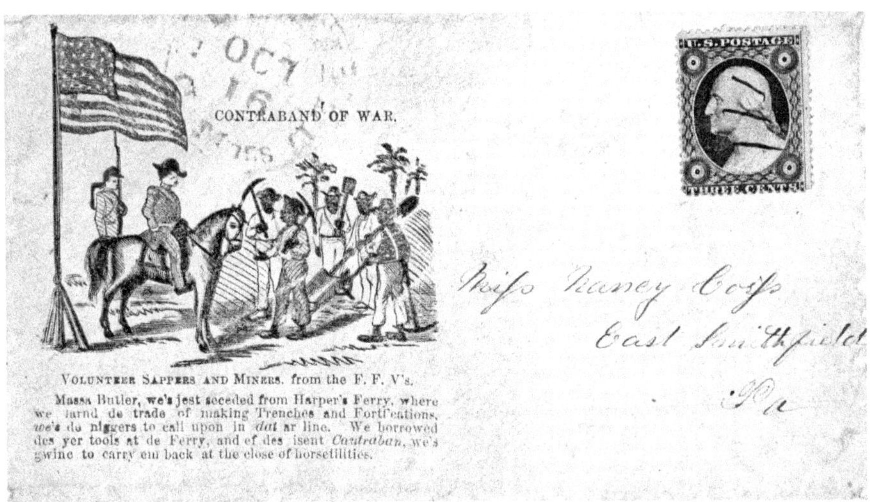

This Civil War envelope bearing the message "Contraband of war," presents fugitive slaves working as sappers and miners for General Benjamin Butler, who is shown astride a horse. The depiction of this scene suggests Butler's association during this period in providing a form of liberation through his contraband declaration. *Library of Congress.*

commanding the New York Zouaves, was approached by the owner of a slave who sought sanctuary in the Union camp. An unnamed Massachusetts colonel stepped into the fray and ordered both out of the camp and said if the owner wanted him, he would have to catch him. After a week, Edwin Stanton responded to Butler that slaves were protected if they were being used to help fight against the Union. Those at peace should be allowed to keep their slaves. Butler interpreted this liberally, allowing all freedom seekers to remain as contraband who arrived at the Fort.[289]

Soon, news of sanctuary at Fortress Monroe reached the ears of many area blacks. On Hampton's May 25 evacuation day, eight enslaved people sought refuge at the fort, followed by forty-seven the next day. It was not long afterward that the stream became a flood. In a May 27 letter to Lieutenant General Winfield Scott, Butler wrote that he believed providing sanctuary to runaway slaves, rather than returning them to their owners, was a military necessity for the Union army because it deprived the South of the slaves' services. Consequently, Butler decided to employ all able-bodied African Americans in exchange for food and supplies, as the government did not provide relief for the runaway slaves. By July 1861, more than nine hundred contrabands had sought sanctuary within the walls of Fort Monroe.[290]

An article in *Frank Leslie's Illustrated Newspaper* reported:

> *From Fortress Monroe...gangs of fugitive slaves, in parties of twenty or thirty, were constantly arriving there, over one hundred having reached there on Monday. Some of them said they were about being sent South, and others alleged that they came in to get food. They complained that, whilst they were kept at work in sandhills, the soldiers ate up all the food. Some of them were free negroes who had been compelled to work upon the enemy's fortifications in and near Norfolk.*[291]

Simply declaring runaway slaves contraband, however, was not enough. It was important that a decision be made as to what to do with the former slaves. Would they be sent north? Would they be put to work where they were presently situated? What further responsibility did the government have for the well-being of the contrabands? Butler opposed sending African Americans northward, where he felt they would be neither welcomed nor needed. He suggested instead that "in Virginia there is land enough cultivated and houses enough deserted" that African Americans could be adequately provided for and, indeed, cared for.[292] Although some African Americans felt that this suggested a possible redistribution of land, blacks

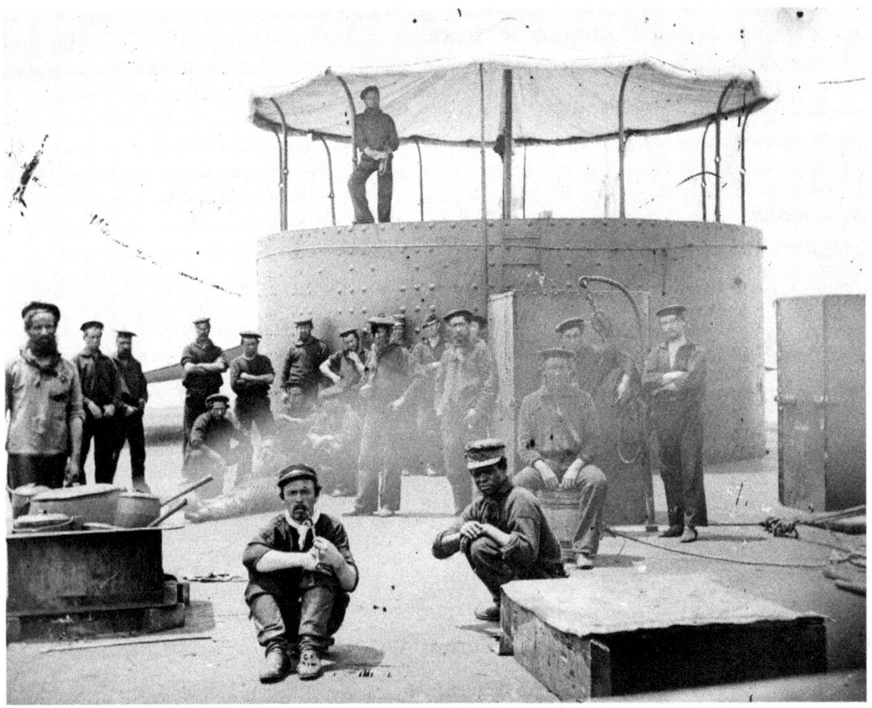

This important picture of the crewmen aboard USS *Monitor* during the Civil War was one of the first to include an image of an African American freedom seeker, Siah Carter, an enslaved man who fled from the Shirley Plantation in Charles City County, Virginia. *Library of Congress.*

were put to work for the government in the area under federal control. In so doing, needed labor was made available for building defenses, and the resulting loss of black labor to Rebel masters hurt the rebellion.[293] Clearly, if blacks thought Butler promised them land, they were mistaken.

Thus, when Butler accepted three runaway slaves seeking their freedom as contrabands of war, he was treading carefully, avoiding the politically charged minefield of anything that smacked of abolitionism. After Butler wrote to Lincoln of his decision, the president remained silent. Yet Congress would validate Butler's move with the first Confiscation Act in August 1861. Prior to that law, however, other commanders took a similar stance regarding slaves owned by the Confederates.[294]

All freedom seekers designated as contrabands of war struggled with finding a permanent safe haven, with most in constant motion either because they followed the Union troops as they moved throughout the South or because they were ejected from the grounds of Union forts. This became policy, even though Butler decided that these freedom seekers were never to be returned to slavery and should be relocated to areas where they could survive and assist the Union government with their labor needs. Yet most agreed that forts were not a place where refugees could live. Instead, officials saw Union lines and forts as transitional areas from which the freedom seekers would be resettled. Most of the time, however, the resettlement areas were unclear and ill-defined. Moreover, most freedom seekers in the first three years of the war fled with only the clothes on their backs. So the problem of feeding, clothing and housing refugees was overwhelming for officials whose focus was fighting a war. In truth, the war's exigencies and the unwanted presence of these refugees led to ongoing deprivation of basic necessities that resulted in large numbers of deaths.[295]

In *Sick from Freedom: African-American Illness and Suffering during the Civil War and Reconstruction*, Jim Downs highlighted that the challenges many Civil War freedom seekers faced significantly contrasted with the trials faced by earlier escapees. Downs observed that many of those fleeing from slavery to Union lines fell within none of the recognized categories of war casualties: gunshots, dysentery, smallpox, pneumonia, prisoners of war or deserters. Instead, these individuals were exposed to polluted conditions that were exacerbated because of a lack of medical care and access to basic needs.

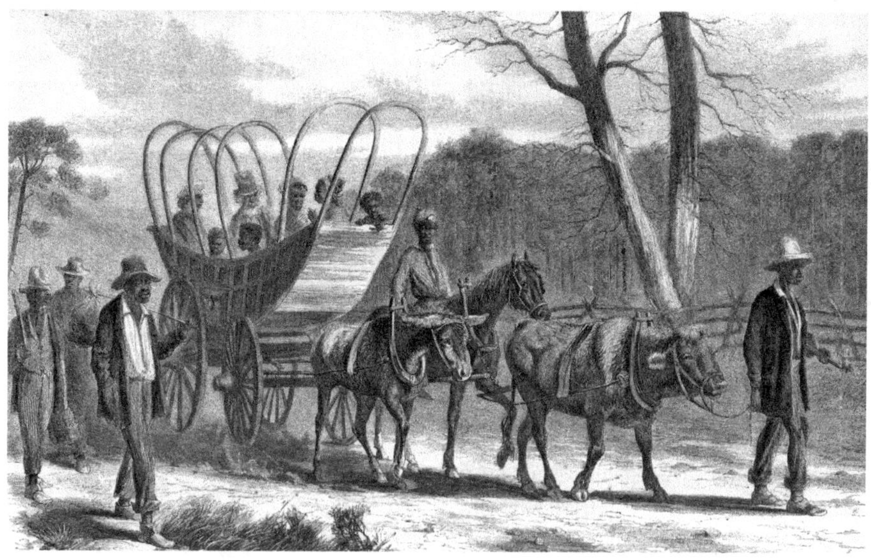

This *Harper's Weekly* illustration depicts freedom seekers journeying with their families and in groups to Union-friendly territories. *Harrison B. Wilson Archives, Norfolk State University.*

Many ex-slaves fleeing toward Union lines journeyed for weeks or months, often without adequate resources to survive. Downs noted that these refugees actually ran toward the battlefronts, placing them directly in the unenviable position between two warring groups.[296]

So who were these Civil War–era seekers of freedom? Did they know what freedom entailed? Did they care? The possibility of freedom meant something better than a life of enslavement that often separated them from their families, forced them to work until their deaths and always involved punishment for the slightest insult, infraction or whim. Facing an uncertain fate, they came by the tens, then hundreds and finally thousands to Union lines. They brought with them a few household items, bundles of food or clothing, but often only the clothes on their backs. They traveled at night through the woods, enduring untold hardships. Sometimes there were hundreds who trekked down to Fort Monroe, with only a few successfully arriving, like the two hundred who left Richmond in 1862, with only three approaching the gates of the fort. Other freedom seekers had better success, reaching Hampton aboard Union riverboats, on small ships and overland in groups. A mass exodus occurred from upcountry plantations, with entire families fleeing to the closest Union lines, willing to risk their lives for freedom. And they came to Fort Monroe; Washington, D.C.; Slabtown, Warrick County; City Point; and Norfolk, just to name a few. Indeed, Virginia had the largest number of contraband camps in the South during the Civil War.[297]

Coming with hope and an expectation of freedom, they faced many of the same prospects from Union officials that confronted them during their enslavement: the probability of hard work in exchange for rations and clothing. These freedom seekers did not sit idly by and wait for freedom; they took it through action, perseverance and force. They pushed the boundaries and limitations established by an unjust and racist system of laws and forced the nation to acknowledge their humanity and apply the ideals of the Declaration of Independence to them and their children. And when they did, the nation began to shed itself of the shackles of hypocrisy and move toward a system of inclusion. It would take another hundred years for that to happen—but that is another story.

Some may say that these contrabands should have been happy to be paid at all. But unlike the world before the Civil War that held no hope for change unless one escaped through the Underground Railroad, this was a new game, and African American slaves were determined to change their world and provide new opportunities for their families. And the first step was freedom.

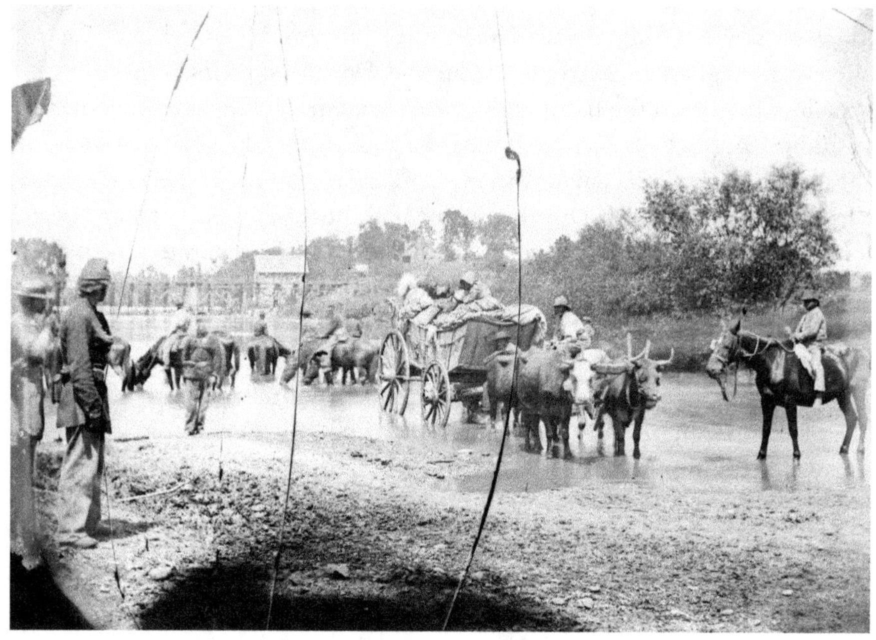

This important picture was taken in August 1862, depicting the flight of freedom seekers crossing the Rappahannock River during the Second Battle of Bull Run. These families were being assisted by Union troops on their way to one of the many contraband camps in Virginia. *Library of Congress.*

These freedom seekers did not take abuses in silence. They complained about being exploited, whether it was by slaveholders or Union officials.[298] In one such case, missionary Lewis C. Lockwood reported that one black man "said that he had worked for [the] gov[ernmen]t since the first of July," expecting money for his efforts, but received "only rations, a pair of shoes [and] a coat."[299]

Other freedom seekers took their complaints about their treatment nationally. William Davis, a contraband from Fort Monroe, took his to an 1862 meeting organized by the American Missionary Association (AMA) and the National Freedmen's Association (NFA). Davis complained that all contributions sent to the fort were actually sent to army officials rather than directly to the contrabands. The result was that they distributed it "wherever needed," opening the door to fraud. The result of his impassioned plea was a shift in how relief was distributed. The AMA sent agents to Fort Monroe and elsewhere who directly distributed clothing, food and books to contrabands and established schools for their general improvement and uplifting.[300]

Despite these and other abuses by Union army officials, these men who were designated as contraband volunteered their services to fight for their freedom and that of their families. Following the issuance of the Emancipation Proclamation on January 1, 1863, President Lincoln authorized the office of the adjutant general to establish the Bureau of Colored Troops. By December 22, 1863, the First Regiment Cavalry had organized at Camp Hamilton, while the Second Regiment Cavalry organized at Fort Monroe. Both were attached to Fort Monroe and later to the First Brigade, Third Division, Eighteenth Corps, Army of the James. Charged with protecting Hampton Roads in the first year of their existence, these regiments would be involved in some of the bloodiest operations in Virginia, including operations against Petersburg and Richmond. These regiments also helped capture Bermuda Hundred and City Point, engaged in operations against Fort Darling and Drury's Bluff and later were dispatched to the Rio Grande in Texas after the war.[301]

Freedom during the Civil War meant the ability to strike at the Confederates who sought to perpetuate their enslavement. In September 1861, a large number of contraband from Fort Monroe, according to the *Morning Leader*, sailed with the naval expedition to capture the Hatteras forts. Employed primarily as coal heavers, firemen and cooks, these brave men demonstrated their loyalty and "fighting propensities" aboard the steam frigate *Minnesota*.

Two months after this event in November 1861, the *Liberator* reported:

> *Since the arrival of the large number of negroes two weeks ago—upwards of one hundred in three days—few have come in through expensive preparations were making among the negroes to follow those who had gone before them. This is owing, probably, to the execution of the purpose among slave owners to destroy the boats accessible to the negroes along the river and inlets of the Chesapeake, its tributaries, and James River. But they will come. The destruction of them may interpose obstacles, and delay their departure, but the negro will find means to make his escape for if he has a talent for anything, it is for running away. It must be confessed that the could not have a much stronger motive than the purpose which is said to exist an Virginia, to sell the negroes to the South—a purpose arising form the necessity on the part of the owners to raise the wind, and the growing insecurity of that description of property.*[302]

Undaunted, their persistence and resistance to slavery in any form forced a shift in their favor, even though that shift was fraught with political limitations and self-serving goals. But it did not matter to these future freedmen because they used their numbers and their insistence on obtaining freedom to force the nation to change.

And the nation was watching.

The AMA had heard of the struggles these freedom seekers were having in the midst of a war and with an army whose priority was to win, not to provide food, clothing and shelter to refugees. To organize efforts, the AMA sent the Reverend Lewis Lockwood from New York to supervise efforts to aid the former slaves. Immediately after his arrival, Lockwood received permission from General John Wool, the new commander of Fort Monroe, to establish schools for those designated as contrabands of war outside the confines of Fort Monroe. Because so many escaped slaves were starving and scattered, numerous northern relief organizations sent people and supplies to the fort. Lockwood solicited funds from his northern brethren and aid from soldiers stationed at Fort Monroe to hold schools for the growing legion of blacks who gathered there seeking sanctuary from slavery.[303]

The Emancipation Proclamation and the reality of service by black men in the military shifted the legalities of quasi-freedom to freedom for those covered under this military directive. But challenges persisted, especially for the families of black soldiers. Rachel Copeland, Delia Carter, Ann Brown and Maria Brooks of Slabtown and Rosa Brooks, Sarah Butler and Hannah Beasley of Camp Hamilton had husbands who served in the First, Tenth, Thirty-Seventh and Thirty-Eighth USCT. These women and their children survived on small portions of army rations and were crowded into makeshift habitations. Even though the rations were paltry, they were provided

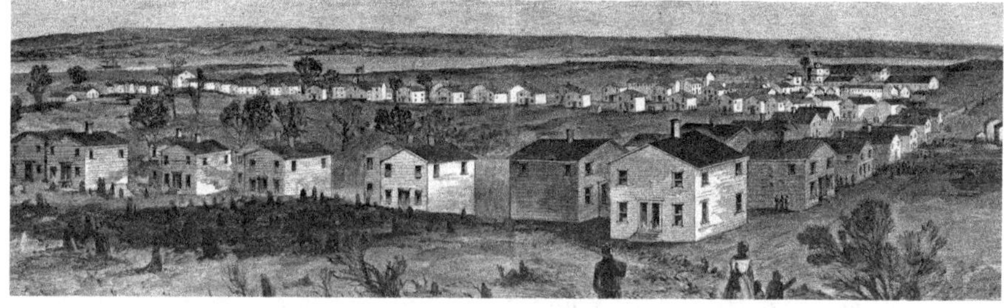

This watercolor of the Freedmen's Village in Arlington was originally published in *Harper's Weekly* on May 7, 1864. The Freedmen's Village was designed as a model community for freed persons while engaging their services as field hands. Lee's Arlington Estate was chosen as a symbolic statement that the leading Confederate general's home would become the site where enslaved people were transformed into free citizens. *Harrison B. Wilson Archives, Norfolk State University.*

assistance as long as a male family member was enlisted. However, if they died from battle wounds or disease, the assistance would only continue for six months. Even so, these families endured, getting work wherever they could and learning to read and write.

Despite these and many other challenges, freed people established new beginnings for themselves and their children. While many died from disease, starvation or battle, others survived, carving a life for themselves and a future for their families. The perception that it was on the federal government to care for the four million souls now free was a false one that framed and perpetuated the stereotype of black dependency. Instead, these freedmen, no longer called contraband, persevered and even flourished, establishing homes, businesses, schools and a future for their children and their communities.

Twenty-three years later, an account was published in Hampton Institute's magazine, the *Southern Workman*, recalling the events surrounding these freedom seekers whom the government labeled contrabands of war. Men, women and children came by the thousands to Fort Monroe begging for protection but with the hope of obtaining freedom. Unlike their counterparts who sought freedom through the Underground Railroad or on their own aboard ships bound for the North, these freedom seekers found little sympathy or compassion for their plight. Until Congress laid out a clear plan for addressing this issue, many were at the mercy of Union officials who saw them as laborers rather than as refugees. The able-bodied men were immediately forced to work on Union defenses or assigned to the quartermaster's department, laboring mostly without pay. Not until the creation of the superintendent of contrabands was any modicum of relief found. However, they continued to pour into camps occupied by Union troops—even an uncertain fate was seen as better than life as a slave.[304]

7

LEGACIES OF THE UNDERGROUND RAILROAD

The true costs that African Americans paid to be free may never be assessed. What is clear is that the choices that freedom seekers made were not always simple or without considerable sacrifice. And at their core was the inexhaustible desire for love, family and the ability to control their own lives. Perhaps more stories of the sacrifices and complicated choices people made just to be free will be revealed so that the record can be corrected about how many people tried to balance their love of family with their desire for freedom.

Following the Civil War, some freedom seekers who fled to northern states or Canada returned to Virginia and became part of the emerging elite. Other freedom seekers who remained in Virginia, fleeing to Union enclaves to gain their freedom as contrabands of war, established themselves within their communities as free people. The euphoria of freedom and the various Constitutional amendments, civil rights acts and court decisions provided hope that full citizenship was possible. But despite their best intentions, by the mid-1880s, these freed people were constrained by increasing racial restrictions in the form of legalized segregation and discrimination. Undaunted by these new challenges, the former freedom seekers embarked on a less direct tactic of self-aggrandizement and turned inward, redefining personal freedom through the creation of institutions that stabilized their communities, such as banks, schools, restaurants, hotels and hospitals.

The 1870 U.S. census records indicated that the majority of these freedom seekers probably returned once the Confederacy was defeated

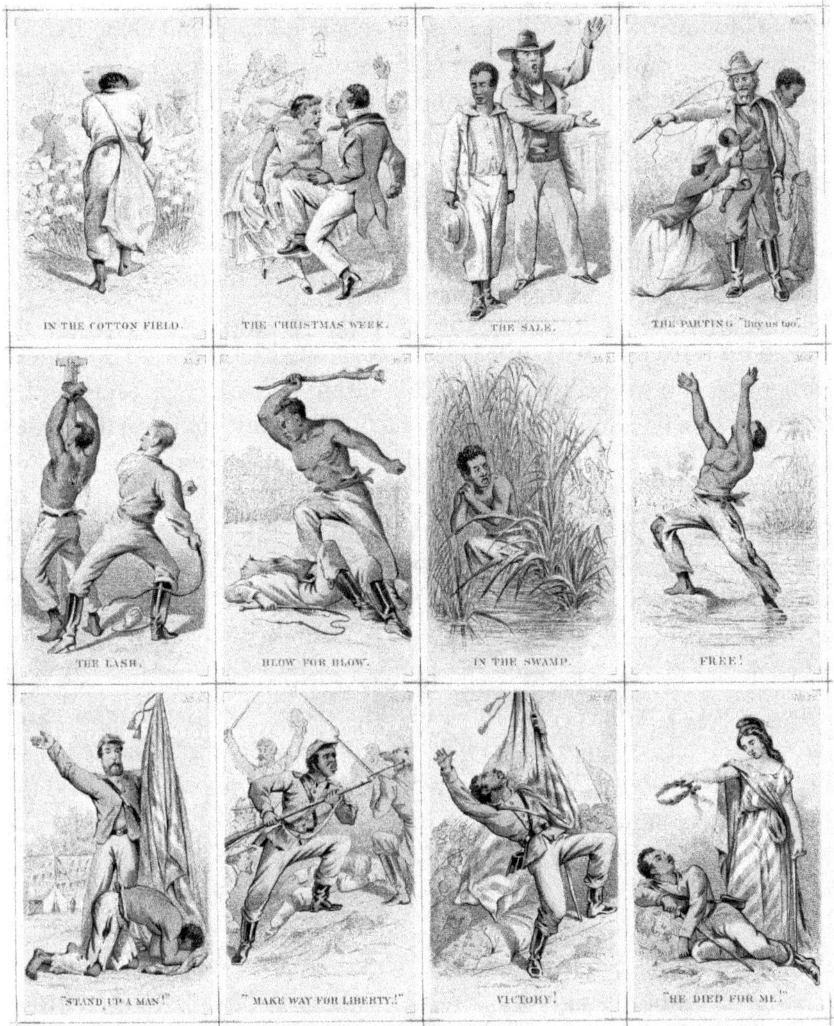

This image of twelve illustrated cards symbolizes the journey of Africans in America from enslavement on the plantations to their struggle for freedom, including black male service as soldiers during the Civil War and the passage of civil rights through the Thirteenth and Fourteenth Amendments. The artist, James Fuller Queen, titled this 1863 illustration "Journey of a slave from the plantation to the battlefield." *Library of Congress.*

and slavery formally abolished. These freedom seekers from Virginia included John Hill and George Teamoh and ex-soldiers Joseph T. Wilson and Thomas Bayne. In the book *Seizing the New Day: African Americans in Post-Civil War Charleston*, Wilbert Jenkins noted that while African Americans were not homogeneous, they aggressively fought for their independence in the years following the Civil War. Almost immediately following the war, churches broke away from national white denominations, either forming their own groups or joining those formed by northern blacks such as the African Methodist Episcopal Church (AME). They also founded political, military, social and pseudo-religious institutions that would guarantee an empowered black leadership.[305] Fragmented accounts of those who returned from Canada or northern areas offer insight and examples about how they continued their quest for full equality in their political and financial activities upon their return to their homes in Virginia.

Freedom seeker John Henry Hill, who escaped in 1853 and lived for a number of years with his family in Hamilton, Canada West, returned to Petersburg shortly after the end of the Civil War. Immediately, Hill entered the political fray as a Republican, becoming an influential leader and serving as a city councilman between 1872 and 1874 in Petersburg. By the late 1870s, when Virginia politics shifted toward the Conservatives, many Republicans like Hill supported the third-party Readjuster candidate, former Confederate general William Mahone, who promised government-appointed jobs for black and white supporters. When Mahone won the gubernatorial election in 1882, he fulfilled his promises. Hill was one of the recipients, serving as the appointed doorkeeper of the Virginia State Senate. Hill also gained distinction for organizing the first free black militia, the Petersburg Blues, in Virginia in 1871. So popular was Hill that he was elected captain of the unit and eventually became a colonel over one of the black state regiments. Hill also opened up a funeral home and a cabinetmaking business. Eventually, he served as a justice of the peace in Petersburg.[306]

Sam Nixon, alias Thomas Bayne, worked the Underground Railroad circuit as a conductor in Norfolk until escaping to New Bedford in 1855. During his time as the slave of Dr. C.F. Martin, a Norfolk dentist, Nixon/Bayne was apprenticed as Martin's assistant. Indeed, he became a conductor because his owner often sent him on night calls, which allowed him to be out at night without anyone suspecting him of "mischief." Eventually, word circulated that he could be involved in helping enslaved people escape, forcing him to leave aboard a steamship. There he became friends with William Still. While in Philadelphia, he completed his dental training and eventually moved to Boston and later New Bedford, where he became an important fixture within the black community, even serving on the New Bedford City Council. At the end of the war, Bayne returned to Norfolk and to the wife and daughter he left in slavery. He quickly established himself as a dentist, opening an office in the downtown area. But politics was his passion. During the 1867–68 Constitutional Convention, Bayne was elected as 1 of 160 black delegates charged with rewriting the state constitution, distinguishing himself as a champion for integrated public schools and the rights of black Virginians.[307]

Another example, George Teamoh, was born into slavery in 1818 and grew up in Portsmouth as the slave of Josiah and Jane Thomas. Josiah Thomas was employed as a carpenter at the Gosport Navy Yard, and like most urban slaveholders, he eventually found it financially necessary to hire out Teamoh, who was a skilled ship's carpenter and caulker, to Captain John Thompson. Thompson owned a brickyard three miles outside of Portsmouth, so Teamoh's skills were important in his industry. But it was while he worked for Thompson that Teamoh got a taste of the harshness of rural slave life. Eventually, he returned to Portsmouth and worked in the Gosport shipyard prior to escaping. According to Teamoh's account, his owners were sympathetic to his dismay about the sale of his family, responding by making it possible for him to return to Portsmouth in 1862 as a shipyard worker. It was while advocating for fair wages of shipyard workers that his taste for politics began. In 1867, Teamoh was elected to the Virginia Constitutional Convention.[308]

Joseph T. Wilson's return to Norfolk from New Bedford set the stage for a second chapter in a remarkable life fraught with intrigue. Because of his familiarity with Virginia, the Union government employed him in the Secret Service. Working with a squadron on the Elizabeth and James Rivers, he assisted the army in reconnaissance work and in the Battles of Petersburg and Fort Fisher. As a reward for his services, Wilson was given an important position as director of the U.S. government's supply store, a job that ended with the Confederacy's surrender. But Wilson's colorful past was only a prelude to a more adventurous future that taught him to create opportunities, whether it was as a freeman, businessman or politician.[309]

Wilson was always seeking out new prospects. In 1865, he founded a mercantile business, managed a fruit store and assumed the position as editor of the *True Southerner* newspaper, originally founded by a white Union officer stationed in Hampton prior to moving to Norfolk. Wilson's energy transformed the newspaper from a weekly that reported on Union activities to a polemic advocating Republican Party mandates—no doubt an unpopular paper with local white Democrats. In 1885, he started another paper, the Democratic *Right Way*. Reports about Mayor William W. Lamb were not appreciated, and the mayor reportedly shut down the press by withholding the printing material through questionable legal means. Ever the publicist, Wilson founded another publication in 1888, the *Industrial Day*, a mouthpiece for the Galileans and an advocate for industrial advancement as a panacea for black economic empowerment. While in Richmond, Wilson published his best-known work, *The Black Phalanx*, a year before he died.[310]

As did the rest of the nation, Virginia quickly sank under the weight of Jim Crow in the final decades of the nineteenth century. Some of the state's fugitives did return to the United States—but not to their point of origin—while others tried to build a new life in New Bedford and Boston, cities that once provided refuge and sustenance after their flight. Even though racial tensions were as prevalent in Boston as in Richmond, the visibility of racism in Virginia kept many from returning to the land of their birth. By 1880, one-third of Boston's black community was composed of Virginians. No doubt some arrived for the first time after the adoption of the Thirteenth Amendment while others were Canadian refugees, returning to America from their adopted home. According to reports, many white Canadians believed that these former fugitives returned to their homelands because of the climate and desire to be among family members. For some, that may have been true. For others, the promise of a better life in America after the war was preferable to the racism and impoverishment that many experienced in Canada.[311]

Most people know that the Underground Railroad in Virginia was a powerful and active operation with a series of secret networks, often working independently of one another and manned by both free blacks and whites. Designed to help enslaved African Americans escape to the North and to Canada, such networks were less necessary in the earliest days of slavery in Virginia because runaways tended to stay relatively close to home. Only after the American Revolution, when northern states outlawed slavery and a new domestic trade began to send thousands of enslaved men, women and children into the Deep South did fugitive slaves cross state lines in great numbers. And even when the federal government took it upon itself to protect the institution using the power of the courts and law enforcement, many Americans fought the institution and its expansion covertly through a loosely devised system called the Underground Railroad, a term that had gained popular currency by the 1840s. Whites, especially Quakers, acted in concert with free blacks and enslaved operatives to smuggle enslaved people to cities and towns in the North and in the Ontario Province in Canada.

Eric Foner's 2015 *Gateway to Freedom: The Hidden History of the Underground Railroad* discussed how many men and women fled slavery, sometimes reluctantly, leaving spouses, children, parents and siblings, in the hope that freedom would allow them the opportunity to reunite in the near future. In powerful, and sometimes incongruous ways, these family connections affected the enslaved persons' decision to flee and their future course. Focusing on representative accounts of fugitives who escaped from Virginia, the center of the southern Underground Railroad, provides a more typical account of the thousands who successfully escaped, finding freedom in the North or Canada. And these individuals escaped despite extreme and coordinated efforts by Virginia slave owners, who used legislation, public and private funds and the force of law to prevent their departures. Examining these complex stories that began in the seventeenth century and continued through the Civil War provides insight about the compelling lives and misadventures of men, women and children who, once they decided to leave slavery, lived boldly under an alias in southern cities or northern locales or in Canada. Yet unless they were accompanied by their families, achieving freedom through flight was often bittersweet.

As America's first nonviolent resistance movement, the Underground Railroad helped countless enslaved people flee to cities and counties in the North and Canada. And while the true numbers of those who successfully escaped may never be known, what is certain is that the clues left about the lives of a few provide an important window into understanding how so many people secretly risked their lives to help those kept in bondage and the risks these freedom seekers took to achieve liberty. In the aftermath of the Civil War, some did return to their homes to build a new life in what they hoped would be a changed society, while others remained in Canada, deciding instead to remain in a society that had a longer commitment to freedom and equality than the land of their birth.

Sixty years after the end of the Civil War and the legal destruction of slavery, poet and intellectual Langston Hughes eloquently articulated the unfulfilled, yet hopeful expectations of African Americans. For years, blacks lived a separate, shadowed existence in America, where their world resembled that of whites but without the ability to control their fates and lives. But the long journey of freedom seekers helped define the nation as no other story in American history. In 1926, Hughes penned "I, Too," defining the struggles and hopes of America's freedom seekers:

I am the darker brother.
They send me to eat in the kitchen
When company comes,
But I laugh,
And eat well,
And grow strong.

Tomorrow,
I'll be at the table
When company comes.
Nobody'll dare
Say to me,
"Eat in the kitchen,"
Then.

Besides,
They'll see how beautiful I am
And be ashamed—

I, too, am America.[312]

NOTES

Introduction

1. William Still, *The Underground Railroad* (Oxford, UK: Benediction Classics, 2008), originally published in Philadelphia by Porter and Coates, 1872, 297; Journal C of Station No. 2 of the Underground Railroad, Agent William Still, 1852–1857, Vigilance Committee of Philadelphia, Pennsylvania Anti-Slavery Society, unpublished document in the Pennsylvania Abolition Society Papers, HSP, edited by Peter P. Hinks, 105 (hereafter Journal C).
2. Still, *Underground Railroad*, 297–98, 560.
3. Ibid., 298.
4. Ibid., 299.
5. Fergus Bordewich, *Bound for Canaan: The Underground Railroad and the War for the Soul of America* (New York: HarperCollins Publishers, 2005), 4, 7.
6. Gary Collinson, *Shadrick Minkins: From Fugitive Slave to Citizen* (Cambridge, MA: Harvard University Press, 1997), 46; Gerald Mullin, *Flight and Rebellion: Slave Resistance in Eighteenth Century Virginia* (New York: Oxford University Press, 1972), 4, 6.
7. Collinson, *Shadrick Minkins*, 45.
8. Vincent Harding, *There Is a River: The Black Struggle for Freedom in America* (New York: Vintage Books, 1983), xix, 27.

Chapter 1

9. *Virginia Magazine of History and Biography* 1 (January 1894): 449–50; *Virginia Magazine of History and Biography* 4 (July 1896): 82–83.
10. Cassandra Pybus, *Epic Journeys of Freedom: Runaway Slaves of the American Revolution and Their Global Quest for Liberty* (Boston: Beacon Press, 2006), 14, 34, 215.
11. John Grant, "Black Immigrants into Nova Scotia, 1776–1815," *Journal of Negro History* 58 (July 1973): 254.
12. Thomas Wertenbaker, *Norfolk: Historic Southern Port*, 2nd ed., edited by Marvin Schlegel (Durham, NC: Duke University Press, 1962), 27–28.
13. David Hackett Fischer and James C. Kelly, *Bound Away: Virginia and the Westward Movement* (Charlottesville: University of Virginia Press, 2000), 18, 27–28.
14. John Thornton, "The African Experience of the '20 and Odd Negroes' Arriving in Virginia in 1619," *William and Mary Quarterly* 55, no. 3 (July 1998): 421; Alden T. Vaughan, "Blacks in Virginia: A Note on the First Decade," *William and Mary Quarterly* 29, no. 3 (July 1972): 471.
15. John Donoghue, "Out of the Land of Bondage: The English Revolution and the Atlantic Origins of Abolition," *American Historical Review* 115 (October 2010): 950; Allan Kulikoff, "The Origins of Afro-American Society in Tidewater Maryland and Virginia, 1700 to 1790," *William and Mary Quarterly* 35 (April 1978): 234.
16. *The Negro in Virginia*, Compiled by workers of the Writers' Program of the Work Projects Administration in the State of Virginia (Winston-Salem, NC: John F. Blair Publishers, 1994; originally published New York: Hastings House, 1940), 14–17.
17. John Coombs, "Beyond the 'Origins Debate': Rethinking the Rise of Virginia Slavery," in *Early Modern Virginia: Reconsidering the Old Dominion*, edited by Douglas Bradburn and John Coombs (Charlottesville: University of Virginia Press, 2011), 247–49; Lorena Walsh, *From Calabar to Carter's Grove: The History of a Virginia Slave Community* (Charlottesville: University Press of Virginia, 1997), 222.
18. Wesley Craven, *The Southern Colonies in the Seventeenth Century, 1607–1689* (Baton Rouge: Louisiana State University Press, 1949), 401–2; Coombs, "Beyond the 'Origins Debate'," 250.
19. Mullin, *Flight and Rebellion*, 6. For a detailed listing of runaways in Virginia, as advertised in Virginia newspapers, see "The Geography of Slavery in Virginia" project sponsored by Tom Costa and the rector and

visitors of the University of Virginia, http://www2.vcdh.virginia.edu/gos/index.html (hereafter cited as "Geography of Slavery").

20. W. Jeffrey Bolster, *Black Jacks: African American Seamen in the Age of Sail* (Cambridge, MA: Harvard University Press, 1997), 24.

21. Wertenbaker, *Norfolk*, 42–43, 47.

22. Bolster, *Black Jacks*, 25; Philip Morgan, *Slave Counterpoint: Black Culture in the Eighteenth Century Chesapeake and Lowcountry* (Chapel Hill: University of North Carolina Press, 1998), 231, 239–40.

23. *Virginia Gazette* (Parks), Williamsburg, February 24 to March 1, 1737 [1738], "Geography of Slavery."

24. *Virginia Gazette* (Parks), Williamsburg, from Friday October 5 to Friday, October 12, 1739, "Geography of Slavery."

25. *Virginia Gazette* (Hunter), Williamsburg, 1751, 1752 and 1767, "Geography of Slavery."

26. *Virginia Gazette* (Hunter), Williamsburg, May 30, 1751; *Virginia Gazette* (Hunter), Williamsburg, September 19, 1751; *Virginia Gazette* (Hunter), Williamsburg, August 21, 1751; *Virginia Gazette* (Hunter), Williamsburg, September 5, 1755.

27. *Runaway Slave Advertisements: A Documentary History from the 1730s to 1790*, vol. 1, *Virginia and North Carolina*, compiled by Lathan Windley (Westport, CT: Greenwood Press, 1983), 35, 118.

28. Walsh, *From Calabar*, 222.

29. Colonel William H. Stewart, ed., *History of Norfolk County, Virginia and Representative Citizens* (Chicago: Biographical Publishing Company, 1902), 22.

30. *Virginia Gazette* or *Norfolk Intelligencer* (Duncan), Norfolk, June 30, 1774.

31. Mullin, *Flight and Rebellion*, 115, 119.

32. Ibid., 129.

33. Alan Taylor, *The Internal Enemy: Slavery and War in Virginia, 1772–1832* (New York: W.W. Norton & Company, 2013), 15; Mullin, *Flight and Rebellion*, 6.

34. Benjamin Quarles, *The Negro in the American Revolution* (Chapel Hill: University of North Carolina Press, 1961), 124, 126, 130.

35. *Book of Negroes*, Black Loyalists Digital Collections, *Black Loyalists: Our People, Our History*, http://www.blackloyalist.info/, accessed June 8, 2006 (hereafter *Book of Negroes*).

36. Quarles emphasized the relevance of the revolutionary rhetoric to blacks. He said that blacks were fast in responding to the revolutionary spirit of the opening passages of the Declaration of Independence, Quarles, *Negro in the American Revolution*, 43.

37. The *Virginia Gazette* made periodic reports on the progress of the trial. For example, see *Virginia Gazette*, May 7, 1772; June 4, 1772; and July 23, 1772. For a brief history of the case see Emory Washburn, "Somerset's Case and the Extinction of Villenage and Slavery in England," *Proceedings of the Massachusetts Historical Society 1863–1864*, 1st, ser., 7, 8 (February 1864): 308–26; Pybus, *Epic Journeys*, 81–82.
38. *Maryland Journal and Baltimore Advertiser* (Goddard) Baltimore, May 11, 1779; *Virginia Gazette* (Dixon & Nicolson), Richmond, November 25, 1780; Taylor, *Internal Enemy*, 26; Windley, *Runaway Slave Advertisements*, 172–73, 203.
39. *Virginia Gazette* (Pinkney), January 20, 1776; *Virginia Gazette* (Dixon & Hunter), October 11, 1776. Quarles, in *Negro in the American Revolution*, estimates that only about eight hundred blacks joined the governor; John Selby, *The Revolution in Virginia, 1775–1783* (Charlottesville: University of Virginia Press, 2007), 73–74; Robert L. Scribner and Brent Tarter, eds., *Revolutionary Virginia, the Road to Independence*, vol. 5, *The Clash of Arms and the Fourth Convention, 1775–1776*, 423–24; *Virginia Gazette* or, *Norfolk Intelligencer*, February 23, 1775; William Pitt Palmer, ed. *Calendar of Virginia State Papers and Other Manuscripts*, vol. 8, 77–79; *Virginia Gazette*, September 8, 1774.
40. George Collier, *A Detail of Some Particular Services Performed in America During the Years 1776–1779* (New York, 1835); "Return of Persons that came off from Virginia with General Mathew in the Fleet August 24, 1779," Records of Colonial Office, 1774–1801, 5/52/63, NA. Pendleton to Woodford, June 21, 1779, in *The Letters and Papers of Edmund Pendleton*, vol. 1, 290–1; Grant, "Black Immigrants," 258.
41. *Book of Negroes.*
42. *Book of Negroes*; Harvey Whitfield, *Blacks on the Board: The Black Refugees in British North America, 1815–1860* (Burlington: University of Vermont Press, 2006), 19–23; Grant, "Black Immigrants," 258.

Chapter 2

43. Bordewich, *Bound for Canaan*, 26; Evelyn Gerson, "Ona Judge Staines: A Thirst for Complete Freedom & Her Escape from President Washington," SeacoastNH, http://www.seacoastnh.com/blackhistory/ona.html, accessed May 1, 2017; Erica Armstrong Dunbar, *Never Caught: The Washingtons' Relentless Pursuit of Their Runaway Slave, Ona Judge* (New York: Atria Books, 2017), 113, 141, 149.

44. Dunbar, *Never Caught*, 141.
45. Bordewich, *Bound for Canaan*, 40.
46. Gerson, "Ona Judge Staines"; Dunbar, *Never Caught*, 149, 157.
47. Steven Deyle, *Carry Me Back: The Domestic Slave Trade in American Life* (Oxford, UK: Oxford University Press, 2005), 39.
48. Ibid., 39.
49. Ibid., 37.
50. Pybus, *Epic Journeys*, x.
51. Darlene Clark Hine et al., *The African American Odyssey*, 7th ed. (New York: Pearson, 2017), 115, 121.
52. *Negro in Virginia*, 108–11.
53. Hine et al., *African American Odyssey*, 121, 124.
54. Tommy Lee Bogger, *Free Blacks in Norfolk, Virginia, 1790–1860: The Darker Side of Freedom* (Charlottesville: University of Virginia Press, 1997), 1, 48, 51; William Hening, ed., *The Statutes at Large Being a Collection of All the Laws of Virginia*, vol. 11 (13 vols., Richmond, VA, 1810–1832), 39–40; Luther P. Jackson, "The Virginia Free Negro Farmer and Property Owner, 1830–1860" *Journal of Negro History* 24 (October 1939): 390.
55. Claudia Goldin, *Urban Slavery in the American South, 1820–1860: A Quantitative History* (Chicago: University of Chicago Press, 1976), 33–36; Richard Wade, *Slavery in the Cities: The South, 1820–1860* (New York: Oxford University Press, 1964), 61.
56. Hine et al., *African American Odyssey*, 126–27.
57. Bordewich, *Bound for Canaan*, 43–45.
58. For example, the USS *Delaware* was built at the Gosport Navy Yard on June 17, 1833.
59. Wertenbaker, *Norfolk*, 88.
60. Bordewich, *Bound for Canaan*, 54.
61. *Norfolk Herald* (Willett and O'Connor), Norfolk, February 6, 1802.
62. "The Civil War and Reconstruction" by Randall and Donald, U.S. Census, 1860, Population, 598–99 (hereafter "Civil War and Reconstruction").
63. Joseph T. Wilson, *The Black Phalanx: A History of the Negro Soldiers of the United States in the War of 1775–1812, 1861–65* (Hartford, CT: American Publishing Company, 1888), 73.
64. Ibid., 74.
65. Ibid.
66. Ibid., 77.
67. Taylor, *Internal Enemy*, 200.
68. Wertenbaker, *Norfolk*, 108–9.

69. Mildred Holladay and Dean Burgess, *History of Portsmouth, Virginia* (Portsmouth, VA: Portsmouth Historical Commission, 2007), 97–98; Wertenbaker, *Norfolk*, 110–11.
70. Grant, "Black Immigrants," 264.
71. Taylor, *Internal Enemy*, 202–3.
72. *Journal and Guide*, January 9, 1971, A18.
73. Taylor, *Internal Enemy*, 98.
74. Ibid., 3–4.
75. Ibid., 4–5.
76. David Cecelski, *The Waterman's Song: Slavery and Freedom in Maritime North Carolina* (Chapel Hill: University of North Carolina Press, 2001), 32, 34, 123.
77. Philip Schwarz, *Slave Laws in Virginia* (Athens: University of Georgia Press, 1996), 128–29.
78. Deyle, *Carry Me Back*, 38.
79. Ibid., 38.
80. Schwarz, *Slave Laws*, 129.
81. Ibid., 129, 131.
82. Ibid., 130.
83. Ibid., 130–31.

Chapter 3

84. Kathryn Grover, *The Fugitives Gibraltar: Escaping Slaves and Abolitionism in New Bedford, Massachusetts* (Amherst: University of Massachusetts Press, 2001), 242–43; Still, *Underground Railroad*, 60–61.
85. Still, *Underground Railroad*, 61; Margaret Berkley was listed as a Portsmouth resident. Interestingly, in the 1840 census she was listed as Burkley and in the 1850 census as Berkley; Grover, *Fugitives Gibraltar*, 243.
86. "Civil War and Reconstruction," 598–99.
87. Bordewich, *Bound for Canaan*, 39; Larry Gara, *The Liberty Line* (Lexington: University of Kentucky Press, 1996), 31–32.
88. Bordewich, *Bound for Canaan*, 135–36; James Horton and Lois Horton, *In Hope of Liberty: Culture, Community and Protest Among Northern Free Blacks, 1700–1860* (New York: Oxford University Press, 1997), 229.
89. June Purcell Guild, *Black Laws of Virginia: A Summary of the Legislative Acts of Virginia Concerning Negroes from Earliest Times to the Present* (New York: Negro Universities Press, 1936), 77–78, 82. See also statutes enacted throughout the 1830s, 1840s and 1850s.

90. Minutes of the Society for the Prevention of the Absconding and Abducting of Slaves, 1833–42, Special Collections, University of Virginia Library; Rodney Dale Green, "Urban Industry, Black Resistance, and Racial Restriction in the Antebellum South: A General Model and a Case Study in Urban Virginia," *Journal of Economic History* 41 (March 1981): 190; Guild, *Black Laws*, 77–78, 82. See also statutes enacted throughout the 1830s, 1840s and 1850s.
91. Bertha-Monica Stearns, "John Greenleaf Whittier, Editor," *New England Quarterly* 13 (June 1940): 280–81, 295.
92. Ibid., 295.
93. Ibid.
94. Bordewich, *Bound for Canaan*, 65.
95. Ibid., 106.
96. Assessment of William Still's records in *Underground Railroad.*
97. Ibid.
98. Ibid., 187–88.
99. Ibid., 187–93.
100. Samuel Howe, *Refugees from Slavery in Canada West: Report to the Freedmen's Inquiry Commission* (Boston: Wright & Potter, 1864), 74.
101. Wilbur Siebert, *The Underground Railroad: From Slavery to Freedom* (London: Forgotten Books, 2012), 118.
102. *Norfolk and Portsmouth Herald*, September 28, 1827, and February 10–11, 1834, compiled by John C. Emmerson Jr. in *Steam Navigation in Virginia and Northeastern North Carolina Waters, 1826–1836* (Portsmouth, VA: self-published, 1949–50), 54–56, 247–48; Guild, *Black Laws*, 84–85.
103. By 1850, the forty-year-old Hatton was listed as a teller at the Farmers' Bank in Norfolk, per ancestry.com.
104. John Capheart was listed in the Norfolk 1850 census as a forty-nine-year-old constable, per ancestry.com; Grover, *Fugitives Gibraltar*, 22–23; *American Beacon*, April 24, 1834, 1. The advertisement for Moses continued to run through May 1, 1834, in the *Beacon*.
105. *Southern Argus*, June 12, 1855, 2.
106. Mullin, *Flight and Rebellion*, 33–34, 38.
107. Clement Eaton, "Slave-Hiring in the Upper South: A Step toward Freedom," *Mississippi Valley Historical Review* 46 (March 1960): 664–65.
108. *American Beacon*, May 27, 1834, 1, 3, and June 7, 1834, 3.
109. *Norfolk and Portsmouth Herald*, September 28, 1827, and February 10–11, 1834; Guild, *Black Laws*, 84–85; Grover, *Fugitives Gibraltar*, 22–23; *American*

Beacon, April 24, 1834, 1. The advertisement for Moses continued to run through May 1, 1834, in the *American Beacon*.

110. Eaton, "Slave-Hiring," 670, 678.

111. Statistics for Hampton Roads can be found in the state's quarterly reports from 1856 to 1860. Although the earlier period is not included, references are made in these reports about the early 1850s. "Quarterly Report of the Chief Inspector Under the Law for the Better Protection of Slave Property in the Commonwealth of Virginia, Passed March 17, 1856 for the Quarter Ending September 30, 1858," Manuscript Division, Library of Virginia; Collinson, *Shadrick Minkins*, 86; Cecelski, *Waterman's Song*, 34.

112. Although not mentioned by name, Nicholson's owner was probably Margaret Hodges, the only Hodges listed as a slaveholder in the 1860 slave schedules. Hodges was also noted as married to a Thomas Hodges in the 1860 census; Thelma Dunston, "The History of the Negro in Portsmouth, Virginia," February 12, 1937, Writers' Project of the Work Projects Administration in the State of Virginia, Library of Virginia; Fannie Nicholson, interview by Thelma Dunston, January 8, 1937, Writers' Project of the Work Projects Administration in the State of Virginia, Library of Virginia, WPA Life Histories database, http://eagle.vsla.edu/cgi-bin/spa.gateway, accessed January 15, 2003.

113. Jeffrey Wilson, the first black reporter to write a weekly column, "The Colored Notes," in the *Portsmouth Star*, stated that the slaves were sold at the corner of High and Court Streets on the first of January each year; *Portsmouth Star*, September 24, 1924.

114. Collinson, *Shadrick Minkins*, 13–16.

115. Ibid., 27.

116 Higgins' wharf, which would later be the primary departure point for many fugitives leaving the area aboard the *City of Richmond*, the *Pennsylvania* and the *Jamestown* steamships, was located on the far end of Widewater Street, beside the Norfolk and Petersburg Railroad tracks and the footbridge to Berkley. Collinson, *Shadrick Minkins*, 24–26, 31–32, 56, 106, 110–12, 116; Still, *Underground Railroad*, 326–27.

117. Collinson, *Shadrick Minkins*, 54, 63.

118. Still, *Underground Railroad*, 559.

119. Collinson, *Shadrick Minkins*, 64–65.

120. Ibid., 65; Siebert, *Underground Railroad*, 448; Bordewich, *Bound for Canaan*, 109–10.

121. Collinson, *Shadrick Minkins*, 64–65; Bordewich, *Bound for Canaan*, 169–72.

122. Collinson, *Shadrick Minkins*, 130–33, 140.
123. Charles Emery Stevens, *Anthony Burns: A History* (Boston: John P Jewett and Company, 1856), 15–18; James Oliver Horton and Lois E. Horton, *Black Bostonians: Family Life and Community Struggle in the Antebellum North* (New York: Holmes and Meier, 1999), 117–20.
124. Jeffrey Ruggles, *The Unboxing of Henry Brown* (Richmond: Library of Virginia, 2003), 3.
125. Ibid., 3, 7–8.
126. Ibid., 15, 20–21.
127. Ibid., 22, 27–30, 35.
128. *Southern Argus*, February 7, 1855, 4, and May 16, 1855, 4.
129. Still, *Underground Railroad*, 161–64.
130. Ibid., 162–63; Don Papson and Tom Calarco, *Secret Lives of the Underground Railroad in New York City: Sydney Howard Gay, Louis Napoleon and the Record of Fugitives* (Jefferson, NC: McFarland and Company, 2015), 145; Still's work provides no evidence suggesting any possible relationship between Thomas and Frederick Nixon except that they were both owned by the Norfolk grocer Benjamin J. Bockover, listed in the Norfolk County 1860 Census. Gray's New Map of Norfolk, Norfolk County, Virginia Drawn from Special Surveys 1877 confirms Still's record that Bockover resided at 12 Brewer Street; Charles E. Stewart, *The African Society Becomes Emanuel African Methodist Episcopal Church, Portsmouth, Virginia* (Norfolk, VA: Guide Quality Press, 1944), 44; W. Eugene Ferslew, *Vickery's Directory for the City of Norfolk, to Which Is Added a Business Directory for 1859* (Norfolk, VA: Vickery & Company, 1859), 39, 164.
131. Still, *Underground Railroad*, 557–59.
132. Ibid., 560.
133. John Kneebone, "A Break Down on the Underground Railroad: Captain B. and the Capture of the *Keziah*, 1858," *Virginia Calvacade* (Spring 1999), 77–79.
134. Unlike their brother, Peter and John Baylis, who also transported fugitives for a fee, were able to leave Virginia without being caught with escaped slaves aboard. They would retire to Wilmington and work as a grocer and painter, respectively. William Baylis would eventually work as a grocer and die in 1881. Kneebone, "Break Down," 82–82; *Williamsburg Weekly Gazette*, June 30, 1858; Midori Takagi, *"Rearing Wolves to Our Own Destruction": Slavery in Richmond, Virginia, 1782–1865* (Charlottesville: University of Virginia Press, 2002), 103–4, 121.

135. Virginia Statutes for 1856 included chapters 47 through 49. Guild, *Black Laws*, 86, 89–90; State of Virginia Penitentiary Inmates, 1860 US Census Records, County of Henrico, City of Richmond, Manuscript Division, Library of Virginia; Schwarz, *Slave Laws*, 137, 145.
136. Collinson, *Shadrick Minkins*, 45; Schwarz, *Slave Laws*, 127–28, 134, 137, 145; Siebert, *Underground Railroad*, 447; list of individuals recorded as inmates in the State of Virginia Penitentiary, 1860 U.S. Census, County of Henrico, City of Richmond; "Fugitive Slave Fund Claims for Payment, 1857–1860," RG 48, APA 689, Box 1801, Manuscript Division, State Library of Virginia; Guild, *Black Laws*, 91.
137. Wertenbaker, *Norfolk*, 29; Tommy Bogger, "Maroons and Laborers in the Great Dismal Swamp," in *Readings in Black and White: Lower Tidewater*, edited by Jane Kobelski (Portsmouth, VA: Portsmouth Public Library, 1982), 1; Bolster, *Black Jacks*, 40, 97.
138. Guild, *Black Laws*, 71–72, 77–78, 82.
139 Still, *Underground Railroad*, 36–40, 117–19.
140. Marion Blackburn, "Letter from Virginia: American Refugees" *Archeology* 64 (September/October 2011), archive.archaeology.org/1109/letter/great_dismal_swamp_slavery_maroons.html, accessed January 15, 2017; Virginia Foundation for the Humanities, "Dismal Swamp," African American Historic Sites Database, accessed May 1, 2017, http://www.aahistoricsitesva.org/items/show/421.
141. Michael Blaakman, "Dismal Swamp Company," Digital Encyclopedia of George Washington, accessed June 1, 2017, http://www.mountvernon.org/digital-encyclopedia/article/dismal-swamp-company; Daniel Sayers, *A Desolate Place for a Defiant People: The Archeology of Maroons, Indigenous Americans, and Enslaved Laborers in the Great Dismal Swamp* (Gainesville: University Press of Florida, 2014, 2015), 88–89.
142. Brent Morris, "'Running Servants and All Other': The Diverse and Elusive Maroons of the Great Dismal Swamp," in *Voices from Within the Veil: African Americans and the Experience of Democracy*, edited by William Alexander, Cassandra Newby-Alexander and Charles Ford (Newcastle upon Tyne, UK: Cambridge Scholars Publishing, 2008), 94–95; Sayers, *Desolate Place*, 2–3, 89, 92; *Virginia Gazette*, June 23, 1768; October 6, 1768; December 13, 1770; and December 5, 1771.
143. Sayers, *Desolate Place*, 89–90.
144. Ibid., 94.
145. Ibid., 94–95; Morris, "'Running Servants,'" 100, 102.

146. Moses Grandy, *Narrative of the Life of Moses Grandy; Late a Slave in the United States of America* (London: C. Gilpin, 1843), 24–26, 38, 69; Morris, "'Running Servants,'" 102.
147. *The North-Carolinian*, April 26, 1845, 2; David Hunter Strother, "The Dismal Swap," *Harper's New Monthly Magazine* 13 (September 1856), 451–53.
148. *The Liberator*, December 30, 1842; *The North Star*, March 31, 1848.
149. *Frederick Douglass Paper*, January 27, 1854.
150. Ibid.
151. William Switala, *Underground Railroad in Delaware, Maryland, and West Virginia* (Mechanicsburg, PA: Stackpole Books, 2004), 109.
152. Ibid., 110.
153. Ibid., 113; Peter Kolchin, *American Slavery, 1619–1877* (New York: Farrar, Straus and Giroux, 2003), 69–70.
154. Switala, *Underground Railroad*, 114; Charles Blockson, *The Underground Railroad in Pennsylvania* (Jacksonville, FL: Flame International, 1981), 60.
155. Switala, *Underground Railroad*, 114–16; Siebert, *Underground Railroad*, 82.
156. Switala, *Underground Railroad*, 123.
157. Levi Coffin, *Reminiscences of Levi Coffin: The Reputed President of the Underground Railroad* (New York: Augustus Kelley, 1968), 438–39.
158. Grover, *Fugitives Gibraltar*, 1, 6, 8; Kathryn Grover, "Fugitive Slave Traffic and the Maritime World of New Bedford," prepared for New Bedford Whaling National Historic Park and the Boston Support Office of the National Park Service (New Bedford, MA, 1998), 5–6.

Chapter 4

159. Bordewich, *Bound for Canaan*, 50.
160. Ibid., 51–52, 53, 57
161. Ibid., 51, 58.
162. Ibid., 59–60.
163. Blockson, *Underground Railroad*, 12–13; Bordewich, *Bound for Canaan*, 59–60.
164. Still, *Underground Railroad*, 335; Siebert, *Underground Railroad*, 8; William and Ellen Craft, *Running a Thousand Miles to Freedom* (London: William Tweedie, 1860), 39–50.
165. Blockson, *Underground Railroad*, 12–13.
166. Ibid., 14–17.

167. Coffin, *Reminiscences,* 429, 431, 433.
168. Ibid., 431–32, 434–35.
169. Ibid., 432, 435–36.
170. Still, *Underground Railroad*, 84–85.
171. Ibid., 85–88.
172. Ibid., 31.
173. Wilbur Seibert, "The Underground Railroad in Massachusetts," *New England Quarterly* 9 (September 1936), 457.
174. Bordewich, *Bound for Canaan*, 168–71.
175. Ibid., 172; Tom Calarco, *The Underground Railroad in the Adirondack Region* (Jefferson, NC: McFarland and Company, 2004), 136–37.
176. Wilbur Siebert, "Light on the Underground Railroad," *American Historical Review* 1 (April 1896): 463.
177. Siebert, *Underground Railroad*, 456; Grover, *Fugitives Gibraltar*, 238.
178. Grover, *Fugitives Gibraltar*, 238; Siebert, *Underground Railroad*, 81, 118, 435.
179. Donald Jacobs, ed., *Courage and Conscience: Black and White Abolitionists in Boston* (Bloomington: Indiana University Press, 1993), ix, 41, 44, 92–93.
180. Collinson, *Shadrick Minkins*, 80, 84–85.
181. Although there is no listing for a Mary Sayer in the census records of this period, there is a thirty-five-year-old William Sayre listed in the 1850 Portsmouth census records. He is also listed as owning five slaves who ranged in ages from seven to fifty-five. More than likely, William is the son of Mary Sayre, although there is no census information available to support that position, except that it would seem, from George Latimer's autobiographical sketch, that one morning after he had spent time visiting his wife, his owner caught him on the streets on his return. Therefore, both Rachel and George were probably living in Portsmouth, although the general accounts referred to the area of departure as Norfolk; Asa J. Davis, "The George Latimer Case: A Benchmark in the Struggle for Freedom," Blueprint for Change: The Life and Times of Lewis H. Latimer, accessed July 6, 2006, http://edison.rutgers.edu/latimer/glatcase.htm.
182. The Portsmouth census records did not confirm the existence of a Mitchell Latimer; however, a Samuel M. Latimer was documented to have lived in Portsmouth as early as the 1830 census and as late as the 1840 census. Moreover, records indicated a sibling connection between Edward and Samuel, the only Latimers living in Portsmouth. In 1820, Samuel M. Latimer lived in Hampton, a town on the peninsula in Hampton Roads.; Davis, "George Latimer Case"; Collinson, *Shadrach Minkins*, 87; James B.

Gray was listed in the 1850 census with a wife, Jane, who was born in Massachusetts; four boys, ages seven to thirteen; one thirty-year-old white female; and a twenty-three year old mulatto laborer named Thomas Sparrow in his household; *Proceedings of the Citizens of the Borough of Norfolk, on the Boston Outrage, in the Case of the Runaway Slave George Latimer.* (Norfolk, VA: T.G. Broughton and Son, 1843), 5; C.N. Drie, Norfolk & Portsmouth, Virginia, map, 1873, Library of Congress.

183. Wilbur Siebert, *The Underground Railroad in Massachusetts* (Worcester, MA: American Antiquarian Society, 1935), 17.

184. *American Beacon*, October 15, 1842; *Negro in Virginia*, 143.

185. *Negro in Virginia*, 143.

186. *American Beacon*, October 15, 1842, 3; *Proceedings*, 5, 10–13.

187. *Proceedings*, 12; Siebert, *Underground Railroad in Massachusetts*, 18.

188. Grover argued that an analysis of the 1855 Massachusetts census revealed that the majority of people of color who claimed free states as their birthplaces actually came from the South. William Ferguson was an example of a fugitive claiming birth in northern free states. Not until the late 1850s would Ferguson and his wife, Nancy, admit to their status as runaway slaves who left Virginia in 1847. Grover, *Fugitives Gibraltar*, 57, 59, 85.

189. Bordewich, *Bound for Canaan*, 256–57; *Southern Argus*, December 22, 1854, 3; January 11, 1855, 2.

190. Bordewich, *Bound for Canaan*, 177–79.

191. Ibid., 300–302; Bogger, *Free Blacks*, 251–52; Still, *Underground Railroad*, 308–9.

192. U.S. Bureau of the Census, Seventh Census of Virginia, 1850, Whites and Free Blacks, Norfolk County, Virginia, (Microfilm Series M432, Roll 964), 94; William S. Forrest, *The Norfolk Directory for 1851–1852* (Norfolk: William S. Forrest, 1851), 44, 90, 96; *Southern Daily Argus*, January 5, 1852, 3; U.S. Bureau of the Census, Seventh Census (1850) Slave Inhabitants Virginia, 132; Still, *Underground Railroad*, 51; Elmwood and Cedar Grove Cemeteries, Database of Interments, Bureau of Cemeteries, Norfolk, VA.

193. State of Virginia Penitentiary, 1860 U.S. Census, County of Henrico, City of Richmond; "Fugitive Slave Fund Claims for Payment, 1857–1860," RG 48, APA 689, Box 1801, Manuscript Division, State Library of Virginia; Virginia Statute 1860, Chapter 42; Still, *Underground Railroad*, 74, 80, 111, 213, 235, 250, 265; Bordewich, *Bound for Canaan*, 138.

194. Virginia Penitentiary records; Still, *Underground Railroad*, 76; Blockson, *Underground Railroad*, 18.

195. *Negro in Virginia*, 149; Still, *Underground Railroad*, 61, 563,
196. The 1850 U.S. Census records for the City of Norfolk indicated that John Minkins worked as an omnibus driver in Norfolk. The Norfolk Minkins family was the only free black family recorded in the U.S. census schedules. With the exception of two free black Minkins children who lived in another household, the Minkins family was likely the only one from whom the mysterious free black steward identified in William Still's work as "Minkins" may have come. A close examination of Virginia's ship inspection records provided circumstantial evidence that John Minkins was the infamous steward Minkins because he was listed as a captain of a schooner that was stopped for violating the inspection laws and suspected of harboring fugitives; Still, *Underground Railroad*, 60–61, 64, 67–68, 81, 163, 191, 202, 228, 230–31, 268–70, 299–300, 308, 316–17; Bogger, *Free Blacks*, 61, 78–79; Captain John Minkins was charged a twenty-five-dollar fee on August 10, 1859, for violating the inspection law, "Fugitive Slave Fund Claims for Payment, 1857–1860," RG 48, APA 689, Box 1801, Manuscript Division, Library of Virginia.
197. Still, *Underground Railroad*, 47, 51, 53, 55, 65–67, 89.
198. Ibid., 64–65; Journal C, 40–41.
199. Still, *Underground Railroad*, 66; Journal C, 40.
200. Still, *Underground Railroad*, 228.
201. Although the 1850 Norfolk County Census did not list an Abigail Wheeler living in Portsmouth, it did note that an Eliza H. Wheeler, age forty-seven, lived in a boardinghouse along with thirty-five others. The slave schedules, however, did not list anyone by the name of Wheeler. This was not an indication that Moses Wines's story had no merit, since many slaveholders are absent from mention in the slave schedules for Hampton Roads; Still, *Underground Railroad*, 230–31.
202. Still, *Underground Railroad*, 48.
203. Ibid., 27–28; Petition, Kanawha Company to General Assembly, January 1, 1861, Halifax County, SLP/RSPP; Richmond Hustings Court, E.P., August 2, 1856; *Richmond Whig*, July 24, 1856; Takagi, *Rearing Wolves*, 121; *Richmond Whig*, July 19, 1853; *Acts of General Assembly*, 1856, 41–43; "Kidnapping at Norfolk," *Richmond Enquirer*, June 1, 1858; "City Jottings," *Petersburg South-Side Democrat*, October 25, 1854.
204. Janine V. da Silva and Kathryn Grover, "Historic Resource Study" (Boston: Boston African American National Historic Site, 2002), 142; Still, *Underground Railroad*, 293, 563; Siebert, "Underground Railroad in

Massachusetts," 449, see also *The Liberator*, March 20, 1846, and *Boston Commonwealth*, March 16, 1846; Stewart, *History of Norfolk County*, 33, 40–41, 44, 49.

205. Thomas Parramore et al., *Norfolk: The First Four Centuries* (Charlottesville: University Press of Virginia, 1994), 183.

206. *American Beacon*, May 1, 1854, 2; *Southern Argus*, May 5, 1858, 2; July 7, 1858, 3; July 9, 1858, 3; July 10, 1858, 3; July 12, 1858, 3; Bogger, *Free Blacks*, 167.

207. Still, *Underground Railroad*, 106; *Richmond Whig*, July 24, 1856; "Kidnapping at Norfolk," *Richmond Enquirer*, June 1, 1858; "City Jottings," *Petersburg South-Side Democrat*, October 25, 1854.

208. *American Beacon*, May 1, 1854, 2.

209 Virginia Statutes for 1856 included Chapters 47 through 49, Guild, *Black Laws*, 86, 89–90. State of Virginia Penitentiary Inmates, 1860 US Census Records, County of Henrico, city of Richmond, Manuscript Division, Library of Virginia; Schwarz, *Slave Laws*, 137, 145.

210. Statistics for Hampton Roads can be found in the state's quarterly reports from 1856 to 1860. Although the earlier period is not included, references are made in these reports about the early 1850s. "Quarterly Report of the Chief Inspector Under the Law for the Better Protection of Slave Property in the Commonwealth of Virginia, Passed March 17, 1856 for the Quarter Ending September 30, 1858," Manuscript Division, Library of Virginia; Collinson, *Shadrick Minkins*, 86; Cecelski, *Waterman's Song*, 34.

211. Collinson, *Shadrick Minkins*, 45; Schwarz, *Slave Laws*, 127–28, 134, 137, 145; Siebert, "Underground Railroad in Massachusetts," 447; Guild, *Black Laws*, 91; list of individuals recorded as inmates in the State of Virginia Penitentiary, 1860 U.S. Census, County of Henrico, City of Richmond; "Fugitive Slave Fund Claims for Payment, 1857–1860," RG 48, APA 689, Box 1801, Manuscript Division, State Library of Virginia; Virginia Statute 1860.

Chapter 5

212. Still, *Underground Railroad*, 44–45.

213. Ibid., 45.

214. Ibid., 46–48.

215. Siebert, *Underground Railroad*, 28, 301.

216. Ibid., 28, 30, 180.
217. Ibid., 181.
218. Ibid.
219. Ibid., 182.
220. Karolyn Frost and Veta Tucker, eds., *A Fluid Frontier: Slavery, Resistance, and the Underground Railroad in the Detroit River Borderland* (Detroit, MI: Wane State University Press, 2016), 67.
221. Ibid., 15, 28.
222. Jason Silverman, *Unwelcome Guests: Canada West's Response to American Fugitive Slaves, 1800–1865* (Millwood, NY: Associated Faculty Press, 1985), 7, 10–11; Frost and Tucker, *Fluid Frontier*, 9–10.
223. Silverman, *Unwelcome Guests*, 11–12.
224. Ibid., 8; Frost and Tucker, *Fluid Frontier*, 9, 48–49.
225. Frost and Tucker, *Fluid Frontier*, 11.
226. Siebert, *Underground Railroad*, 196–197.
227. Frost and Tucker, *Fluid Frontier*, 10, 50.
228. Ibid., 83–84.
229. Benjamin Drew, *A North-Side View of Slavery, The Refugee, or, The Narratives of Fugitive Slaves in Canada. Related by Themselves, with an Account of the History and Condition of the Colored Population of Upper Canada* (Boston: John P. Jewett and Company, 185l; NY: Sheldon, Lamport and Blakeman, London: Trubner and Co., 1856), 19–20, 27–28.
230. Siebert, *Underground Railroad*, 198–100.
231. Ibid., 200.
232. Ibid. 202–203.
233. Frost and Tucker, *Fluid Frontier*, 83.
234. Drew, *Refugee*, 79–83.
235. Frost and Tucker, *Fluid Frontier*, 84–85; Bordewich, *Bound for Canaan*, 370.
236. Frost and Tucker, *Fluid Frontier*, 85.
237. Ibid., 86.
238. Ibid., 86–87, 103.
239. W.R. Riddell, "The Slave in Upper Canada," *Journal of Negro History* 4 (October 1919): 387–88.
240. Still, *Underground Railroad*, 28–29; Adrienne Shadd, Afua Cooper and Karolyn Frost, *The Underground Railroad: Next Stop, Toronto!* (Toronto: Natural Heritage Books, 2002), 20.
241. Drew, *Refugee*, 19–30, 43–91; Bordewich, *Bound for Canaan*, 255.
242. Drew, *Refugee*, 43.
243. Ibid., 46–50; Still, *Underground Railroad*, 260, 299–300.

244. Robin W. Winks, *The Blacks in Canada: A History* (New Haven, CT: Yale University Press, 1971), 142–43;
Frost and Tucker, *Fluid Frontier*, 94, 96.
245. Frost and Tucker, *Fluid Frontier*, 8, 14.
246. Siebert, *Underground Railroad*, 199; Frost and Tucker, *Fluid Frontier*, 49.
247. Frost and Tucker, *Fluid Frontier*, 49.
248. Riddell, "Slave in Upper Canada," 387–88.
249. Still, *Underground Railroad*, 64, 66, 299–300, 316–317; *Southern Argus*, January 25, 1860.
250. Siebert, *Underground Railroad*, 153–54.
251. Ibid., 154.
252. Ibid.
253. Howe, *Refugees from Slavery*, 16–17.
254. Winks, *Blacks in Canada*, 142–145.
255. Still, *Underground Railroad*, 319.
256. Howe, *Refugees from Slavery*, 28.
257. Still, *Underground Railroad*, 317.
258. Silverman, *Unwelcome Guests*, 22.
259. Shadd, Cooper and Frost, *Underground Railroad*, 39, 40, 42, 46.
260. Ibid., 2–3.
261. Ibid., 27.
262. Silverman, *Unwelcome Guests*, 23; Bordewich, *Bound for Canaan*, 114–15; Still, *Underground Railroad*, 64–65.
263. Still, *Underground Railroad*, 302–3; Drew, *Refugee*, 97–98.
264. Still, *Underground Railroad*, 58.
265. Drew, *Refugee*, 43–44.
266. Ibid., 43–44.
267. Still, *Underground Railroad*, 300–302, 308–9; Bogger, *Darker Side*, 251–52; Siebert, *Underground Railroad*, 126.
268. Still, *Underground Railroad*, 287, 291–93.
269. Ibid., 27–28.
270. Ibid., 190.
271. Howe, *Refugees from Slavery*, 74.
272. Ibid., 74–75.
273. A week afterward, several Bostonians were accused and arrested for assisting in Minkins's escape, including Elizur Wright, Charles Davis, John Foye and James Scott. The judge ruled that no evidence existed that proved any of the defendants were part of a conspiracy, and all were released. Shortly thereafter, others were arrested, including Lewis

Hayden, Paul Smith, John Coburn and Robert Morris. After some time, all were eventually freed and cleared of the charges. Collinson, *Shadrick Minkins*, 125–26, 128, 132, 140–42, 146–48, 164, 185, 187, 189–90, 194–95, 197, 199–200, 209–11.

274. Silverman, *Unwelcome Guests*, 13–14, 21–22.
275. Winks, *Blacks in Canada*, 142–45.
276. Shadd, Cooper and Frost, *Underground Railroad*, 52–54.
277. Ibid., 59–60.

Chapter 6

278. Edward Pierce, "The Contrabands at Fortress Monroe," *Atlantic Monthly* 49 (November 1861): 626–27; Robert Engs, *Freedom's First Generation: Black Hampton, Virginia, 1861–1890* (New York: Fordham University Press, 2004), 18–19; "Fort Monroe in the Civil War," Fort Monroe, Civil War, 1861–1865 box, Hampton University Archives, Hampton, Virginia, 1.
279. Engs, *Freedom's First Generation*, 18–19.
280. Workers of the Writers' Program of the Work Projects Administration in the State of Virginia, compiler, *The Negro in Virginia* (Winston-Salem, NC: John Blair Publisher, 1994), 210.
281. Pierce, "Contrabands," 626–27; Engs, *Freedom's First Generation*, 18–19; "Fort Monroe in the Civil War," 1.
282. Engs, *Freedom's First Generation*, 25.
283. *Southern Argus*, "Editorial," March 10, 1860.
284. Gideon Wells to Abraham Lincoln, letter, July 4, 1861. Letters Sent by the Secretary of the Navy to the President and Executive Agencies, 1821–1886, vol. 13, National Archives Microfilm Publishers, 1963, Washington, D.C., 358.
285. Engs, *Freedom's First Generation*, 7; George Holbert Tucker, *Norfolk Highlights, 1584–1881* (Norfolk, VA: Norfolk Historical Society, 1972), 94; H.W. Burton, *The History of Norfolk, Virginia: A Review of Important Events and Incidents which Occurred from 1736 to 1877; Also a Record of Personal Reminiscences and Political, Commercial, and Curious Facts* (Norfolk: Norfolk Virginian Job Print, 1877), 47.
286. Chester Bradley, "Controversial Ben Butler," Fort Monroe, Civil War, 1861–1865 box, Hampton University Archives, Hampton, Virginia, 1.
287. Engs, *Freedom's First Generation*, 17–18; Betsy L. Fahlman, Beth N.

Rossheim, David W. Steadman and Peter Stewart, *A Tricentennial Celebration: Norfolk 1682–1982* (Norfolk, VA: Chrysler Museum, 1982), 70.

288. Benjamin Butler to Lewis Tappan, letter, August 10, 1861, in American Missionary Association Manuscripts, Roll 1, microfilm, Collis P. Huntington Library, Hampton University (hereafter cited AMA MSS); Pierce, "Contrabands of Fortress Monroe," 627. See also Steven Frank Petrine, "Benjamin Butler and the Bureau of Negro Affairs in Tidewater, Virginia 1861–1865" (master's thesis, Old Dominion University, 1975), 8; *Official Records of the Union and Confederate Navies in the War of the Rebellion*, series I, vol. 4, (Washington, D.C.: Government Printing Office, 1911), 604.

289. *Negro in Virginia*, 210.

290. Engs, *Freedom's First Generation*, 46–47; Sandra Gallop and Margo Gaither, "First Steps to Freedom," Fort Monroe, Civil War, 1861–1865 box, Hampton University Archives, Hampton, Virginia, 2; "Fort Monroe in the Civil War," 2.

291. "Negroes Taking Refuge at Fort Monroe," *Frank Leslie's Illustrated Newspaper*, June 8, 1861, 55.

292. Butler to Tappan, AMA MSS.

293. Louis S. Gerteis, *From Contraband to Freedmen: Federal Policy Toward Southern Blacks, 1861–1865* (Westport, CT: Greenwood Press, 1973), 14–17.

294. Engs, *Freedom's First Generation*, 15, 25; James McPherson, *Battle Cry of Freedom: The Civil War Era* (New York: Oxford University Press, 1988), 353.

295. *Negro in Virginia*, 210.

296. Jim Downs, *Sick from Freedom: African-American Illness and Suffering during the Civil War and Reconstruction* (New York: Oxford University Press, 2012), 22, 24, 26.

297. Ibid., 138; Engs, *Freedom's First Generation*, 53.

298. Lewis C. Lockwood to AMA, letter, January 4, 1862, AMA MSS.

299. "Among the Contrabands: Reminiscences of a Veteran Missionary," *Southern Workman* 13 (April 1884): 46.

300. *Cleveland Morning Leader*, November 4, 1862.

301. Cassandra Newby-Alexander, *An African American History of the Civil War in Hampton Roads* (Charleston, SC: The History Press, 2010), 52, 59–60, 71.

302. *The Liberator*, November 29, 1861.

303. Joe Richardson, *Christian Reconstruction: The American Missionary Association and Southern Blacks, 1861–1890* (Athens: University of Georgia Press, 1986), 4–3; *American Missionary Magazine*, supplement 5 (October 1861): 241–42.

304. "Among the Contrabands," 46.

Chapter 7

305. Wilbert L. Jenkins, *Seizing the New Day: African Americans in Post–Civil War Charleston* (Bloomington: Indiana University Press, 1998), 133, 152; "Reorganization of Civil Government, Speech of Governor Pierpont [sic], Delivered at Mechanics' Hall in the City of Norfolk on Thursday Evening, February 16th, 1865" (Courtesy of Kirn Memorial Library, Norfolk), 1, 3–5; Maxwell Whiteman, ed., "Equal Suffrage. Address from the Colored Citizens of Norfolk, Virginia, June 5, 1865," *Afro-American History Series* III (Wilmington, DE: Scholarly Resources Inc., 1970), 9.
306. Still, *Underground Railroad*, 203; "Exploring a Common Past: Researching and Interpreting the Underground Railroad," accessed July 21, 2006, http://www.cr.nps.gov/history/online_books/ugrr/ exugrr4.htm; Cassandra Newby, "'The World Was All Before Them': A Study of the Black Community in Norfolk, Virginia, 1861–1884" (PhD dissertation, College of William and Mary, 1992), 336; *Journal and Guide* (Norfolk, VA), February 27, 1932, 7; Luther P. Jackson, *Negro Office-Holders in Virginia, 1865–1895* (Norfolk, VA: Guide Quality Press, 1945), 86.
307. *New Journal and Guide* (Norfolk, VA), April 1, 1998, 1, 7; Newby, "'World Was All Before Them,'" 151, 187, 187.
308. Cassandra Newby-Alexander, Mae Breckenridge-Haywood and the African American Historical Society of Portsmouth, *Black America Series: Portsmouth, Virginia* (Charleston, SC: Arcadia Publishing, 2003), 83.
309. I. Garland Penn, *The Afro-American Press and Its Editors* (Springfield, MA: Willey & Company, 1891), 176.
310. Ibid., 176; Newby, "'World Was All Before Them,'" 163, 165–66, 176.; Robert Ewell Greene, *Black Defenders of America, 1775–1973: A Reference and Pictorial History* (Chicago: Johnson Publishing Company, 1974), 101; Rayford Logan and Michael Winston, eds., *Dictionary of African American Biography* (New York: W.W. Norton, 1982), 234; Penn, *Afro-American Press*, 178–79.
311. Winks, *Blacks in Canada*, 231.
312. Langston Hughes, "I, Too," Poetry Foundation, https://www.poetryfoundation.org/poems-and-poets/poems/detail/47558, accessed June 20, 2017.

INDEX

K

L

M

N

O

P

Q

R

S

T

U

V

W

Y

ABOUT THE AUTHOR

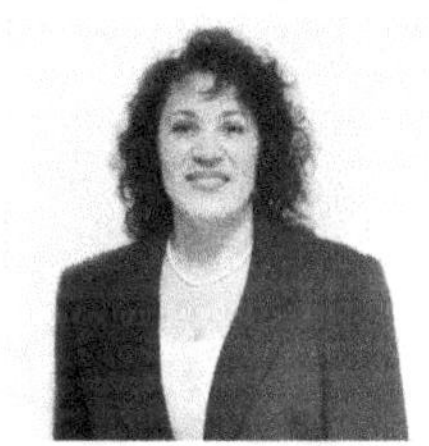

Cassandra Newby-Alexander currently serves as a professor of history and the director of the Joseph Jenkins Roberts Center for the African Diaspora at Norfolk State University. She has spearheaded the 1619 Making of America conference, which seeks to transform the narrative about the role of early Africans in the evolution of America. Her books include *An African American History of the Civil War in Hampton Roads*, *Hampton Roads: Remembering Our Schools* and *Voices from within the Veil: African Americans and the Experience of Democracy*.

www.ingramcontent.com/pod-product-compliance
Lightning Source LLC
LaVergne TN
LVHW010944100826
845153LV00002B/140
9781540227829